CASEBOOK SERIES

JANE AUSTEN: *'Northanger Abbey' & 'Persuasion'* B.C. Southam
JANE AUSTEN: *'Sense and Sensibility', 'Pride and Prejudice' & 'Mansfield Park'* B. C. Southam
BECKETT: *Waiting for Godot* Ruby Cohn
WILLIAM BLAKE: *Songs of Innocence and Experience* Margaret Bottrall
CHARLOTTE BRONTE: *'Jane Eyre' & 'Villette'* Miriam Allott
EMILY BRONTE: *Wuthering Heights* (Revised) Miriam Allott
BROWNING: *'Men and Women' & Other Poems* J. R. Watson
CHAUCER: *The Canterbury Tales* J. J. Anderson

C̶O̶L̶E̶R̶I̶D̶G̶E̶: 'The Ancient Mariner' & Other Poems Alun R. Jones & W. Tydeman
C̶ ...ox
D̶
D̶ ...an Page
D̶
G̶EORGE ELIOT ...
T̶. S. ELIOT: Four Quartets
T̶. S. ELIOT ...B. C. Southam
T̶. S. ELIOT: The Waste Land C. B. Cox & Arnold P. Hinchliffe
H̶ENRY FIELDING ...
E̶. M. FORSTER: A Passage to India ...
H̶ARDY ...
H̶ARDY: Poems James Gibson & Trevor Johnson
G̶ERARD MANLEY HOPKINS ...
H̶ENRY JAMES ...on
J̶OHNSON ...
J̶AMES JOYCE ...rris Beja
K̶EATS ...
K̶EATS ...
D̶. H. LAWRENCE ...
D̶. H. LAWRENCE ...
L̶OWRY ...
M̶ARLOWE: Doctor Faustus John Jump
M̶ARLOWE ...Brown
M̶ILTON: Paradise Lost ...
O̶'CASEY ...v of a
J̶OHN OSBORNE ...
P̶INTER ...
POPE: *The Rape of the Lock* John Dixon Hunt
SHAKESPEARE: *A Midsummer Night's Dream* Antony Price
SHAKESPEARE: *Antony and Cleopatra* (Revised) John Russell Brown
SHAKESPEARE: *Coriolanus* B. A. Brockman

Browning

'Men and Women' and Other Poems

A CASEBOOK

EDITED BY

J. R. WATSON

palgrave
macmillan

First published 1974 by
THE MACMILLAN PRESS LTD
Houndmills, Basingstoke, Hampshire RG21 2XS
and London
Companies and representatives
throughout the world

ISBN 0–333–14966–1

A catalogue record for this book is available
from the British Library.

Transferred to digital printing 2002

Printed and bound in Great Britain by
Antony Rowe Ltd, Chippenham and Eastbourne

CONTENTS

ACKNOWLEDGEMENTS

Richard D. Altick, 'Andrea del Sarto: The Kingdom of Heaven is Within', from *Browning's Mind and Art*, ed. Clarence Tracy, by permission of Oliver & Boyd, Edinburgh and London; Patricia M. Ball, 'Browning's Godot', from *Victorian Poetry*, III (1965), by permission; G. K. Chesterton, chapter IV from *Robert Browning*, Macmillan, London; E. D. H. Johnson, extract from *The Alien Vision of Victorian Poetry: Sources of the Poetic Imagination in Tennyson, Browning and Arnold*, copyright © 1952 by Princeton University Press, reprinted by permission of Princeton University Press; Roma A. King Jr, chapter IV from *The Bow and the Lyre*, by permission of the University of Michigan Press; Robert Langbaum, extracts from *The Poetry of Experience*, by permission of Chatto & Windus, London, and Random House, New York; J. Hillis Miller, extracts from *The Disappearance of God: Five Nineteenth-Cenurty Writers*, copyright © 1963 by the President and Fellows of Harvard College, reprinted by permission of The Belknap Press of Harvard University Press; W. O. Raymond, chapter 12 from *The Infinite Moment*, copyright © 1965 by the University of Toronto Press, reprinted by permission of the University of Toronto Press; extract from *The Correspondence of Gerard Manley Hopkins and Richard Watson Dixon*, ed. C. C. Abbott, by permission of the Oxford University Press and by arrangement with the Society of Jesus.

GENERAL EDITOR'S PREFACE

Each of this series of Casebooks concerns either one well-known and influential work of literature or two or three closely linked works. The main section consists of critical readings, mostly modern, brought together from journals and books. A selection of reviews and comments by the author's contemporaries is also included, and sometimes comments from the author himself. The Editor's Introduction charts the reputation of the work from its first appearance until the present time.

The critical forum is a place of vigorous conflict and disagreement, but there is nothing in this to cause dismay. What is attested is the complexity of human experience and the richness of literature, not any chaos or relativity of taste. A critic is better seen, no doubt, as an explorer than as an 'authority', but explorers ought to be, and usually are, well equipped. The effect of good criticism is to convince us of what C. S. Lewis called 'the enormous extension of our being which we owe to authors'. This Casebook will be justified if it helps to promote the same end.

A single volume can represent no more than a small selection of critical opinions. Some critics have been excluded for reasons of space, and it is hoped that readers will follow up the further suggestions in the Select Bibliography. Other contributions have been severed from their original context, to which some readers may wish to return. Indeed, if they take a hint from the critics represented here, they certainly will.

A. E. Dyson

INTRODUCTION

The title of this volume, *'Men and Women' and Other Poems*, refers to three collections of Browning's shorter poems: *Dramatic Lyrics* (1842), *Dramatic Romances and Lyrics* (1845), and *Men and Women* (1855). Browning later redistributed the contents of these three books: thus many of the original poems from *Men and Women* appeared in 1863, and subsequently, under the heading of 'Dramatic Lyrics'. Others moved differently: for instance, 'My Last Duchess' from *Dramatic Lyrics* to 'Dramatic Romances', and 'The Bishop Orders his Tomb' from *Dramatic Romances and Lyrics* to 'Men and Women'. A list of the poems, as they originally appeared, will be found on p. 31; their present location can easily be found by consulting the contents page of any complete edition of Browning's poetry.

With the exception of certain poems from the later *Dramatis Personae* (1864), the three collections contain the most celebrated examples of Browning's shorter poetry, both in the form of the dramatic monologue and of the lyric. It is tempting to see them as a steady development, from the discovery of his true talent in 1842, through its maturing in 1845, to the great climax of *Men and Women*; but such a growth pattern does not fit the facts. After 1842 Browning returned to the writing of full-length dramas, and brought out the 1845 pamphlet only at the urging of his publisher. This was followed by another drama, *Luria*, and then by a period of what appears to be, by Browning's standards, remarkable indolence. There is no apparent realisation of what, with hindsight, seems so obvious to the reader of Browning – that in 1842 he had at last hit upon the form best suited to his genius; though it must also be said that he had little help from the critics, most of whom received the 1842 and 1845 collections with as much indifference as they had done his plays.

In 1842 Browning was thirty, ambitious, anxious to justify his parents' continued support, and frustrated by his failure with *Pauline*, his play *Strafford*, and *Sordello*. It was true that *Paracelsus* had enjoyed a modest success, but this had been obliterated by the ridicule heaped upon the difficult *Sordello*. During the six years after its failure in 1840, Browning worked with a tenacious energy to re-establish himself. He published a series of eight pamphlets under the title of *Bells and Pomegranates* – *Dramatic Lyrics* and *Dramatic Romances and Lyrics* were the third and seventh. By the side of such creative industry, the silence of the years which followed the elopement with Elizabeth Barrett in 1846 is extraordinary. *Christmas-Eve and Easter-Day*, published in 1850, was the first instance of a continued serious poetic activity; and in 1855 *Men and Women* presented the accumulated riches of these comparatively unproductive years. They were the years in which Browning completed his somewhat unorthodox education, which may have been one reason for his inactivity in poetry: his celebrated assertion that 'Italy was my university' was not just an epigram. He was also looking after a wife whose health was never strong, with the consciousness (particularly in the early years of the marriage) that he would be widely held to blame if she died. The sense that he had just acted out his favourite myth of Perseus rescuing Andromeda may also have helped to still his restless search for fame. Throughout these years, too, his wife was so much better known and more successful a poet than himself, that he may have deliberately spent time on helping her and sacrificing time which might have been spent on his own work. Certainly the reception of *Christmas-Eve and Easter-Day* would have given him no cause to change his mind; published in the same year as *In Memoriam*, and struggling with the same modern themes of faith and doubt, it was totally eclipsed by the success of Tennyson's poem. Seen against this background of neglect by critics and public, the completion of such a vigorous and individual book as *Men and Women* was an act of faith in his own judgement and that of his supporters, such as Landor, Carlyle and Rossetti.

The contents page of the 1842 *Dramatic Lyrics* betrays a certain nervousness: most of the poems are shepherded into groups, as though Browning was diffident about presenting them on their own. He described them, in a sentence which he was to use again and which has become famous as a description of his dramatic monologues, as 'for the most part Lyric in expression, always Dramatic in principle, and so many utterances of so many imaginary persons, not mine'.[1] No doubt he had Mill's detection of an 'intense and morbid self-consciousness' in *Pauline* at the back of his mind;[2] but again this suggests a nervousness, which was to some extent shown to have been justified by the pamphlet's critical reception. While it received warm praise from John Forster in *The Examiner*, the reviewer in *The Athenaeum* picked on what was considered to be Browning's besetting sin :

The inaptitude for giving intelligible expression to his meanings, whether unconscious or artificial, whether its cause be affectation or incapacity, is a defect, lessening the value, in any available sense, of the meanings themselves; and the riches which can be turned to no account lose their character of riches.[3]

At this time Browning was sometimes compared to the painter J. M. W. Turner, as an artist of great power who was thought to have a certain perverse and deliberate obscurity; yet it seems amazing that any critic should have written thus about 'Incident of the French Camp' and 'The Pied Piper of Hamelin', or even about 'My Last Duchess', harder though it may be. Browning's own reaction to the critics is seen in an astonishing paragraph of one of the early letters to Elizabeth Barrett :

I write from a thorough conviction that it is the duty of me, and with the belief that, after every drawback and shortcoming, I do my best, all things considered – that is for *me*, and, so being, the not being listened to by one human creature would, I hope, in nowise affect me. But of course I must, if for merely scientific purposes, know all about this 1845, its ways and doings, and something I do know, as that for a dozen cabbages, if I pleased to grow them in the garden here, I might demand, say, a dozen pence at Covent Garden Market, – and that for a dozen scenes, of the average goodness, I may challenge as many plaudits at the theatre close by; and a dozen pages of verse, brought to the Rialto where verse-merchants most do

congregate, ought to bring me a fair proportion of the Reviewers'
gold-currency, seeing the other traders pouch their winnings, as I
do see : well, when they won't pay me for my cabbages, nor praise
me for my poems, I may, if I please, say 'more's the shame', and
bid both parties 'decamp to the crows', in Greek phrase, and YET
go very lighthearted back to a garden-full of rose-trees, and a soul-
full of comforts; if they had bought my greens I should have been
able to buy the last number of 'Punch', and go thro' the toll-gate
of Waterloo Bridge, and give the blind clarionet-player a trifle, and
all without changing my gold – if they had taken to my books, my
father and mother would have been proud of this and the other
'favourable critique', and . . . at least so folks hold . . . I should have
to pay Mr. Moxon less by a few pounds – whereas . . . but you see !
Indeed, I force myself to say ever and anon, in the interest of the
market-gardeners regular, and Keats's proper, – 'It's nothing to *you*,
– critics & hucksters, all of you, if I *have* this garden and this conscience, – I might go die at Rome, or take to gin and the newspaper,
for what *you* would care !' So I don't quite lay open my resources
to everybody. But it does so happen, that I have met with much
more than I could have expected in this matter of kindly and prompt
recognition. I never wanted a real set of good hearty praisers – and
no bad reviewers – I am quite content with my share.[4]

The convolutions of this letter may have been due to Browning's
struggle to conceal his frustration and disappointment; but they
also reveal something of the crowded mind which he possessed at
this time. The actual answer to Elizabeth Barrett's question about
his reaction to criticism weaves its way between the cabbages, and
the Rialto, and Waterloo Bridge, and the rose trees, and the
blind clarinet player. Ideas and images tumble over one another
in riotous fertility. It is a very good example, in style and
content, of the Browning described by J. Hillis Miller : the poet
who needs to hear all sides of life, the recorder of a world
swarming with people, the artist of an existential kind of inner
fluidity. Reading this one is amazed, not at the variety and range
of his poetry, but at the control which he managed to exercise
over his teeming imagination.

More than any other of Browning's collections, perhaps,
Dramatic Romances and Lyrics is informed with the spirit of
place. Not only is there 'Claret and Tokay', later called

'Nationality in Drinks', but there are several poems about exiles, and a pair ('The Laboratory' and 'The Confessional') entitled 'France and Spain'. 'Pictor Ignotus' and 'The Tomb at St. Praxed's' (as it was called) were the result of Browning's visit to Italy in the second half of 1844. It was this sense of place, as well as of time, that Ruskin observed in his praise of 'The Bishop Orders his Tomb', when he said that Browning, 'living much in Italy, and quit of the Renaissance influence, is able fully to enter into the Italian feeling'.[5] Unfortunately this praise came later, and Browning had to be content with less enthusiasm in 1845; not everyone had as expert an eye for authenticity as Ruskin. Nevertheless, there were favourable comments in *The Examiner* and *The Athenaeum*, while *The English Review* and *The Critic* mingled praise with reservation.[6] The greatest delight for Browning came from the lines which Landor sent to *The Morning Chronicle*, and which the young poet's father caused to be reprinted and circulated to his friends :

> Browning ! Since Chaucer was alive and hale,
> No man hath walkt along our road with step
> So active, so inquiring eye, or tongue
> So varied in discourse.[7]

On the whole, however, the reception of *Dramatic Romances and Lyrics* was disappointing. When she was shown the proofs, Elizabeth Barrett had written that 'their various power & beauty will be striking and surprising to your most accustomed readers. . . . Now if people do not cry out about these poems, what are we to think of the world?'[8] But the world grumbled on, like the author of *The Poets and Poetry of England in the Nineteenth Century* (1846), who thought Browning's poems 'deformed by so many novelties of construction, and affectations of various kinds, that few will have patience to wade through his marshes to cull the flowers with which they are scattered'.[9] Charles Kingsley, entirely missing Browning's talent for portraying a variety of places, wanted him to be more English.[10] By way of reply in *Men and Women*, Browning contented himself with the fiercely riddling 'Popularity', in which it is the unoriginal

who are successful. The true poet knows how to extract and refine
the blue dye from the Tyrian shell, and others grow fat on his
labours :

> And there's the extract, flasked and fine,
>   And priced and saleable at last !
> And Hobbs, Nobbs, Stokes and Nokes combine
>   To paint the future from the past,
> Put blue into their line.
>
> Hobbs hints blue, – straight he turtle eats :
>   Nobbs prints blue, – claret crowns his cup :
> Nokes outdares Stokes in azure feats, –
>   Both gorge. Who fished the murex up?
> What porridge had John Keats?

The sense of exile in these poems, of the poet abroad and independent after the manner of Byron, may have contributed its
own kind of originality to *Men and Women*. Certainly in 1846
Browning had crossed his Rubicon, and some poems, notably
'The Statue and the Bust' with its unorthodox moral, may have
been influenced by a new and defiant life style. Yet his careful
accumulation of the fifty poems, his return to England with them,
and his composition and dedication of the final poem to 'E.B.B.',
all suggest that it was important for Browning to bring back
triumphantly the fruits of his exile. 'One Word More' is a
curious poem, public yet intimate, declaring the importance of
the book to its author and its token of his love – all the more
curious because of Browning's habitual reticence :

> Love, you saw me gather men and women,
> Live or dead or fashioned by my fancy,
> Enter each and all, and use their service,
> Speak from every mouth, – the speech, a poem.
> Hardly shall I tell my joys and sorrows,
> Hopes and fears, belief and disbelieving :
> I am mine and yours – the rest be all men's,
> Karshish, Cleon, Norbert and the fifty.
> Let me speak this once in my true person,

Not as Lippo, Roland or Andrea,
Though the fruit of speech be just this sentence :
Pray you, look on these my men and women,
Take and keep my fifty poems finished;
Where my heart lies, let my brain lie also !

Not only was this a public announcement of the book's value, as
the author saw it; but he had been at great pains to make
it more acceptable to the readers of poetry. In 1853 he wrote to
his French champion, Joseph Milsand, to say that he was
writing '– a first step towards popularity for me – lyrics with
more music and painting than before, so as to get people to
hear and see'.[11] The failure of the book, therefore, was a bitter
disappointment to Browning. The reviewer in *The Saturday
Review* described it as 'another book of madness and mysticism';
no doubt remembering 'Porphyria's Lover' and 'Johannes
Agricola in Meditation', he had, in all abusive intention, touched
on two of Browning's favourite themes. Unfortunately the perception was lost in the general disparagement : it was, according
to *The Saturday Review*, 'another specimen of power wantonly
wasted, and talent deliberately perverted – another act of self-
prostration before that demon of bad taste who now seems to
hold in absolute possession the fashionable masters of our ideal
literature'. Quoting from 'Master Hugues of Saxe-Gotha', the
reviewer commented :

Do our readers exclaim, 'But where's poetry – the dickens ! – in all
this rigmarole?' We confess we can find none – we can find nothing
but a set purpose to be obscure, and an idiot captivity to the jingle
of Hudibrastic rhyme. This idle weakness really appears to be at the
bottom of half the daring nonsense in this most daringly nonsensical book . . . why should a man who, with so little apparent labour,
can write naturally and well, take so much apparent labour to write
affectedly and ill?[12]

The Athenaeum ('Who will not grieve over energy wasted and
power misspent'[13]) agreed, and so did *Fraser's*. In the latter,
Browning was cruelly contrasted with Tennyson, who was thought
to have made his poems as perfect as he could, while Browning,

it was implied, did his work in the way that gave him least
trouble; and while Tennyson supplied the great Victorian public
with beauty, Browning belonged to a perverse literary clique :

And as for fame, or its counterfeit, popularity, there are silly people
enough in English society, who look on this carelessness as the fitting
and only garb of genius; who, if a poet will but be slovenly, will
applaud his graceful audacity, and if obscure, will worship his pro-
fundity. And thus laziness and vanity – the two most fatal forms of
selfishness – do their worst, and the cliques are in admiration at one
of the saddest sights under God's sky, when the light that came
from heaven burns murkier and murkier in a poet's soul; . . .[14]

No doubt *Men and Women* was condemned, in part, because it
was not for the lazy, as George Eliot saw. 'These poems', she
wrote, quoting Heinsius, 'have a "majestic obscurity", which
repels not only the ignorant but the idle.'[15] Mrs Oliphant, for
instance, decided feebly that 'only very few of his *Men and
Women* is it possible to make out'.[16] But there seems also to have
been a real measure of agreement that Browning had not given
enough consideration to making his poems regular and beautiful,
and that the striking moments were obscured by 'barnacle words,
and long trails of entangled sea weed sentences'.[17] Even George
Eliot, who could not possibly be accused of being either ignorant
or idle, discovered a 'garb of whimsical mannerism' in Browning's
work; and Clough, whose own originality might have made him
sympathetic, thought that he was 'dashing at anything and
insisting that it would do'.[18] The true comparison here is not
with Turner but with Constable, whose pictures were often considered by his contemporaries to be rough and unfinished, and
whose success, like Browning's, came only after his wife's death.
Indeed Browning, like Constable, could have used Dr Johnson's
words about his later fame : 'it has been delayed until I am
solitary, and cannot impart it.'[19]

The bitterness of Browning's disappointment can be seen in
the letters he wrote at the time concerning the critics' 'zoological
utterances' : ' "Whoo-oo-oo-oo" mouths the big monkey –
"Whee-ee-ee-ee" squeaks the little monkey.'[20] Yet he was probably more fortunate than it appeared. Ten years later, Swinburne

was to seize the hearts of the young and rebellious; in 1855 Browning was just in time to become the chief poet for those to whom the literary establishment meant little or nothing : William Allingham, D. G. Rossetti (who converted Ruskin) and William Morris, who asked angrily : 'I wonder what the critics would have said to *Hamlet, Prince of Denmark*, if it had been first published by Messrs. Chapman and Hall in the year 1855.'[21] The comparison was a good one, for *Hamlet* is a play which is particularly subject to the same kind of charge of artistic irregularity that was aimed at Browning, as readers of T. S. Eliot will know. Besides this irregularity, which was usually ascribed to laziness or carelessness, there were two other charges which the advocates of Browning's excellence had to answer : one was his apparent disregard of the need to shape and organise his material into a whole that held meaning and instruction; the other was his apparent lack of the elevation which was expected of the finest poetry.

The first of these is found in the review in *Fraser's* by G. Brimley, which has already been referred to. Brimley noted, correctly, Browning's delight in the multifarious forms of human activity, and went on :

To fill his mind with the elements of dramas, to enter by sympathy into the lives, characters and conduct of others, has plainly been the business of his life. What we complain of him for is, that he has been satisfied with this; that the stir, and business, and passion of the scene has been all he cared for; that what it all meant has seldom seemed to occur to him as worth asking.[22]

After *Men and Women*, Browning's poetry certainly became more philosophical and didactic. Whether because of this, or because it came to be thought that there was significance to be extracted from the welter of human activity, Brimley's criticism died away, until it was revived in a more sophisticated form by George Santayana. With the founding of the Browning Society in 1881, and the publication of Mrs Sutherland Orr's *A Handbook to the Works of Robert Browning* (a work which had the poet's approval and help) in 1886, Browning began to be valued chiefly for his 'wisdom'. This development reached its most influential moment with Sir Henry Jones's *Browning as a Philosophical and Religious Teacher* (1891), which saw art as implicit philosophy and celebrated Carlyle and Browning as 'the prophets of our age'. To some extent all subsequent Browning criticism has been struggling to escape from the idea of his poetry which was put forward in this influential book – not only by querying the belief that Browning was an optimist, but also by trying to restore the fine relationship between meaning and expression, and asserting the fundamental inseparability of form and content; for one of the drawbacks of both Jones and Mrs Sutherland Orr is that they treat Browning as if he were a writer of rather exceptional prose.

The charge that Browning was closer to being a prose writer than a poet was related to the charge of laziness. To many of his earlier readers it seemed that he had not taken the trouble, as Tennyson had, to acquire that noble beauty, and elevation of spirit which seemed necessary for the finest poetry. George Eliot, for instance, thought that Browning had 'a footing between the level of prose and the topmost heights of poetry',[23] and Gilbert, in Oscar Wilde's dialogue 'The Critic as Artist', declared that Browning would be remembered 'as a writer of fiction, as the most supreme writer of fiction, it may be, that we have ever had . . . He used poetry as a medium for writing in prose'.[24] Such a criticism, in the great age of the novel, is tribute enough : but it misses the point that was seen so well by Chesterton, who energetically responded to Browning's individuality, and thought that the question was 'whether in any other style except Browning's you could have achieved the precise artistic effect'. Chesterton delighted in Browning's idiosyncrasies : nature to Browning, he thought, meant the odd, the grotesque, the Behemoth-like world. He noted 'a kind of demented ingenuity', presenting Browning in a near-paradox which might have pleased the poet himself, as 'a particularly perfect artist in the use of the grotesque'.[25]

Chesterton's exhilarating admiration for Browning, however agreeable to read, does not fully answer a critic such as George Santayana, whose essay, 'The Poetry of Barbarism' (1900), linked Browning with Whitman as an example of a poet whose multitudinous world was too actual and pressing to allow a 'clarification of ideas and disentanglement of values'. Browning 'threw himself too unreservedly into his creations', and this is evidence of 'some profound incapacity in the poet'.[26] No doubt this criticism was valuable as a reaction against Sir Henry Jones; but it is not easy to see why Santayana's conception of Browning's work as a barbaric muddle has been so often described as 'devastating',[27] for it is little more than G. Brimley again, in rather more detail and with a more refined critical vocabulary. Nevertheless, Chesterton's robust 'I like it' is more helpful only in the sense that it is concerned to point out the individual splendours of the poetry. At this stage in the history of Browning criticism, opinions fall sharply into 'liking' and 'disliking'; as two American scholars have written, 'disinterestedness is lacking'. In their view, this was because Browning was still 'a living force, a power not to be ignored'. Since then, they observe, Browning criticism has become more professional and academic, and at the same time his reputation has declined: 'From being a comfort to his century, a stay against confusion, he has become an irritant to ours.'[28]

This last sentence seems to me to be disputable. Certainly between the two world wars there was little significant Browning criticism, apart from W. C. DeVane's masterly *Handbook* (which is informative rather than critical) and his work on the 'Parleyings'; in England, particularly, F. R. Leavis's dismissal of Browning in *New Bearings in English Poetry* crossed him off the list of considerable poets for thirty years. Leavis's summation once more concerned Browning's relationship to his age. His poetry 'belongs to the world he lives in, and he lives happily in the Victorian world with no sense of disharmony . . . so inferior a mind and spirit as Browning's could not provide the impulse needed to bring back into poetry the adult intelligence'.[29] The Browning who appears here sounds curiously like the public Browning, the cheerful diner-out whose ordinariness so puzzled Henry James; in this Browning may have been consistently deceptive, his courage and self-discipline concealing a spirit which ached with longing and uncertainty. His poetry is certainly deceptive, and it is easy to take the high spirits of Browning's inventiveness – both in subject matter and technique – for the poetical centre of his work; and to charge Browning with not being adult is to ignore the probing, questioning mind, and his knowledge of

>   the pain
> Of finite hearts that yearn.
>   ('Two in the Campagna')

It is necessary to see the 'ideas' in Browning's work, and the exploration of the world through character or situation, as attempts to find a way through a dark universe which is, at best, incomplete, imperfect and unknowable; and which is, at worst, represented by the landscape of ' "Childe Roland to the Dark Tower Came" ' :

> Now blotches rankling, coloured gay and grim,
> Now patches where some leanness of the soil's
> Broke into moss or substances like boils;
> Then came some palsied oak, a cleft in him
> Like a distorted mouth that splits its rim
> Gaping at death, and dies while it recoils. (xxvi)

It is the exploration of the hitherto ignored subtleties of Browning's poetry, seen in relation to his questionings and difficulties, that has given Browning studies such an impetus during the last twenty years. E. D. H. Johnson, for instance, has considered Browning in relation to his age, arguing that he was often at odds with it and preferred to trust his intuitive and individual apprehension rather than the received ideas of the time. Johnson's distinction between intuition and rationalism is reminiscent of Sir Henry Jones's between head and heart; but Johnson relates it to the age with a developed historical sense and a sophisticated critical apparatus. Thus Browning's ideas of love, which Jones rightly sees as central to his 'philosophy', are seen by Johnson in their unorthodox position relative to the age. Another approach, by Robert Langbaum, has greatly deepened our understanding of the dramatic monologue, and indeed of all romantic and post-romantic poetry; Browning is one of the chief beneficiaries of this understanding, and Langbaum has carefully shown the subtle and complex ways in which a poem like 'My Last Duchess' works. An essay which brilliantly combines an acute observation of Browning's technique with his fundamental interpretation of existence is that by J. Hillis Miller. Miller is fascinated by what he sees as Browning's 'indeterminacy of selfhood', and he relates this to the poet's use of language, with its extraordinary tumbling flow of verbal effects, catching the movement and pulse of energy and excitement. Further still in the discovery of the new existentialist Browning is Patricia M. Ball, who makes a stimulating comparison between Browning and Samuel Beckett. Where previous critics have seen God, she sees Godot. Significantly, her work is related not only to Miller's but also to Langbaum's when she argues that the 'message' of 'Abt Vogler' or 'Karshish' is not primarily a Christian one, but is concerned with 'a man undergoing his own special kind of revelation, the experience which exposes him to himself by the shock of its unfamiliarity and its demand that he assimilate it into his universe, whether he accepts it or not'.[30] Thus the poetry of what she calls 'the sustained query' is also the poetry of experience, and form and meaning are indissolubly joined. All of this new critical exploration has given Browning a remarkable place among Victorian poets: 'He is', says Philip Drew, 'our man in the nineteenth century.'[31]

It is possible to think of other candidates for this dubious honour: Clough in particular, and perhaps Arnold. But Drew's description, particularly when compared with the earlier opinion that Browning was a comfort to his own age but an irritant to ours, indicates how far the pendulum has swung. We are in the process of discovering a new poet: the old one seems to have been pulling the wool over our eyes for a long time, with his attractive Renaissance figures, his ebullient technique, and the tenderness of his lyrics; but we now recognise the way in which the brave outside concealed something more doubting, sensitive and mature. Two features of his poetry in particular have prevented him from being seriously considered as an adult intelligence. The first is the Byronic energy (one remembers Goethe's remark about Byron, quoted by Arnold, that 'the moment he reflects, he is a child') which is responsible for much of the immediate delight and force of his poems. It is a force which comes from two things : firstly, his use of language, that amazing word-spinning so brilliantly described by Swinburne in his phrase about Browning's 'spider-like swiftness and sagacity', with its 'building spirit' which 'leaps and lightens to and fro and backward and forward as it lives along the animated line of its labour'.[32] J. Hillis Miller has described it as 'heavy language' :

Grotesque metaphors, ugly words heavy with consonants, stuttering alliteration, strong active verbs, breathless rhythms, onomatopoeia, images of rank smells, rough textures, and of things fleshy, viscous, sticky, nubbly, slimy, shaggy, sharp, crawling, thorny, or prickly – all these work together in Browning's verse to create an effect of unparalleled thickness, harshness, and roughness.[33]

One might add to this Browning's use of heavy punctuation, with its high density of exclamation marks and question marks :

Already how am I so far
    Out of that minute? Must I go
Still like the thistle-ball, no bar,
    Onward, whenever light winds blow,
Fixed by no friendly star?

Just when I seemed about to learn !
    Where is the thread now? Off again !
The old trick ! Only I discern –
    Infinite passion, and the pain
Of finite hearts that yearn.
                                        ('Two in the Campagna')

This makes the moments of stillness and repose all the more effective :

So, earth has gained by one man the more,
    And the gain of earth must be heaven's gain too;
And the whole is well worth thinking o'er
    When autumn comes : which I mean to do
One day, as I said before.
                                        ('By the Fire-Side')

But Browning's language is not just 'heavy'; often its force comes from a sparkle and lightness:

> Not that I expect the great Bigordi,
>   Nor Sandro to hear me, chivalric, bellicose;
> Nor the wronged Lippino; and not a word I
>   Say of a scrap of Fra Angelico's:
> But are you too fine, Taddeo Gaddi,
>   To grant me a taste of your intonaco,
> Saint Jerome that seeks the heaven with a sad eye?
>   Not a churlish saint, Lorenzo Monaco?
>
> ('Old Pictures in Florence')

In different ways the variety and energy of Browning's language provides a surface which is liable to dominate the reader's impressions of the poem. But secondly, the fine vigour of his verse depends on his use of situation. In this (to borrow a phrase from Richard Hoggart, who used it of Graham Greene) Browning's poetry frequently has 'the force of caricature'. Naturally Browning chooses striking and significant moments for his dramatic monologues; what is not so obvious is his use of extreme characters and situations. The duke in 'My Last Duchess' is not just a tyrannical husband, but an appalling monster; the monk in the Spanish cloister is not just irritated, but violently spiteful and angry; the bishop, ordering his tomb, is not moderately sensual and worldly, but exceptionally and outrageously so. In 'The Statue and the Bust' the duke and the lady meet, and it is love at first sight:

> He looked at her, as a lover can;
> She looked at him, as one who awakes:
> The past was a sleep, and her life began.

The husband's reaction is extreme:

> Calmly he said that her lot was cast,
> That the door she had passed was shut on her
> Till the final catafalque repassed.

In this poem the element of melodrama is obscured by the

inaction which follows; but much of the force, here as elsewhere, is due to the violence of the passions which are denied.

Together with the force and vigour of its surface, the other great feature which has held back an understanding of Browning's poetry is its robust refusal to be 'poetical' and imaginative by withdrawing from the circumstances of human life. It was this which the refined perceptions of Gerard Manley Hopkins did not like;[34] it can be seen in a letter which Browning wrote about Rossetti's *Poems*:

Yes, I have read Rossetti's Poems, and poetical they are – *scented* with poetry, as it were, like trifles of various sorts you take out of a cedar or sandal-wood box. You know I hate the *effeminacy* of his school; the men that dress up like women; . . . Then, how I hate 'Love', as a lubberly naked young man putting his arms here and his wings there, about a pair of lovers; a fellow they would like to kick away in the reality.[35]

Browning's own work prefers, as this letter implies, to remain vigorously rooted 'in the reality', in common human experience: lovers meet, and grow old, or visit an old church, or sit by the fire; wives are unfaithful, husbands tyrannical; men lie dying, or talk to night-watchmen, or gallop horses. Only rarely do his characters move in an imaginative and symbolist landscape, as Childe Roland does; the others are emphatically men and women in society, representative, sinful, unpoetical men and women. Browning's fascination with their human behaviour, however unpleasant and unheroic, is another reason why his poetry has seemed, for so long, to be less subtle and imaginative than in fact it is. A poem like 'Up at a Villa – Down in the City' is a good example of the kind of poetic experience which it can offer:

Ere you open your eyes in the city, the blessed church-bells
   begin :
No sooner the bells leave off than the diligence rattles in;
You get the pick of the news, and it costs you never a pin.

No one would claim that this was one of Browning's more pro-found poems, though it is certainly original: not only does it reverse the usual town–country preference, but it also deals with the unusual (for Victorian poetry) subject of money :

> But bless you, it's dear – it's dear! fowls, wine, at double the rate.
> They have clapped a new tax upon salt, and what oil pays
> passing the gate
> It's a horror to think of. And so, the villa for me, not the city !
> Beggars can scarcely be choosers : but still – ah, the pity, the
> pity !

In its unpretentious interest in the trivial details of human life, there is an imagination at work which is quite different from the kind of poetic imagination represented by Rossetti. Browning has an extraordinary ability to enter into the feelings of this 'Italian Person of Quality', with his almost childish delight in the procession, and its drum and fife ('No keeping one's haunches still : it's the greatest pleasure in life'). This is the imagination of humanity, seen at its finest, perhaps, in 'Andrea del Sarto'; yet even in 'Up at a Villa – Down in the City', with the decayed hedonist struggling to make ends meet and longing for a little excitement, Browning is able to show heartache and boredom and human longing. Like many of Browning's greatest poems, it penetrates the deepest part of human experience in an unspectacular way : to use a phrase that the Brownings were fond of, 'the lamp is trimmed behind the wall',[36] and in life, as in poetry, the effort goes on unseen.

It is out of this concern for everyday experience, the pressing multiplicity of detail so disliked by Santayana, that the essential insights of Browning's poems emerge : not through the grand statement, but through the trivial incident, the brief moment. And, in the end, what we know is often what we do not know : we see the misery of unhappy marriages, but no reason why; we experience the worldliness and greed, without understanding its cause; we behold human nature in all its bewildering variety, but are given no prescriptive interpretation of it. We can carve out for ourselves, as Lippi does, a certain brief truth – but this is only a personal insight, with no guarantee of its permanent or universal truth. The world has beauty, captured in music and painting, and love, experienced by human beings; it also has

squalor, hatred and confusion. Thus Browning's poetry seems
chameleon-like, because he is aware of all sides and seems to have
no fixity : yet, even if the centre of his world is Godot and not
God, he is determined to live life well. Unsure of the ultimate
answers, he places himself in a Camus-like stance of rebellion
against the unmeaning universe; and before Sartre, he knew the
importance of the self-defining action :

> How the world is made for each of us !
>   How all we perceive and know in it
> Tends to some moment's product thus,
>   When a soul declares itself – to wit,
> By its fruit, the thing it does !
>   ('By the Fire-Side')

And in a world of 'broken arcs' where the ultimate laws are not
clear, Browning held to his own lesser lights which may seem to
us relevant and authentic : the keeping of promises, the hiding
of disappointment, the enjoyment of happiness, the delight in
other human beings; and, above all, the importance and tenderness of human love.

J. R. WATSON

NOTES

1. W. C. DeVane, *A Browning Handbook,* 2nd ed. (New York,
1955) p. 96.
2. See below, p. 51.
3. Boyd Litzinger and Donald Smalley (eds), *Browning: the
Critical Heritage* (London, 1970) p. 84.
4. Elvan Kintner (ed.), *The Letters of Robert Browning and
Elizabeth Barrett Barrett* (Cambridge, Mass., 1969) I, 18–19.
5. See below, p. 58.
6. *Critical Heritage,* pp. 104–10.
7. Ibid. p. 108.
8. Kintner, *Letters of R.B. and E.B.B.,* I, 244.
9. *Critical Heritage,* p. 128.
10. Ibid. pp. 146–8.

11. DeVane, *Handbook*, p. 187.
12. *Critical Heritage*, pp. 158–60.
13. Ibid. p. 155.
14. Ibid. p. 166.
15. See below, p. 53.
16. *Critical Heritage*, p. 188.
17. Ibid. p. 189.
18. Ibid. preface, p. 16.
19. C. R. Leslie, *Memoirs of the Life of John Constable*, ed. J. Mayne (London, 1951) p. 171.
20. *Critical Heritage*, preface, p. 14.
21. Ibid. p. 196.
22. Ibid. pp. 167–8.
23. See below, p. 56.
24. From *Intentions* (1891). Reprinted in *The Critic as Artist, Critical Writings of Oscar Wilde*, ed. Richard Ellman (London, 1970) p. 346.
25. See below, p. 91.
26. Philip Drew (ed.), *Robert Browning, A Collection of Critical Essays* (London, 1966) pp. 19, 21, 31.
27. See Philip Drew, *The Poetry of Browning* (London, 1970) p. 396.
28. Boyd Litzinger and K. L. Knickerbocker (eds), *The Browning Critics* (Lexington, Kentucky, 1965) pp. ix–xi.
29. F. R. Leavis, *New Bearings in English Poetry* (1932), new ed. (London, 1950) pp. 19–20.
30. See below, p. 179.
31. Drew, *The Poetry of Browning*, p. 432.
32. See below, p. 62.
33. See below, p. 163.
34. See below, pp. 66–7.
35. W. C. DeVane, 'The Harlot and the Thoughtful Young Man', in *The Browning Critics*, p. 165.
36. Kintner, *Letters of R.B. and E.B.B.*, I, 21.

BROWNING'S POEMS AS ORIGINALLY PUBLISHED

The following is a list of Browning's poems, as they were originally published in the three collections from 1842 to 1855. The titles are printed in their later forms:

Dramatic Lyrics (1842)

Marching Along
Give a Rouse
Boot and Saddle
My Last Duchess
Count Gismond
Incident of the French Camp
Soliloquy of the Spanish Cloister
In a Gondola
Artemis Prologuizes

Waring
Rudel to the Lady of Tripoli
Christina
Johannes Agricola in
  Meditation
Porphyria's Lover
Through the Metidja to
  Abd-el-Kadr – 1842
The Pied Piper of Hamelin

Dramatic Romances and Lyrics (1845)

How They Brought the Good
  News from Ghent to Aix (16—)
Pictor Ignotus
The Italian in England
The Englishman in Italy
The Lost Leader
The Lost Mistress
Home Thoughts from Abroad
The Bishop Orders his Tomb
  at St Praxed's Church

The Flower's Name
Sibrandus Schafnaburgensis
The Laboratory
The Confessional
The Flight of the Duchess
Earth's Immortalities
Song ('Nay but you, who do not
  love her')
The Boy and the Angel
Meeting at Night

Parting at Morning   Time's Revenges
Nationality in Drinks   The Glove
Saul (first nine sections)

Men and Women (1855)

Volume I

Love among the Ruins
A Lover's Quarrel
Evelyn Hope
Up at a Villa – Down in the City
A Woman's Last Word
Fra Lippo Lippi
A Toccata of Galuppi's
By the Fire-Side
Any Wife to Any Husband
An Epistle Containing the
  Strange Medical Experience of
  Karshish, the Arab Physician
Mesmerism
A Serenade at the Villa
My Star

Instans Tyrannus
A Pretty Woman
'Childe Roland to the Dark
  Tower Came'
Respectability
A Light Woman
The Statue and the Bust
Love in a Life
Life in a Love
How it Strikes a Contemporary
The Last Ride Together
The Patriot
Master Hugues of Saxe-Gotha
Bishop Blougram's Apology
Memorabilia

Volume II

Andrea del Sarto
Before
After
In Three Days
In a Year
Old Pictures in Florence
In a Balcony
Saul
'De Gustibus'
Women and Roses
Protus
Holy-Cross Day

The Guardian-Angel
Cleon
The Twins
Popularity
The Heretic's Tragedy
Two in the Campagna
A Grammarian's Funeral
One Way of Love
Another Way of Love
'Transcendentalism'
Misconceptions
One Word More. To E.B.B.

PART ONE

Two Sources

Giorgio Vasari[1]

FROM 'THE FLORENTINE PAINTER, FRA FILIPPO LIPPI' (1550)

The Carmelite monk, Fra Filippo di Tommaso Lippi, was born
at Florence in a bye street called Ardiglione, under the Canto
alla Cuculia, and behind the convent of the Carmelites. By the
death of his father he was left a friendless orphan at the age of
two years, his mother having also died shortly after his birth. The
child was for some time under the care of a certain Mona
Lapaccia, his aunt, the sister of his father, who brought him up
with very great difficulty till he had attained his eighth year,
when, being no longer able to support the burden of his main-
tenance, she placed him in the above-named convent of the Carmelites. Here, in proportion as he showed himself dexterous and
ingenious in all works performed by hand, did he manifest the
utmost dulness and incapacity in letters, to which he would never
apply himself, nor would he take any pleasure in learning of any
kind. The boy continued to be called by his worldly name of
Filippo, and being placed with others, who like himself were in
the house of the novices, under the care of the master, to the
end that the latter might see what could be done with him; in
place of studying, he never did any thing but daub his own
books, and those of the other boys, with caricatures, whereupon
the prior determined to give him all means and every opportunity
for learning to draw. The Chapel of the Carmine had then been
newly painted by Masaccio, and this being exceedingly beautiful,
pleased Fra Filippo greatly, wherefore he frequented it daily for
his recreation, and, continually practising there, in company
with many other youths, who were constantly drawing in that
place, he surpassed all the others by very much in dexterity and
knowledge; insomuch that he was considered certain to accom-

plish some marvellous thing in the course of time. For not only in his youth, but when almost in his childhood, he performed so many praiseworthy labours, that it was truly wonderful. While still very young he painted a picture in *terra verde*, in the cloister, near Masaccio's painting of the Consecration; the subject of which was a Pope confirming the Rule of the Carmelites, with others in fresco on several of the walls in different parts of the church : among these was a figure of St. John the Baptist, with stories from the life of that saint. Proceeding thus, and improving from day to day, he had so closely followed the manner of Masaccio, and his works displayed so much similarity to those of the latter, that many affirmed the spirit of Masaccio to have entered the body of Fra Filippo. On one of the pillars of the church, near the organ, he depicted the figure of San Marziale, a work by which he acquired great fame, seeing that it was judged to bear a comparison with those executed by Masaccio. Whereupon, hearing himself so highly commended by all, he formed his resolution at the age of seventeen, and boldly threw off the clerical habit.

Some time after this event, and being in the march of Ancona, Filippo was one day amusing himself with certain of his friends in a boat on the sea, when they were all taken by a Moorish galley which was cruising in that neighbourhood, and led captives into Barbary, where he remained, suffering many tribulations, for eighteen months. But, having frequent opportunities of seeing his master, it came into his head one day to draw his portrait; and finding an opportunity, he took a piece of charcoal from the fire, and with that delineated his figure at full length on a white wall, robed in his Moorish vestments. This being related to the master by the other slaves, to all of whom it appeared a miracle, the arts of drawing and painting not being practised in that country, the circumstance caused his liberation from the chains in which he had so long been held. And truly that was greatly to the glory of that noble art; for here was a man to whom belonged the right of condemning and punishing, but who, in place of inflicting pains and death, does the direct contrary, and is even led to show friendship, and restore the captive to liberty. Having afterwards executed certain works in painting for his master, he was then conducted safely to Naples, where he painted a picture on panel for king Alfonso, then Duke of Calabria, which was placed in the chapel of the castle, where the guard-room now is. But after no long time he conceived a wish to return to Florence, where he remained some months, during which time he painted an altar-piece for the nuns of Sant' Ambrogio, a most beautiful picture, by means of which he became known to Cosimo de' Medici, who was thereby rendered his most assured friend. He likewise executed a painting in the chapter-house of Santa Croce, with a second, which was placed in the chapel of the Medici Palace, and on which he depicted the Nativity of Christ. Fra Filippo likewise painted a picture for the wife of the above-named Cosimo, the subject of which is also a Nativity of Christ, with a figure of St. John the Baptist; this work was intended for one of the cells in the hermitage of Camaldoli which she had caused to be constructed as a mark of devotion, and had dedicated to St. John the Baptist. Other pictures by the same master, containing stories in small figures, were sent as a gift to Pope Eugenius IV, who was a Venetian, by Cosimo de' Medici, and these works caused Fra Filippo to be in great favour with that pontiff.

It is said that Fra Filippo was much addicted to the pleasures of sense, insomuch that he would give all he possessed to secure the gratification of whatever inclination might at the moment be predominant; but if he could by no means accomplish his wishes, he would then depict the object which had attracted his attention, in his paintings, and endeavour by discoursing and reasoning with himself to diminish the violence of his inclination. It was known that, while occupied in the pursuit of his pleasures, the works undertaken by him received little or none of his attention; for which reason Cosimo de' Medici, wishing him to execute a work in his own palace, shut him up, that he might not waste his time in running about; but having endured this confinement for two days, he then made ropes with the sheets of his bed, which he cut to pieces for that purpose, and so having let himself down from a window, escaped, and for several days gave himself up to his amusements. When Cosimo found that the painter had disappeared, he caused him to be sought, and Fra Filippo at last returned to his work, but from that time forward Cosimo gave him liberty to go in and out at his pleasure, repenting greatly of having previously shut him up, when he considered the danger that Fra Filippo had incurred by his folly in descending from the window; and ever afterwards, labouring to keep him to his work by kindness only, he was by this means much more promptly and effectually served by the painter, and was wont to say that the excellencies of rare genius were as forms of light and not beasts of burden.

For the church of Santa Maria Primerana, on the piazza of Fiesole, Fra Filippo painted a picture, wherein he depicted Our Lady receiving the Annunciation from the angel. This work exhibits extraordinary care, and there is so much beauty in the figure of the angel, that it appears to be indeed a celestial messenger. This master executed two pictures for the nuns of the Murate; one, an Annunciation, is placed on the high altar; the other, presenting stories from the lives of San Benedetto and San Bernardo, is on another altar of the same church. In the palace of the Signoria Fra Filippo likewise painted a picture of the Annunciation, which is over a door; with another representing San Bernardo, placed over another door in the same palace. In the sacristy of Santo Spirito, in Florence, is a painting by this master, representing the Virgin surrounded by angels, and with saints on either hand, a work of rare excellence, which has ever been held in the highest esteem by men versed in our arts. In the church of San Lorenzo, Fra Filippo executed a picture, also representing the Annunciation, which is in the chapel of the Superintendents of Works, with a second for the Della Stufa Chapel, which is not finished. For Sant' Apostolo, in the same city, he painted a picture in panel for one of the chapels; it presents the Virgin surrounded by different figures. And in Arezzo he executed one for Messer Carlo Marsuppini, to be placed in the chapel of San Bernardo, belonging to the monks of Monte Oliveto, wherein he depicted the Coronation of the Virgin, surrounded by numerous saints. This work has maintained itself in so remarkable a degree of freshness, that one might suppose it to have but just left the hands of the master. With respect to this picture, the latter was exhorted by Carlo Marsuppini to give particular attention to the hands, his painting of which, in many of his works, had been much complained of; whereupon Fra Filippo, wishing to avoid such blame for the future, ever afterwards sought to conceal the hands of his figures, either by the draperies or by some other contrivance. In the painting we are now describing, the master has given the portrait of Messer Carlo Marsuppini from the life.

In Florence, Fra Filippo painted the picture of a *Presepio*, for the nuns of Annalena, and some of his works are also to be seen in Padua. He sent two stories in small figures to Rome for Cardinal Barbo; they were admirably executed, and finished with extraordinary care. This master certainly displayed most wonderful grace in his works, blending his colours with the most perfect harmony, qualities for which he has ever been held in the highest esteem among artists, and for which he is extolled by modern masters with unlimited commendation; nay, there can be no doubt, that so long as his admirable labours can be preserved from the voracity of time, his name will be held in veneration by all coming ages. In Prato, near Florence, where Fra Filippo had some relations, he took up his abode for some months, and there executed various works for the whole surrounding district, in company with the Carmelite, Fra Diamante, who had been his companion in noviciate. Having then received a commission from the nuns of Santa Margherita, to paint a picture for the high altar of their church, he one day chanced to see the daughter of Francesco Buti, a citizen of Florence, who had been sent to the Convent, either as a novice or boarder. Fra Filippo, having given a glance at Lucrezia, for such was the name of the girl, who was exceedingly beautiful and graceful, so persuaded the nuns, that he prevailed on them to permit him to make a likeness of her, for the figure of the Virgin in the work he was executing for them. The result of this was, that the painter fell violently in love with Lucrezia, and at length found means to influence her in such a manner, that he led her away from the nuns, and on a certain day, when she had gone forth to do honour to the Cintola of our Lady, a venerated relic preserved at Prato and exhibited on that occasion, he bore her from their keeping. By this event the nuns were deeply disgraced, and the father of

Lucrezia was so grievously afflicted thereat, that he never more
recovered his cheerfulness, and made every possible effort to
regain his child. But Lucrezia, whether retained by fear or by
some other cause, would not return, but remained with Filippo,
to whom she bore a son, who was also called Filippo, and who
eventually became a most excellent and very famous painter like
his father.

In the church of San Domenico, in this same Prato, are two
pictures by this master, and in the transept of the church of
San Francesco is another, a figure of the Virgin namely. Desiring
to remove this work from its original place, the superintendents,
to save it from injury, had the wall on which it was depicted cut
away, and having secured and bound it with wood-work, thus
transported it to another wall of the church, where it is still to
be seen. Over a well, in the court-yard of the Ceppo of Francesco
di Marco, there is a small picture on panel by this master,
representing the portrait of the above-named Francesco di
Marco, the author and founder of that pious establishment. In
the Capitular Church of Prato, on a small tablet which is over
the side door as one ascends the steps, Fra Filippo depicted the
death of San Bernardo, by the touch of whose bier many lame
persons are restored to health. In this work are monks bewailing
the loss of their master; and the exquisite grace of their heads,
the truth and beauty with which their grief, and the plaintive
expression of their weeping, are conveyed to the spectator, is a
thing marvellous to behold. Some of the hoods and draperies of
these monks have most beautiful folds, and the whole work
merits the utmost praise for the excellence of its design, composition, and colouring, as well as for the grace and harmony of
proportion displayed in it, completed as it is by the most delicate
hand of Filippo. He was also appointed by the wardens of the
same church, who desired to retain a memorial of him, to paint
the chapel of the High Altar, and here we have likewise good
evidence of his power, for besides the excellence of the picture
as a whole, there are certain heads and draperies in it which are
most admirable. In this work Fra Filippo made the figures larger
than life, and hereby instructed later artists in the mode of giving
true grandeur to large figures. There are likewise certain figures

clothed in vestments but little used at that time, whereby the minds of others were awakened, and artists began to depart from that sameness which should rather be called obsolete monotony than antique simplicity. In the same work are stories from the life of Santo Stefano, to whom the church is dedicated; they cover the wall on the right side, and consist of the Disputation, the Stoning and the Death of the Protomartyr. In the first of these, where St. Stephen is disputing with the Jews, the countenance of the saint exhibits so much zeal and fervour, that it is difficult even to imagine; how much more then to give it expression : while, in the faces and attitudes of these Jews, their hatred and rage, with the anger they feel at finding themselves vanquished by the saint, are equally manifest. Still more forcibly has he depicted the brutal rage of those who slew the martyr with stones, which they grasp, some large, others smaller ones, with grinding teeth, horrible to behold, and with gestures of demoniac rage and cruelty. St. Stephen, calm and steadfast in the midst of their terrible violence, is seen with his face towards heaven, imploring the pardon of the Eternal Father for those who thus attack him, with the utmost piety and fervour. This variety of expression is certainly very fine, and is well calculated to teach students of art the value of imitative power, and the importance of being able to express clearly the affections and emotions of the characters represented. Fra Filippo devoted the most earnest attention to this point, as is seen in this work; he has given the disciples who are burying St. Stephen attitudes so full of dejection, and faces so deeply afflicted, so drowned in tears, that it is scarcely possible to look at them without feeling a sense of sorrow. On the other side of the chapel is the History of St. John the Baptist, his Birth, that is to say, his Preaching in the Wilderness, his Baptism, the Feast of Herod, and the Decapitation of the Saint. In the picture of the Preaching, the Divine Spirit inspiring the speaker is most clearly manifest in his face, while the different emotions of hope, anxiety, gladness, and sorrow, of the crowd, women as well as men, who are listening around him, charmed and mastered by the force of his words, are equally well expressed. In the Baptism are beauty and goodness exemplified, and in the Feast of Herod, the splendour of the banquet, the address of

Herodias, the astonishment of the guests, and their inexpressible sorrow when the head is presented on the charger, are rendered with admirable truth and effect. Among those present at the banquet are numerous figures in fine attitudes, exhibiting beautiful draperies and exquisite expressions of countenance. A portrait of Fra Filippo himself, taken with his own hand by help of a mirror, is one of them, and among the persons who bewail the death of St. Stephen, is the portrait of his disciple Fra Diamante, in a figure robed in black, and bearing the vestments of a bishop. This work is indeed the best of all that he produced, as well for the many fine qualities displayed in it, as for the circumstance, that having made the figures somewhat larger than life, he encouraged those who came after him to enlarge their manner. Fra Filippo was indeed so highly estimated for his great gifts, that many circumstances in his life which were very blameable received pardon, and were partly placed out of view, in consideration of his extraordinary abilities.

SOURCE: *Lives of the Most Eminent Painters, Sculptors, and Architects*, translated by Mrs Jonathan Foster (London, 1851) II, 73–82.

NOTE

1. Giorgio Vasari was a Florentine painter (1511–74), pupil of Andrea del Sarto, and historian of Italian Renaissance art. His *Lives of the Most Eminent Painters, Sculptors, and Architects* was first published in 1550 and enlarged in 1568. [Editor.]

Giorgio Vasari

FROM 'THE MOST EXCELLENT FLORENTINE PAINTER, ANDREA DEL SARTO' (1550)

At length then we have come, after having written the lives of many artists who have been distinguished, some for colouring, some for design, and some for invention; we have come, I say, to that of the truly excellent Andrea del Sarto, in whom art and nature combined to show all that may be done in painting, when design, colouring, and invention unite in one and the same person. Had this master possessed a somewhat bolder and more elevated mind, had he been as much distinguished for higher qualifications as he was for genius and depth of judgment in the art he practised, he would beyond all doubt, have been without an equal. But there was a certain timidity of mind, a sort of diffidence and want of force in his nature, which rendered it impossible that those evidences of ardour and animation, which are proper to the more exalted character, should ever appear in him; nor did he at any time display one particle of that elevation which, could it but have been added to the advantages wherewith he was endowed, would have rendered him a truly divine painter: wherefore the works of Andrea are wanting in those ornaments of grandeur, richness, and force, which appear so conspicuously in those of many other masters. His figures are nevertheless well drawn, they are entirely free from errors, and perfect in all their proportions, and are for the most part simple and chaste: the expression of his heads is natural and graceful in women and children, while in youths and old men it is full of life and animation. The draperies of this master are beautiful to a marvel, and the nude figures are admirably executed, the drawing is simple, the colouring is most exquisite, nay, it is truly divine. . . .

These various labours secured so great a name for Andrea in his native city, that among the many artists, old and young, who were then painting, he was accounted one of the best that handled pencil and colours. Our artist then found himself to be not only honoured and admired, but also in a condition, notwithstanding the really mean price that he accepted for his labours, which permitted him to render assistance to his family, while he still remained unoppressed for his own part, by those cares and anxieties which beset those who are compelled to live in poverty.

At that time there was a most beautiful girl in the Via di San Gallo, who was married to a capmaker, and who, though born of a poor and vicious father, carried about her as much pride and haughtiness as beauty and fascination. She delighted in trapping the hearts of men, and among others ensnared the unlucky Andrea, whose immoderate love for her soon caused him to neglect the studies demanded by his art, and in great measure to discontinue the assistance which he had given to his parents.

Now it chanced that a sudden and grievous illness seized the husband of this woman, who rose no more from his bed, but died thereof. Without taking counsel of his friends therefore; without regard to the dignity of his art or the consideration due to his genius, and to the eminence he had attained with so much labour; without a word, in short, to any of his kindred, Andrea took this Lucrezia di Baccio del Fede, such was the name of the woman, to be his wife; her beauty appearing to him to merit thus much at his hands, and his love for her having more influence over him than the glory and honour towards which he had begun to make such hopeful advances. But when this news became known in Florence, the respect and affection which his friends had previously borne to Andrea changed to contempt and disgust, since it appeared to them that the darkness of this disgrace had obscured for a time all the glory and renown obtained by his talents.

But he destroyed his own peace as well as estranged his friends by this act, seeing that he soon became jealous, and found that he had besides fallen into the hands of an artful woman, who made him do as she pleased in all things. He abandoned his own poor father and mother, for example, and adopted the father and sisters of his wife in their stead; insomuch that all who knew the facts, mourned over him, and he soon began to be as much avoided as he had previously been sought after. His disciples still remained with him, it is true, in the hope of learning something useful, yet there was not one of them, great or small, who was not maltreated by his wife, both by evil words and despiteful actions: none could escape her blows, but although Andrea lived in the midst of all that torment, he yet accounted it a high pleasure. . . .

Andrea now began to feel, not that the beauties of his wife had become wearisome, but that the mode of his life was an oppression to him; his error had become in part apparent to his perceptions; he saw that he could never lift himself from the earth; though perpetually toiling, he did so to no purpose. He had the father and all the sisters of his wife devouring every thing he gained, and though well-accustomed to that burthen, he could not be insensible to the weight thereof, and he finally became tired of the life he was leading. Knowing this, some friend, who still loved him, though more perhaps as an artist than as a man, advised him to change his dwelling, leaving his wife in some more secure abode for a time, that so he might at a future period receive her again, when they might live in a manner more creditable to him. He had hardly been brought to a conviction of his error, and to the persuasion that something should be done towards the discovery of a remedy, when such an occasion for re-instating himself was presented to him as he had never had before, since the time when he had taken a wife. The two pictures, which he had sent into France, were obtaining much admiration from King Francis, and among the many others which had been despatched to him from Rome, Venice, and Lombardy, these had been adjudged to be by far the best. That monarch therefore, praising them very highly, was told that he might easily prevail on Andrea to visit France, when he might enter the service of His Majesty; this proposal was exceedingly agreeable to the king, who therefore gave orders that everything needful should be done for that purpose, and that a sum of money for the expenses of the journey, should be paid to Andrea in Florence. The latter gladly set forth on his way to France accordingly, taking with him his scholar Andrea Sguazzella.

Having in due time arrived at the French court, they were received by the monarch very amicably and with many favours, even the first day of his arrival was marked to Andrea by proofs of that magnanimous sovereign's liberality and courtesy, since he at once received not only a present of money, but the added gift of very rich and honourable vestments. He soon afterwards commenced his labours, rendering himself so acceptable to the king as well as to the whole court, and receiving so many proofs of good-will from all, that his departure from his native country soon appeared to our artist to have conducted him from the extreme of wretchedness to the summit of felicity. One of Andrea's first works in France was the portrait of the Dauphin, the son of the king, a child born but a few months previously, and still in his swathing bands; wherefore, having taken this painting to the king, he received in return three hundred ducats of gold.

Continuing his labours, he afterwards painted a figure of Charity for King Francis, this was considered an exceedingly beautiful picture, and was held by that monarch in all the estimation due to so admirable a work. From that time the king commanded that a very considerable income should be annually paid to Andrea, doing his utmost to induce the painter to remain contentedly at his court, and promising that he should never want for anything that he could desire; and this happened because the promptitude of Andrea in his works, and the easy character of the man, who was satisfied with everything around him, were both agreeable to King Francis; he gave very great satisfaction to the whole court also, painting numerous pictures and executing various works of different kinds for the nobles.

And now, had Andrea del Sarto only reflected on all that he had escaped from, and duly weighed the advantageous character of that position to which fate had conducted him, I make no doubt but that, to say nothing of riches, he might have attained to great honours. But one day being employed on the figure of a St. Jerome doing penance, which he was painting for the mother of the king, he received a letter, after having had many others, from Lucrezia his wife, whom he had left disconsolate for his

departure, although she wanted for nothing. Andrea had even
ordered a house to be built for them behind the Nunziata, giving
her hopes that he might return at any moment; yet as she could
not give her money to her kindred connexions, as she had previously done, she wrote with bitter complaints to Andrea, declaring that she never ceased to weep, and was in perpetual
affliction at his absence; dressing all this up with sweet words,
well calculated to move the heart of the luckless man, who loved
her but too well, she drove the poor soul half out of his wits; above
all, when he read her assurance that if he did not return speedily,
he would certainly find her dead. Moved by all this, he resolved
to resume his chain, and preferred a life of wretchedness with
her to the ease around him, and to all the glory which his art
must have secured to him. He was then too so richly provided
with handsome vestments by the liberality of the king and his
nobles, and found himself so magnificently arrayed that every hour
seemed a thousand years to him, until he could go to show himself in his bravery to his beautiful wife. Taking the money which
the king confided to him for the purchase of pictures, statues,
and other fine things, he set off therefore, having first sworn on
the gospels to return in a few months. Arrived happily in
Florence, he lived joyously with his wife for some time, making
large presents to her father and sisters, but doing nothing for his
own parents, whom he would not even see, and who at the end
of a certain period, ended their lives in great poverty and misery.
But when the period specified by the king, and that at which he
ought to have returned, had come and passed, he found himself at the end, not only of his own money, but what with building,
indulging himself in various pleasures and doing no work, of that
belonging to the French monarch also, the whole of which he
had consumed. He was nevertheless determined to return to
France, but the prayers and tears of his wife had more power
than his own necessities, or the faith which he had pledged to the
king : he remained therefore in Florence, and the French
monarch was so greatly angered thereby, that for a long time
after he would not look at the paintings of Florentine masters,
and declared that if Andrea ever fell into his hands he would
have no regard to the distinction of his endowments, but would

do him more harm than he had before done him good. Andrea del Sarto remained in Florence therefore, as we have said, and from a highly eminent position he sank to the very lowest, procuring a livelihood and passing his time as he best might. . . .

We conclude, then, with the opinion, that if Andrea displayed no great elevation of mind in the actions of his life, and contented himself with little, yet, it is not to be denied, that he manifested considerable elevation of genius in his art, or that he gave proof of infinite promptitude and ability in every kind of labour connected therewith; nor will any refuse to admit, that his works form a rich ornament to every place wherein they are found; nay, more, it is most certain that he conferred great benefits on his contemporaries in art, by the examples he left them in manner, design, and colouring; his works exhibiting fewer errors than those of any other Florentine; seeing that Andrea, as I have said before, understood the management of light and shade most perfectly, causing the objects depicted to take their due degree of prominence, or to retire within the shadows, with infinite ability, and painting his pictures with the utmost grace and animation. He likewise taught the method of working in fresco with perfect harmony, and without much retouching *a secco*, which causes all his pictures in that manner to appear as if they were executed in a day; wherefore this master may serve as an example to the Tuscan artists on all occasions. He is entitled to the highest praise among the most eminent of their number, and well merits to receive the palm of honour.

SOURCE: *Lives of the Most Eminent Painters, Sculptors, and Architects*, translated by Mrs Jonathan Foster (London, 1851) III, 180–1, 193–4, 204–7, 235–6.

PART TWO

Some Victorian Assessments

John Stuart Mill

A NOTE ON *PAULINE* (1833)

With considerable poetic powers, the writer seems to me possessed with a more intense and morbid self-consciousness than I
ever knew in any sane human being. I should think it a sincere
confession, though of a most unlovable state, if the 'Pauline' were
not evidently a mere phantom. All about her is full of inconsistency – he neither loves her nor fancies he loves her, yet insists
upon *talking* love to her. If she *existed* and loved him, he treats
her most ungenerously and unfeelingly. All his aspirings and
yearnings and regrets point to other things, never to her; then he
pays her off toward the end by a piece of flummery, amounting
to the modest request that she will love him and live with him
and give herself up to him *without* his *loving her – moyennant
quoi* he will think her and call her everything that is handsome,
and he promises her that she shall find it mighty pleasant. Then
he leaves off by saying he knows he shall have changed his mind
by tomorrow, and despite 'these intents which seem so fair', but
that having been thus visited once no doubt he will be again –
and is therefore 'in perfect joy', bad luck to him! as the Irish
say. A cento of most beautiful passages might be made from this
poem, and the psychological history of himself is powerful and
truthful – *truth-like* certainly, all but the last stage. *That*, he
evidently has not yet got into. The self-seeking and self-wor-
shipping state is well described – beyond that, I should think the
writer had made, as yet, only the next step, viz. into despising
his own state. I even question whether part even of that self-
disdain is not *assumed*. He is evidently *dissatisfied*, and feels part
of the badness of his state; he does not write as if it were purged
out of him. If he once could muster a hearty hatred of his selfishness it would *go*; as it is, he feels only the *lack* of *good*, not the

positive evil. He feels not remorse, but only disappointment; a mind in that state can only be regenerated by some new passion, and I know not what to wish for him but that he may meet with a *real* Pauline.

Meanwhile he should not attempt to show how a person may be *recovered* from this morbid state – for *he* is hardly convalescent, and 'what should we speak of but that which we know?'

SOURCE : John Forster's copy of *Pauline*, now in the Victoria and Albert Museum, London.

George Eliot

MEN AND WOMEN (1856)

We never read Heinsius – a great admission for a reviewer – but we learn from M. Arago that that formidably erudite writer pronounces Aristotle's works to be characterized by a *majestic obscurity which repels the ignorant*. We borrow these words to indicate what is likely to be the first impression of a reader who, without any previous familiarity with Browning, glances through his two new volumes of poems. The less acute he is, the more easily will he arrive at the undeniable criticism, that these poems have a 'majestic obscurity', which repels not only the ignorant but the idle. To read poems is often a substitute for thought : finesounding conventional phrases and the sing-song of verse demand no co-operation in the reader; they glide over his mind with the agreeable unmeaningness of 'the compliments of the season', or a speaker's exordium on 'feelings too deep for expression'. But let him expect no such drowsy passivity in reading Browning. Here he will find no conventionality, no melodious commonplace, but freshness, originality, sometimes eccentricity of expression; no didactic laying-out of a subject, but dramatic indication, which requires the reader to trace by his own mental activity the underground stream of thought that jets out in elliptical and pithy verse. To read Browning he must exert himself, but he will exert himself to some purpose. If he finds the meaning difficult of access, it is always worth his effort – if he has to dive deep, 'he rises with his pearl'. Indeed, in Browning's best poems he makes us feel that what we took for obscurity in him was superficiality in ourselves. We are far from meaning that all his obscurity is like the obscurity of the stars, dependent simply on the feebleness of men's vision. On the contrary, our admiration for his genius only makes us feel the more acutely that its inspirations are too often straitened by the garb of whimsical mannerism with which he clothes them. This mannerism is even irritating sometimes, and should at least be kept under restraint in *printed* poems, where the writer is not merely indulging his own vein, but is avowedly appealing to the mind of his reader.

Turning from the ordinary literature of the day to such a writer as Browning, is like turning from Flotow's music, made up of well-pieced shreds and patches, to the distinct individuality of Chopin's Studies or Schubert's Songs. Here, at least, is a man who has something of his own to tell us, and who can tell it impressively, if not with faultless art. There is nothing sickly or dreamy in him : he has a clear eye, a vigorous grasp, and courage to utter what he sees and handles. His robust energy is informed by a subtle, penetrating spirit, and this blending of opposite qualities gives his mind a rough piquancy that reminds one of a russet apple. His keen glance pierces into all the secrets of human character, but, being as thoroughly alive to the outward as to the inward, he reveals those secrets, not by a process of dissection, but by dramatic painting. We fancy his own description of a poet applies to himself :

> He stood and watched the cobbler at his trade,
> The man who slices lemons into drink,
> The coffee-roaster's brazier, and the boys
> That volunteer to help him at the winch.
> He glanced o'er books on stalls with half an eye,
> And fly-leaf ballads on the vendor's string,
> And broad-edge bold-print posters by the wall.
> *He took such cognizance of men and things,*
> *If any beat a horse, you felt he saw;*
> *If any cursed a woman, he took note;*
> *Yet stared at nobody, – they stared at him,*
> *And found, less to their pleasure than surprise,*
> *He seemed to know them and expect as much.*

Browning has no soothing strains, no chants, no lullabys; he rarely gives voice to our melancholy, still less to our gaiety; he sets our thoughts at work rather than our emotions. But though eminently a thinker, he is as far as possible from prosaic; his mode of presentation is always concrete, artistic, and where it is most felicitous, dramatic. Take, for example, 'Fra Lippo Lippi', a poem at once original and perfect in its kind. The artist-monk, Fra Lippo, is supposed to be detected by the night-watch roaming the streets of Florence, and while sharing the wine with which he makes amends to the Dogberrys for the roughness of his tongue, he pours forth the story of his life and his art with the racy conversational vigour of a brawny genius under the influence of the Care-dispeller. . . .

Extracts cannot do justice to the fine dramatic touches by which Fra Lippo is made present to us, while he throws out this instinctive Art-criticism. And extracts from 'Bishop Blougram's Apology', an equally remarkable poem of what we may call the dramatic-psychological kind, would be still more ineffective. 'Sylvester Blougram, styled *in partibus Episcopus*', is talking

> Over the glass's edge when dinner's done,
> And body gets its sop and holds its noise
> And leaves soul free a little,

with 'Gigadibs the literary man', to whom he is bent on proving by the most exasperatingly ingenious sophistry, that the theory of life on which he grounds his choice of being a bishop, though a doubting one is wiser in the moderation of its ideal, with the certainty of attainment, than the Gigadibs theory, which aspires after the highest and attains nothing. The way in which Blougram's motives are dug up from below the roots, and laid bare to the very last fibre, not by a process of hostile exposure, not by invective or sarcasm, but by making himself exhibit them with a self-complacent sense of supreme acuteness, and even with a crushing force of worldly common sense, has the effect of masterly satire. But the poem is too strictly consecutive for any fragments of it to be a fair specimen. Belonging to the same order of subtle yet vigorous writing are the 'Epistle of Karshish, the Arab Physician', 'Cleon', and 'How it Strikes a Contemporary'. 'In a Balcony', is so fine, that we regret it is not a complete drama instead of being merely the suggestion of a drama. One passage especially tempts us to extract.

All women love great men
If young or old – it is in all the tales –
Young beauties love old poets who can love –
Why should not he the poems in my soul,
The love, the passionate faith, the sacrifice,
The constancy? I throw them at his feet.
Who cares to see the fountain's very shape
And whether it be a Triton's or a Nymph's
That pours the foam, makes rainbows all around?
You could not praise indeed the empty conch;
But I'll pour floods of love and hide myself.

These lines are less rugged than is usual with Browning's blank verse; but generally, the greatest deficiency we feel in his poetry is its want of music. The worst poems in his new volumes are, in our opinion, his lyrical efforts; for in these, where he engrosses us less by his thought, we are more sensible of his obscurity and his want of melody. His lyrics, instead of tripping along with easy grace, or rolling with a torrent-like grandeur, seem to be struggling painfully under a burthen too heavy for them; and many of them have the disagreeable puzzling effect of a charade, rather than the touching or animating influence of song. We have said that he is never prosaic; and it is remarkable that in his blank verse, though it is often colloquial, we are never shocked by the sense of a sudden lapse into prose. Wordsworth is, on the whole, a far more musical poet than Browning, yet we remember no line in Browning so prosaic as many of Wordsworth's, which in some of his finest poems have the effect of bricks built into a rock. But we must also say that though Browning never flounders helplessly on the plain, he rarely soars above a certain tableland – a footing between the level of prose and the topmost heights of poetry. He does not take possession of our souls and set them aglow, as the greatest poets – the greatest artists do. We admire his power, we are not subdued by it. Language with him does not seem spontaneously to link itself into song, as sounds link themselves into melody in the mind of the creative musician; he rather seems by his commanding powers to compel language into verse. He has *chosen* verse as his medium; but of our greatest poets we feel that they had no choice : Verse chose them. Still we are grateful that Browning chose this medium : we would rather have 'Fra Lippo Lippi' than an essay on Realism in Art; we would rather have 'The Statue and the Bust' than a three-volumed novel with the same moral; we would rather have 'Holy-Cross Day' than 'Strictures on the Society for the Emancipation of the Jews'.

SOURCE : *Westminster Review* (January 1856) pp. 290–6.

John Ruskin

BROWNING AND THE RENAISSANCE
IN ITALY (1856)

Robert Browning is unerring in every sentence he writes of the Middle Ages: always vital, right, and profound; so that in the matter of art, with which we have been specially concerned, there is hardly a principle connected with the mediæval temper, that he has not struck upon in those seemingly careless and too rugged rhymes of his. There is a curious instance, by the way, in a short poem referring to this very subject of tomb and image sculpture; and illustrating just one of those phases of local human character which, though belonging to Shakespere's own age, he never noticed, because it was specially Italian and un-English; connected also closely with the influence of mountains on the heart, and therefore with our immediate inquiries. I mean the kind of admiration with which a southern artist regarded the *stone* he worked in; and the pride which populace or priest took in the possession of precious mountain substance, worked into the pavements of their cathedrals, and the shafts of their tombs.

Observe, Shakespere, in the midst of architecture and tombs of wood, or freestone, or brass, naturally thinks of *gold* as the best enriching and ennobling substance for them; – in the midst also of the fever of the Renaissance he writes, as every one else did, in praise of precisely the most vicious master of that school – Giulio Romano; but the modern poet, living much in Italy, and quit of the Renaissance influence, is able fully to enter into the Italian feeling, and to see the evil of the Renaissance tendency, not because he is greater than Shakespere, but because he is in another element, and has *seen* other things. I miss fragments here and there not needed for my purpose in the passage quoted,

without putting asterisks, for I weaken the poem enough by the
omissions, without spoiling it also by breaks.

'The Bishop Orders his Tomb in St. Praxed's Church'

As here I lie
In this state chamber, dying by degrees,
Hours, and long hours, in the dead night, I ask
Do I live – am I dead? Peace, peace seems all :
St. Praxed's ever was the church for peace.
And so, about this tomb of mine. I fought
With tooth and nail to save my niche, ye know;
Old Gandolf cozened me, despite my care.
Shrewd was that snatch from out the corner south
He graced his carrion with.
Yet still my niche is not so cramped but thence
One sees the pulpit o' the epistle-side,
And somewhat of the choir, those silent seats :
And up into the aery dome where live
The angels, and a sunbeam's sure to lurk.
And I shall fill my slab of basalt there,
And 'neath my tabernacle take my rest,
With those nine columns round me, two and two,
The odd one at my feet, where Anselm stands;
Peach-blossom marble all.
Swift as a weaver's shuttle fleet our years :
Man goeth to the grave, and where is he?
Did I say basalt for my slab, sons? Black –
'Twas ever antique-black I meant ! How else
Shall ye contrast my frieze to come beneath?
The bas-relief in bronze ye promised me,
Those Pans and Nymphs ye wot of, and perchance
Some tripod, thyrsus, with a vase or so,
The Saviour at His sermon on the mount,
St. Praxed in a glory, and one Pan,
And Moses with the tables . . . but I know
Ye marked me not ! What do they whisper thee,
Child of my bowels, Anselm? Ah, ye hope
To revel down my villas while I gasp,
Bricked o'er with beggar's mouldy travertine,
Which Gandolf from his tomb-top chuckles at !
Nay boys, ye love me – all of jasper, then !

There's plenty jasper somewhere in the world –
And have I not St. Praxed's ear to pray
Horses for ye, and brown Greek manuscripts?
That's if ye carve my epitaph aright,
Choice Latin, picked phrase, Tully's every word,
No gaudy ware like Gandolf's second line –
Tully, my masters? Ulpian serves *his* need.

I know no other piece of modern English, prose or poetry, in
which there is so much told, as in these lines, of the Renaissance
spirit, – its worldliness, inconsistency, pride, hypocrisy, ignorance
of itself, love of art, of luxury, and of good Latin. It is nearly
all that I said of the central Renaissance in thirty pages of the
Stones of Venice put into as many lines, Browning's being also
the antecedent work. The worst of it is that this kind of concentrated writing needs so much *solution* before the reader can fairly
get the good of it, that people's patience fails them, and they give
the thing up as insoluble; though, truly, it ought to be to the
current of common thought like Saladin's talisman, dipped in
clear water, not soluble altogether, but making the element
medicinal.

SOURCE : *Modern Painters*, vol. IV, in *The Works of John
Ruskin*, ed. E. T. Cook and Alexander Wedderburn (London,
1904) VI, 446–9.

A. C. Swinburne

BROWNING'S CLARITY (1875)

The charge of obscurity is perhaps of all charges the likeliest to impair the fame or to imperil the success of a rising or an established poet. It is often misapplied by hasty or ignorant criticism as any other on the roll of accusations; and was never misapplied more persistently and perversely than to an eminent writer of our own time. The difficulty found by many in certain of Mr. Browning's works arises from a quality the very reverse of that which produces obscurity properly so called. Obscurity is the natural product of turbid forces and confused ideas; of a feeble and clouded or of a vigorous but unfixed and chaotic intellect. Such a poet as Lord Brooke, for example – and I take George Chapman and Fulke Greville to be of all English poets the two most genuinely obscure in style upon whose works I have ever adventured to embark in search of treasure hidden beneath the dark gulfs and crossing currents of their rocky and weedy waters, at some risk of my understanding being swept away by the ground-swell – such a poet, overcharged with overflowing thoughts, is not sufficiently possessed by any one leading idea, or attracted towards any one central point, to see with decision the proper end and use with resolution the proper instruments of his design.

Now if there is any great quality more perceptible than another in Mr. Browning's intellect it is his decisive and incisive faculty of thought, his sureness and intensity of perception, his rapid and trenchant resolution of aim. To charge him with obscurity is about as accurate as to call Lynceus purblind or complain of the sluggish action of the telegraphic wire. He is something too much the reverse of obscure; he is too brilliant and subtle for the ready reader of a ready writer to follow with any certainty the track of an intelligence which moves with such incessant rapidity, or even to realise with what spider-like swiftness and sagacity his building spirit leaps and lightens to and fro and backward and forward as it lives along the animated line of its labour, springs from thread to thread and darts from centre to circumference of the glittering and quivering web of living thought woven from the inexhaustible stores of his perception and kindled from the inexhaustible fire of his imaginatinon. He never thinks but at full speed; and the rate of his thought is to that of another man's as the speed of a railway to that of a wagon or the speed of a telegraph to that of a railway. It is hopeless to enjoy the charm or to apprehend the gist of his writings except with a mind thoroughly alert, an attention awake at all points, a spirit open and ready to be kindled by the contact of the writer's.

To do justice to any book which deserves any other sort of justice than that of the fire or the waste-paper basket, it is necessary to read it in the fit frame of mind; and the proper mood in which to study for the first time a book of Mr. Browning's is the freshest, clearest, most active mood of the mind in its brightest and keenest hours of work. Read at such a time, and not 'with half-shut eyes falling asleep in a half-dream', it will be found (in Chapman's phrase) 'pervial' enough to any but a sluggish or a sand-blind eye; but at no time and in no mood will a really obscure writer be found other than obscure. The difference between the two is the difference between smoke and lightning; and it is far more difficult to pitch the tone of your thought in harmony with that of a foggy thinker than with that of one whose thought is electric in its motion. To the latter we have but to come with an open and pliant spirit, untired and undisturbed by the work or the idleness of the day, and we cannot but receive a vivid and active pleasure in following the swift and fine radiations, the subtle play and keen vibration of its sleepless fires; and the more steadily we trace their course the more surely do we see that all these forked flashes of fancy and changing lights of thought move unerringly around one centre and strike straight in the end to one point. Only random thinking and random writing produce obscurity; and these are the radical faults of Chapman's style of poetry. We find no obscurity in the lightning, whether it play about the heights of metaphysical speculation or the depths of character and motive; the mind derives as much of vigorous enjoyment from the study by such light of the one as of the other. The action of so bright and swift a spirit gives insight as it were to the eyes and wings to the feet of our own; the reader's apprehension takes fire from the writer's, and he catches from a subtler and more active mind the infection of spiritual interest; so that any candid and clear-headed student finds himself able to follow for the time in fancy the lead of such a thinker with equal satisfaction on any course of thought or argument; when he sets himself to refute Renan through the dying lips of St. John or to try conclusions with Strauss in his own person, and when he flashes at once the whole force of his illumination full upon the inmost thought and mind of the most infamous criminal, a Guido Franceschini or a Louis Bonaparte, compelling the black and obscene abyss of such a spirit to yield up at last the secret of its profoundest sophistries, and let forth the serpent of a soul that lies coiled under all the most intricate and supple reasonings of self-justified and self-conscious crime. And thanks to this very quality of vivid spiritual illumination we are able to see by the light of the author's mind without being compelled to see with his eyes, or with the eyes of the living mask which he assumes for his momentary impersonation of saint or sophist, philosopher or malefactor; without accepting one conclusion, conceding one point, or condoning one crime.

It is evident that to produce any such effect requires above all things brightness and decision as well as subtlety and pliancy of genius; and this is the supreme gift and distinctive faculty of Mr. Browning's mind. If indeed there be ever any likelihood of error in his exquisite analysis, he will doubtless be found to err rather through excess of light than through any touch of darkness; we may doubt, not without a sense that the fittest mood of criticism might be that of a self-distrustful confidence in the deeper intuition of his finer and more perfect knowledge, whether the perception of good or evil would actually be so acute in the mind of the supposed reasoner; whether, for instance, a veritable household assassin, a veritable saviour of society or other incarnation of moral pestilence, would in effect see so clearly and so far, with whatever perversion or distortion of view, into the recesses of the pit of hell wherein he lives and moves and has his being; recognising with quick and delicate apprehension what points of vantage he must strive to gain, what outposts of self-defence he may hope to guard, in the explanation and vindication of the motive forces of his nature and the latent mainspring of his deeds. This fineness of intellect and dramatic sympathy which is ever on the watch to anticipate and answer the unspoken imputations and prepossessions of his hearer, the very movements of his mind, the very action of his instincts, is perhaps a quality hardly compatible with a nature which we might rather suppose, judging from public evidence and historic indication, to be sluggish and short-sighted, 'a sly slow thing with circumspective eye' that can see but a little way immediately around it, but neither before it nor behind, above it nor beneath; and whose introspection, if ever that eye were turned inward, would probably be turbid, vacillating, cloudy and uncertain as the action of a spirit incapable of self-knowledge but not incapable of self-distrust, timid and impenitent, abased and unabashed, remorseless but not resolute, shameless but not fearless.

If such be in reality the public traitor and murderer of a nation, we may fairly infer that his humbler but not viler counterpart in private life will be unlikely to exhibit a finer quality of mind or a clearer faculty of reason. But this is a question of realism which in no wise affects the spiritual value and interest of such work as Mr. Browning's. What is important for our present purpose is to observe that this work of exposition by soliloquy and apology by analysis can only be accomplished or undertaken by the genius of a great special pleader, able to fling himself with all his heart and all his brain, with all the force of his intellect and all the strength of his imagination, into the assumed part of his client; to concentrate on the cause in hand his whole power of illustration and illumination, and bring to bear upon one point at once all the rays of his thought in one focus. Apart from his gift of moral imagination, Mr. Browning has in the supreme degree the qualities of a great debater or an eminent leading counsel; his finest reasoning has in its expression and development something of the ardour of personal energy and active interest which inflames the argument of a public speaker; we feel, without the reverse regret of Pope, how many a first-rate barrister or parliamentary tactician has been lost in this poet.

SOURCE : from *George Chapman* (1875), in *The Complete Works of Algernon Charles Swinburne*, ed. Sir Edmund Gosse and T. J. Wise, *Prose Works*, II, 144–9.

Gerard Manley Hopkins

REMARKS ON BROWNING (1881)

But Browning has, I think, many frigidities. Any untruth to nature, to human nature, is frigid. Now he has got a great deal of what came in with Kingsley and the Broad Church school, a way of talking (and making his people talk) with the air and spirit of a man bouncing up from table with his mouth full of bread and cheese and saying that he meant to stand no blasted nonsense. There is a whole volume of Kingsley's essays which is all a kind of munch and a not standing of any blasted nonsense from cover to cover. Do you know what I mean? The 'Flight of the Duchess', with the repetition of 'My friend', is in this vein. Now this is *one* mood or vein of human nature, but they would have it all and look at all human nature through it. And Tennyson in his later works has been 'carried away with their dissimulation'.[1] The effect of this style is a frigid bluster. A true humanity of spirit, neither mawkish on the one hand nor blustering on the other, is the most precious of all qualities in style, and this I prize in your poems, as I do in Bridges'. After all it is the breadth of his human nature that we admire in Shakespeare.

I read some, not much, of *The Ring and the Book*, but as the tale was not edifying and one of our people, who had been reviewing it, said that further on it was coarser, I did not see, without a particular object, sufficient reason for going on with it. So far as I read I was greatly struck with the skill in which he displayed the facts from different points of view: this is masterly, and to do it through three volumes more shews a great body of genius. I remember a good case of 'the impotent collection of particulars' of which you speak in the description of the market place at Florence where he found the book of the trial: it is a pointless photograph of still life, such as I remember in Balzac, minute upholstery description; only that in Balzac, who besides is writing prose, all tells and is given with a reserve and simplicity of style which Browning has not got. Indeed I hold with the old-fashioned criticism that Browning is not really a poet, that he has all the gifts but the one needful and the pearls without the string; rather one should say raw nuggets and rough diamonds. I suppose him to resemble Ben Jonson, only that Ben Jonson has more real poetry.

SOURCE: from a letter to W. R. Dixon (12 October 1881), in *The Correspondence of Gerard Manley Hopkins and Richard Watson Dixon*, ed. C. C. Abbott (London, 1935) pp. 74–5.

NOTE

1. Galatians 2 : 13.

Henry James

BROWNING IN WESTMINSTER ABBEY
(1891)

The lovers of a great poet are the people in the world who are
most to be forgiven a little wanton fancy about him, for they have
before them, in his genius and work, an irresistible example of
the application of the imaginative method to a thousand subjects.
Certainly, therefore, there are many confirmed admirers of
Robert Browning to whom it will not have failed to occur that the
consignment of his ashes to the great temple of fame of the
English race was exactly one of those occasions in which his own
analytic spirit would have rejoiced, and his irrepressible faculty
for looking at human events in all sorts of slanting coloured lights
have found a signal opportunity. If he had been taken with it as
a subject, if it had moved him to the confused yet comprehensive
utterance of which he was the great professor, we can immediately guess at some of the sparks he would have scraped from it,
guess how splendidly, in the case, the pictorial sense would
have intertwined itself with the metaphysical. For such an occasion would have lacked, for the author of *The Ring and the Book*,
none of the complexity and convertibility that were dear to him.
Passion and ingenuity, irony and solemnity, the impressive and
the unexpected, would each have forced their way through; in a
word, the author would have been sure to take the special, cir-
cumstantial view (the inveterate mark of all his speculation)
even of so foregone a conclusion as that England should pay her
greatest honour to one of her greatest poets. As they stood in the
Abbey, at any rate, on Tuesday last, those of his admirers and
mourners who were disposed to profit by his warrant for in-
quiring curiously may well have let their fancy range, with its
muffled step, in the direction which *his* fancy would probably not
have shrunk from following, even perhaps to the dim corners

where humour and the whimsical lurk. Only, we hasten to add, it would have taken Robert Browning himself to render the multifold impression.

One part of it on such occasion is, of course, irresistible – the sense that these honours are the greatest that a generous nation has to confer and that the emotion that accompanies them is one of the high moments of a nation's life. The attitude of the public, of the multitude, at such hours, is a great expansion, a great openness to ideas of aspiration and achievement; the pride of possession and of bestowal, especially in the case of a career so complete as Mr. Browning's, is so present as to make regret a minor matter. We possess a great man most when we begin to look at him through the glass plate of death; and it is a simple truth, though containing an apparent contradiction, that the Abbey never takes us so benignantly as when we have a valued voice to commit to silence there. For the silence is articulate after all, and in worthy instances the preservation great. It is the other side of the question that would pull most the strings of irresponsible reflection – all those conceivable postulates and hypotheses of the poetic and satiric mind to which we owe the picture of how the bishop ordered his tomb in St. Praxed's. Macaulay's 'temple of silence and reconciliation' – and none the less perhaps because he himself is now a presence there – strikes us, as we stand in it, not only as local but as social – a sort of corporate company; so thick, under its high arches, its dim transepts and chapels, is the population of its historic names and figures. They are a company in possession, with a high standard of distinction, of immortality, as it were; for there is something serenely inexpugnable even in the position of the interlopers. As they look out, in the rich dusk, from the cold eyes of statues and the careful identity of tablets, they seem, with their converging faces, to scrutinise decorously the claims of each new recumbent glory, to ask each other how he is to be judged as an accession. How difficult to banish the idea that Robert Browning would have enjoyed prefiguring and playing with the mystifications, the reservations, even perhaps the slight buzz of scandal, in the Poets' Corner, to which his own obsequies might give rise! Would not his great relish, in so characteristic an interview with his crucible,

have been his perception of the bewildering modernness, to much
of the society, of the new candidate for a niche? That is the
interest and the fascination, from what may be termed the inside
point of view, of Mr. Browning's having received, in this direction
of becoming a classic, the only official assistance that is ever conferred upon English writers.

It is as classics on one ground and another – some
members of it perhaps on that of not being anything else –
that the numerous assembly in the Abbey holds together, and it is
as a tremendous and incomparable modern that the author of
Men and Women takes his place in it. He introduces to his prede-
cessors a kind of contemporary individualism which surely for
many a year they had not been reminded of with any such force.
The tradition of the poetic character as something high, detached
and simple, which may be assumed to have prevailed among
them for a good while, is one that Browning has broken at every
turn; so that we can imagine his new associates to stand about
him, till they have got used to him, with rather a sense of failing
measures. A good many oddities and a good many great writers
have been entombed in the Abbey; but none of the odd ones have
been so great and none of the great ones so odd. There are plenty
of poets whose right to the title may be contested, but there is no
poetic head of equal power – crowned and recrowned by almost
importunate hands – from which so many people would with-
hold the distinctive wreath. All this will give the marble phantoms
at the base of the great pillars and the definite personalities of
the honorary slabs something to puzzle out until, by the quick
operation of time, the mere fact of his lying there among the
classified and protected makes even Robert Browning lose a
portion of the bristling surface of his actuality.

For the rest, judging from the outside and with his contemporaries, we of the public can only feel that his very modernness –
by which we mean the all-touching, all-trying spirit of his work,
permeated with accumulations and playing with knowledge –
achieves a kind of conquest, or at least of extension, of the rigid
pale. We cannot enter here upon any account either of that or of
any other element of his genius, though surely no literary figure
of our day seems to sit more unconsciously for the painter. The

very imperfections of this original are fascinating, for they never present themselves as weaknesses; they are boldnesses and over-growths, rich roughnesses and humours, and the patient critic need not despair of digging to the primary soil from which so many disparities and contradictions spring. He may finally even put his finger on some explanation of the great mystery, the im-perfect conquest of the poetic form by a genius in which the poetic passion had such volume and range. He may successfully say how it was that a poet without a lyre – for that is practically Browning's deficiency : he had the scroll, but not often the sounding strings – was nevertheless, in his best hours, wonderfully rich in the magic of his art, a magnificent master of poetic emo-tion. He will justify on behalf of a multitude of devotees the great position assigned to a writer of verse of which the nature or the fortune has been (in proportion to its value and quantity) to be treated rarely as quotable. He will do all this and a great deal more besides; but we need not wait for it to feel that something of our latest sympathies, our latest and most restless selves, passed the other day into the high part – the show-part, to speak vul-garly – of our literature. To speak of Mr. Browning only as he was in the last twenty years of his life, how quick such an imagination as his would have been to recognise all the latent or mystical suitabilities that, in the last resort, might link to the great Valhalla by the Thames a figure that had become so conspicu-ously a figure of London! He had grown to be intimately and inveterately of the London world; he was so familiar and recur-rent, so responsive to all its solicitations, that, given the endless incarnations he stands for to-day, he would have been missed from the congregation of worthies whose memorials are the special pride of the Londoner. Just as his great sign to those who knew him was that he was a force of health, of temperament, of tone, so what he takes into the Abbey is an immense expression of life – of life rendered with large liberty and free experiment, with an unprejudiced intellectual eagerness to put himself in other people's place, to participate in complications and conse-quences; a restlessness of psychological research that might well alarm any pale company for their formal orthodoxies.

But the illustrious whom he rejoins may be reassured, as they

will not fail to discover : in so far as they are representative it will
clear itself up that, in spite of a surface unsuggestive of marble
and a reckless individualism of form, he is quite as representative
as any of them. For the great value of Browning is that at bottom,
in all the deep spiritual and human essentials, he is unmistakably
in the great tradition – is, with all his Italianisms and cosmopoli-
tanisms, all his victimisation by societies organised to talk about
him, a magnificent example of the best and least dilettantish
English spirit. That constitutes indeed the main chance for his
eventual critic, who will have to solve the refreshing problem of
how, if subtleties be not what the English spirit most delights in,
the author of, for instance, 'Any Wife to any Husband' made them
his perpetual pasture, and yet remained typically of his race. He
was indeed a wonderful mixture of the universal and the alem-
bicated. But he played with the curious and the special, they never
submerged him, and it was a sign of his robustness that he could
play to the end. His voice sounds loudest, and also clearest, for
the things that, as a race, we like best – the fascination of faith,
the acceptance of life, the respect for its mysteries, the endurance
of its charges, the vitality of the will, the validity of character,
the beauty of action, the seriousness, above all, of the great
human passion. If Browning had spoken for us in no other way,
he ought to have been made sure of, tamed and chained as a
classic, on account of the extraordinary beauty of his treatment
of the special relation between man and woman. It is a complete
and splendid picture of the matter, which somehow places it at
the same time in the region of conduct and responsibility. But
when we talk of Robert Browning's speaking 'for us' we go to the
end of our privilege, we say all. With a sense of security, perhaps
even a certain complacency, we leave our sophisticated modern
conscience, and perhaps even our heterogeneous modern vocabulary, in his charge among the illustrious. There will possibly
be moments in which these things will seem to us to have widened
the allowance, made the high abode more comfortable, for some
of those who are yet to enter it.

SOURCE : *The Speaker* (4 January 1891) pp. 11–12.

PART THREE

Twentieth-Century Views:
1. General Essays

G. K. Chesterton

BROWNING AS A LITERARY ARTIST
(1903)

Mr. William Sharp, in his *Life* of Browning, quotes the remarks of another critic to the following effect : 'The poet's processes of thought are scientific in their precision and analysis; the sudden conclusion that he imposes upon them is transcendental and inept.'

This is a very fair but a very curious example of the way in which Browning is treated. For what is the state of affairs? A man publishes a series of poems, vigorous, perplexing, and unique. The critics read them, and they decide that he has failed as a poet, but that he is a remarkable philosopher and logician. They then proceed to examine his philosophy, and show with great triumph that it is unphilosophical, and to examine his logic and show with great triumph that it is not logical, but 'transcendental and inept'. In other words, Browning is first denounced for being a logician and not a poet, and then denounced for insisting on being a poet when they have decided that he is to be a logician. It is just as if a man were to say first that a garden was so neglected that it was only fit for a boys' playground, and then complain of the unsuitability in a boys' playground of rockeries and flower-beds.

As we find, after this manner, that Browning does not act satisfactorily as that which we have decided that he shall be – a logician – it might possibly be worth while to make another attempt to see whether he may not, after all, be more valid than we thought as to what he himself professed to be – a poet. And if we study this seriously and sympathetically, we shall soon come to a conclusion. It is a gross and complete slander upon Browning to say that his processes of thought are scientific in their precision and analysis. They are nothing of the sort; if they were, Browning could not be a good poet. The critic speaks of the conclusions of a poem as 'transcendental and inept'; but the conclusions of a poem, if they are not transcendental, must be inept. Do the people who call one of Browning's poems scientific in its analysis realise the meaning of what they say? One is tempted to think that they know a scientific analysis when they see it as little as they know a good poem. The one supreme difference between the scientific method and the artistic method is, roughly speaking, simply this – that a scientific statement means the same thing wherever and whenever it is uttered, and that an artistic statement means something entirely different, according to the relation in which it stands to its surroundings. The remark, let us say, that the whale is a mammal, or the remark that sixteen ounces go to a pound, is equally true, and means exactly the same thing, whether we state it at the beginning of a conversation or at the end, whether we print it in a dictionary or chalk it up on a wall. But if we take some phrase commonly used in the art of literature – such a sentence, for the sake of example, as 'the dawn was breaking' – the matter is quite different. If the sentence came at the beginning of a short story, it might be a mere descriptive prelude. If it were the last sentence in a short story, it might be poignant with some peculiar irony or triumph. Can any one read Browning's great monologues and not feel that they are built up like a good short story, entirely on this principle of the value of language arising from its arrangement. Take such an example as 'Caliban upon Setebos', a wonderful poem designed to describe the way in which a primitive nature may at once be afraid of its gods and yet familiar with them. Caliban in describing his deity starts with a more or less natural and obvious parallel between the deity and himself, carries out the comparison with consistency and an almost revolting simplicity, and ends in a kind of blasphemous extravaganza of anthropomorphism, basing his conduct not merely on the greatness and wisdom, but also on the manifest weaknesses and stupidities, of the Creator of all things. Then suddenly a thunderstorm breaks over Caliban's island, and the profane speculator falls flat upon his face :

Lo! 'Lieth flat and loveth Setebos!
'Maketh his teeth meet through his upper lip,
Will let those quails fly, will not eat this month
One little mess of whelks, so he may 'scape!

Surely it would be very difficult to persuade oneself that this thunderstorm would have meant exactly the same thing if it had occurred at the beginning of 'Caliban upon Setebos'. It does not mean the same thing, but something very different; and the deduction from this is the curious fact that Browning is an artist, and that consequently his processes of thought are not 'scientific in their precision and analysis'.

No criticism of Browning's poems can be vital, none in the face of the poems themselves can be even intelligible, which is not based upon the fact that he was successfully or otherwise a conscious and deliberate artist. He may have failed as an artist, though I do not think so; that is quite a different matter. But it is one thing to say that a man through vanity or ignorance has built an ugly cathedral, and quite another to say that he built it in a fit of absence of mind, and did not know whether he was building a lighthouse or a first-class hotel. Browning knew perfectly well what he was doing; and if the reader does not like his art, at least the author did. The general sentiment expressed in the statement that he did not care about form is simply the most ridiculous criticism that could be conceived. It would be far nearer the truth to say that he cared more for form than any other English poet who ever lived. He was always weaving and modelling and inventing new forms. Among all his two hundred to three hundred poems it would scarcely be an exaggeration to say that there are half as many different metres as there are different poems.

The great English poets who are supposed to have cared more for form than Browning did, cared less at least in this sense – that they were content to use old forms so long as they were certain that they had new ideas. Browning, on the other hand, no sooner had a new idea than he tried to make a new form to express it. Wordsworth and Shelley were really original poets; their attitude of thought and feeling marked without doubt certain great changes in literature and philosophy. Nevertheless, the 'Ode on the Intimations of Immortality' is a perfectly normal and traditional ode, and *Prometheus Unbound* is a perfectly genuine and traditional Greek lyrical drama. But if we study Browning honestly, nothing will strike us more than that he really created a large number of quite novel and quite admirable artistic forms. It is too often forgotten what and how excellent these were. *The Ring and the Book*, for example, is an illuminating departure in literary method – the method of telling the same story several times and trusting to the variety of human character to turn it into several different and equally interesting stories. *Pippa Passes*, to take another example, is a new and most fruitful form, a series of detached dramas connected only by the presence of one fugitive and isolated figure. The invention of these things is not merely like the writing of a good poem – it is something like the invention of the sonnet or the Gothic arch. The poet who makes them does not merely create himself – he creates other poets. It is so in a degree long past enumeration with regard to Browning's smaller poems. Such a pious and horrible lyric as 'The Heretic's Tragedy', for instance, is absolutely original, with its weird and almost bloodcurdling echo verses, mocking echoes indeed –

> And clipt of his wings in Paris square,
>   They bring him now to be burned alive.
>   *And wanteth there grace of lute or clavicithern,*
>   *ye shall say to confirm him who singeth –*
>   We bring John now to be burned alive.

A hundred instances might, of course, be given. Milton's 'Sonnet on his Blindness', or Keats's 'Ode on a Grecian Urn', are both thoroughly original, but still we can point to other such sonnets and other such odes. But can any one mention any poem of exactly the same structural and literary type as 'Fears and Scruples', as 'The Householder', as 'House' or 'Shop', as 'Nationality in Drinks', as 'Sibrandus Schafnaburgensis', as 'My Star', as 'A Portrait', as any of 'Ferishtah's Fancies', as any of the 'Bad Dreams'.

The thing which ought to be said about Browning by those who do not enjoy him is simply that they do not like his form; that they have studied the form, and think it a bad form. If more people said things of this sort, the world of criticism would gain almost unspeakably in clarity and common honesty. Browning put himself before the world as a good poet. Let those who think he failed call him a bad poet, and there will be an end of the matter. There are many styles in art which perfectly competent æsthetic judges cannot endure. For instance, it would be perfectly legitimate for a strict lover of Gothic to say that one of the monstrous rococo altar-pieces in the Belgian churches with bulbous clouds and oaken sun-rays seven feet long, was, in his opinion, ugly. But surely it would be perfectly ridiculous for any one to say that it had no form. A man's actual feelings about it might be better expressed by saying that it had too much. To say that Browning was merely a thinker because you think 'Caliban upon Setebos' ugly, is precisely as absurd as it would be to call the author of the old Belgian altar-piece a man devoted only to the abstractions of religion. The truth about Browning is not that he was indifferent to technical beauty, but that he invented a particular kind of technical beauty to which any one else is free to be as indifferent as he chooses.

There is in this matter an extraordinary tendency to vague and unmeaning criticism. The usual way of criticising an author, particularly an author who has added something to the literary forms of the world, is to complain that his work does not contain something which is obviously the speciality of somebody else. The correct thing to say about Maeterlinck is that some play of his in which, let us say, a princess dies in a deserted tower by the sea, has a certain beauty, but that we look in vain in it for that robust geniality, that really boisterous will to live which may be found in *Martin Chuzzlewit*. The right thing to say about *Cyrano de Bergerac* is that it may have a certain kind of wit and spirit, but that it really throws no light on the duty of middle-aged married couples in Norway. It cannot be too much insisted upon that at least three-quarters of the blame and criticism commonly directed against artists and authors falls under this general objection, and is essentially valueless. Authors both great and small

are, like everything else in existence, upon the whole greatly
under-rated. They are blamed for not doing, not only what they
have failed to do to reach their own ideal, but what they have
never tried to do to reach every other writer's ideal. If we can
show that Browning had a definite ideal of beauty and loyally
pursued it, it is not necessary to prove that he could have written
In Memoriam if he had tried.

Browning has suffered far more injustice from his admirers
than from his opponents, for his admirers have for the most part
got hold of the matter, so to speak, by the wrong end. They
believe that what is ordinarily called the grotesque style of
Browning was a kind of necessity boldly adopted by a great genius
in order to express novel and profound ideas. But this is an entire
mistake. What is called ugliness was to Browning not in the least
a necessary evil, but a quite unnecessary luxury, which he enjoyed
for its own sake. For reasons that we shall see presently in discussing the philosophical use of the grotesque, it did so happen
that Browning's grotesque style was very suitable for the expression of his peculiar moral and metaphysical view. But the whole
mass of poems will be misunderstood if we do not realise first of
all that he had a love of the grotesque of the nature of art for
art's sake. Here, for example, is a short distinct poem merely
descriptive of one of those elfish German jugs in which it is to be
presumed Tokay had been served to him. This is the whole poem,
and a very good poem too :

Up jumped Tokay on our table,
Like a pigmy castle-warder,
Dwarfish to see, but stout and able,
Arms and accoutrements all in order;
And fierce he looked North, then, wheeling South
Blew with his bugle a challenge to Drouth,
Cocked his flap-hat with the tosspot-feather,
Twisted his thumb in his red moustache,
Jingled his huge brass spurs together,
Tightened his waist with Buda sash,
And then, with an impudence nought could abash,
Shrugged his hump-shoulder, to tell the beholder,
For twenty such knaves he would laugh but the bolder :

And so, with his sword-hilt gallantly jutting,
And dexter-hand on his haunch abutting,
Went the little man, Sir Ausbruch, strutting!

I suppose there are Browning students in existence who would think that this poem contained something pregnant about the Temperance question, or was a marvellously subtle analysis of the romantic movement in Germany. But surely to most of us it is sufficiently apparent that Browning was simply fashioning a ridiculous knick-knack, exactly as if he were actually moulding one of these preposterous German jugs. Now before studying the real character of this Browningesque style, there is one general truth to be recognised about Browning's work. It is this – that it is absolutely necessary to remember that Browning had, like every other poet, his simple and indisputable failures, and that it is one thing to speak of the badness of his artistic failures, and quite another thing to speak of the badness of his artistic aim. Browning's style may be a good style, and yet exhibit many examples of a thoroughly bad use of it. On this point there is indeed a singularly unfair system of judgment used by the public towards the poets. It is very little realised that the vast majority of great poets have written an enormous amount of very bad poetry. The unfortunate Wordsworth is generally supposed to be almost alone in this; but any one who thinks so can scarcely have read a certain number of the minor poems of Byron and Shelley and Tennyson.

Now it is only just to Browning that his more uncouth effusions should not be treated as masterpieces by which he must stand or fall, but treated simply as his failures. It is really true that such a line as 'Irks care the crop-full bird? Frets doubt the maw-crammed beast?' is a very ugly and a very bad line. But it is quite equally true that Tennyson's 'And that good man, the clergyman, has told me words of peace', is a very ugly and very bad line. But people do not say that this proves that Tennyson was a mere crabbed controversialist and metaphysician. They say that it is a bad example of Tennyson's form; they do not say that it is a good example of Tennyson's indifference to form. Upon the whole, Browning exhibits far fewer instances of this failure in his own

style than any other of the great poets, with the exception of one
or two like Spenser and Keats, who seem to have a mysterious
incapacity for writing bad poetry. But almost all original poets,
particularly poets who have invented an artistic style, are subject
to one most disastrous habit – the habit of writing imitations of
themselves. Every now and then in the works of the noblest
classical poets you will come upon passages which read like extracts from an American book of parodies. Swinburne, for
example, when he wrote the couplet

> From the lilies and languors of virtue
> To the raptures and roses of vice,

wrote what is nothing but a bad imitation of himself, an imitation
which seems indeed to have the wholly unjust and uncritical
object of proving that the Swinburnian melody is a mechanical
scheme of initial letters. Or again, Mr. Rudyard Kipling when he
wrote the line 'Or ride with the reckless seraphim on the rim of a
red-maned star', was caricaturing himself in the harshest and
least sympathetic spirit of American humour. This tendency is,
of course, the result of the self-consciousness and theatricality of
modern life in which each of us is forced to conceive ourselves as
part of a *dramatis personæ* and act perpetually in character.
Browning sometimes yielded to this temptation to be a great deal
too like himself.

> Will I widen thee out till thou turnest
> From Margaret Minnikin mou' by God's grace,
> To Muckle-mouth Meg in good earnest.

This sort of thing is not to be defended in Browning any more
than in Swinburne. But, on the other hand, it is not to be attributed in Swinburne to a momentary exaggeration, and in
Browning to a vital æsthetic deficiency. In the case of Swinburne,
we all feel that the question is not whether that particular preposterous couplet about lilies and roses redounds to the credit of
the Swinburnian style, but whether it would be possible in any
other style than the Swinburnian to have written the Hymn to

Proserpine. In the same way, the essential issue about Browning as an artist is not whether he, in common with Byron, Wordsworth, Shelley, Tennyson, and Swinburne, sometimes wrote bad poetry, but whether in any other style except Browning's you could have achieved the precise artistic effect which is achieved by such incomparable lyrics as 'The Patriot' or 'The Laboratory'. The answer must be in the negative, and in that answer lies the whole justification of Browning as an artist.

The question now arises, therefore, what was his conception of his functions as an artist? We have already agreed that his artistic originality concerned itself chiefly with the serious use of the grotesque. It becomes necessary, therefore, to ask what is the serious use of the grotesque, and what relation does the grotesque bear to the eternal and fundamental elements in life?

One of the most curious things to notice about popular æsthetic criticism is the number of phrases it will be found to use which are intended to express an æsthetic failure, and which express merely an æsthetic variety. Thus, for instance, the traveller will often hear the advice from local lovers of the picturesque, 'The scenery round such and such a place has no interest; it is quite flat.' To disparage scenery as quite flat is, of course, like disparaging a swan as quite white, or an Italian sky as quite blue. Flatness is a sublime quality in certain landscapes, just as rockiness is a sublime quality in others. In the same way there are a great number of phrases commonly used in order to disparage such writers as Browning which do not in fact disparage, but merely describe them. One of the most distinguished of Browning's biographers and critics says of him, for example, 'He has never meant to be rugged, but has become so in striving after strength.' To say that Browning never tried to be rugged is to say that Edgar Allan Poe never tried to be gloomy, or that Mr. W. S. Gilbert never tried to be extravagant. The whole issue depends upon whether we realise the simple and essential fact that ruggedness is a mode of art like gloominess or extravagance. Some poems ought to be rugged, just as some poems ought to be smooth. When we see a drift of stormy and fantastic clouds at sunset, we do not say that the cloud is beautiful although it is ragged at the edges. When we see a gnarled and sprawling oak, we do not say that it is fine although it is twisted. When we see a mountain, we do not say that it is impressive although it is rugged, nor do we say apologetically that it never meant to be rugged, but became so in its striving after strength. Now, to say that Browning's poems, artistically considered, are fine although they are rugged, is quite as absurd as to say that a rock, artistically considered, is fine although it is rugged. Ruggedness being an essential quality in the universe, there is that in man which responds to it as to the striking of any other chord of the eternal harmonies. As the children of nature, we are akin not only to the stars and flowers, but also to the toad-stools and the monstrous tropical birds. And it is to be repeated as the essential of the question that on this side of our nature we do emphatically love the form of the toad-stools, and not merely some complicated botanical and moral lessons which the philosopher may draw from them. For example, just as there is such a thing as a poetical metre being beautifully light or beautifully grave and haunting, so there is such a thing as a poetical metre being beautifully rugged. In the old ballads, for instance, every person of literary taste will be struck by a certain attractiveness in the bold, varying, irregular verse :

> He is either himsell a devil frae hell,
> Or else his mother a witch maun be;
> I wadna have ridden that wan water
> For a' the gowd in Christentie,

is quite as pleasing to the ear in its own way as

> There's a bower of roses by Bendemeer stream,
> And the nightingale sings in it all the night long,

is in another way. Browning had an unrivalled ear for this particular kind of staccato music. The absurd notion that he had no sense of melody in verse is only possible to people who think that there is no melody in verse which is not an imitation of Swinburne. To give a satisfactory idea of Browning's rhythmic originality would be impossible without quotations more copious than entertaining. But the essential point has been suggested.

They were purple of raiment and golden,
Filled full of thee, fiery with wine,
Thy lovers in haunts unbeholden,
In marvellous chambers of thine,

is beautiful language, but not the only sort of beautiful language.
This, for instance, has also a tune in it :

I – 'next poet.' No my hearties,
I nor am, nor fain would be !
Choose your chiefs and pick your parties,
Not one soul revolt to me !

* * * * *

Which of you did I enable
Once to slip inside my breast,
There to catalogue and label
What I like least, what love best,
Hope and fear, believe and doubt of,
Seek and shun, respect, deride,
Who was right to make a rout of
Rarities he found inside?

This quick, gallantly stepping measure also has its own kind of
music, and the man who cannot feel it can never have enjoyed
the sound of soldiers marching by. This, then, roughly is the main
fact to remember about Browning's poetical method, or about
any one's poetical method – that the question is not whether that
method is the best in the world, but the question whether there
are not certain things which can only be conveyed by that method.
It is perfectly true, for instance, that a really lofty and lucid line
of Tennyson, such as 'Thou art the highest, and most human
too' and 'We needs must love the highest when we see it' would
really be made the worse for being translated into Browning. It
would probably become 'High's human; man loves best, best
visible', and would lose its peculiar clarity and dignity and courtly
plainness. But it is quite equally true that any really characteristic
fragment of Browning, if it were only the tempestuous scolding
of the organist in 'Master Hugues of Saxe-Gotha' –

Hallo, you sacristan, show us a light there !
   Down it dips, gone like a rocket.
What, you want, do you, to come unawares,
Sweeping the church up for first morning-prayers,
And find a poor devil has ended his cares
At the foot of your rotten-runged rat-ridden stairs?
   Do I carry the moon in my pocket?

– it is quite equally true that this outrageous gallop of rhymes
ending with a frantic astronomical image would lose in energy
and spirit if it were written in a conventional and classical style,
and ran :

What must I deem then that thou dreamest to find
Disjected bones adrift upon the stair
Thou sweepest clean, or that thou deemest that I
Pouch in my wallet the vice-regal sun?

   Is it not obvious that this statelier version might be excellent
poetry of its kind, and yet would be bad exactly in so far as it was
good; that it would lose all the swing, the rush, the energy of the
preposterous and grotesque original? In fact, we may see how
unmanageable is this classical treatment of the essentially absurd
in Tennyson himself. The humorous passages in *The Princess*,
though often really humorous in themselves, always appear
forced and feeble because they have to be restrained by a
certain metrical dignity, and the mere idea of such restraint is
incompatible with humour. If Browning had written the passage
which opens *The Princess*, descriptive of the 'larking' of the
villagers in the magnate's park, he would have spared us nothing:
he would not have spared us the shrill uneducated voices and
the unburied bottles of ginger beer. He would have crammed
the poem with uncouth similes; he would have changed the
metre a hundred times; he would have broken into doggerel
and into rhapsody; but he would have left, when all is said and
done, as he leaves in that paltry fragment of the grumbling
organist, the impression of a certain eternal human energy.
Energy and joy, the father and the mother of the grotesque,

would have ruled the poem. We should have felt of that rowdy
gathering little but the sensation of which Mr. Henley writes :

> Praise the generous gods for giving,
>   In this world of sin and strife,
> With some little time for living,
>   Unto each the joy of life,

the thought that every wise man has when looking at a Bank
Holiday crowd at Margate.

To ask why Browning enjoyed this perverse and fantastic style
most would be to go very deep into his spirit indeed, probably a
great deal deeper than it is possible to go. But it is worth while
to suggest tentatively the general function of the grotesque in art
generally and in his art in particular. There is one very curious
idea into which we have been hypnotised by the more eloquent
poets, and that is that nature in the sense of what is ordinarily
called the country is a thing entirely stately and beautiful as those
terms are commonly understood. The whole world of the fantastic, all things top-heavy, lop-sided, and nonsensical are conceived as the work of man, gargoyles, German jugs, Chinese
pots, political caricatures, burlesque epics, the pictures of Mr.
Aubrey Beardsley and the puns of Robert Browning. But in truth
a part, and a very large part, of the sanity and power of nature
lies in the fact that out of her comes all this instinct of caricature.
Nature may present itself to the poet too often as consisting of
stars and lilies; but these are not poets who live in the country;
they are men who go to the country for inspiration and could no
more live in the country than they could go to bed in Westminster
Abbey. Men who live in the heart of nature, farmers and peasants,
know that nature means cows and pigs, and creatures more
humorous than can be found in a whole sketch-book of Callot.
And the element of the grotesque in art, like the element of the
grotesque in nature, means, in the main, energy, the energy which
takes its own forms and goes its own way. Browning's verse, in so
far as it is grotesque, is not complex or artificial; it is natural and
in the legitimate tradition of nature. The verse sprawls like the
trees, dances like the dust; it is ragged like the thunder-cloud, it is

top-heavy like the toadstool. Energy which disregards the standard of classical art is in nature as it is in Browning. The same sense of the uproarious force in things which makes Browning dwell on the oddity of a fungus or a jellyfish makes him dwell on the oddity of a philosophical idea. Here, for example, we have a random instance from 'The Englishman in Italy' of the way in which Browning, when he was most Browning, regarded physical nature :

> And pitch down his basket before us,
>   All trembling alive
> With pink and grey jellies, your sea-fruit;
>   You touch the strange lumps,
> And mouths gape there, eyes open, all manner
>   Of horns and of humps,
> Which only the fisher looks grave at.

Nature might mean flowers to Wordsworth and grass to Walt Whitman, but to Browning it really meant such things as these, the monstrosities and living mysteries of the sea. And just as these strange things meant to Browning energy in the physical world, so strange thoughts and strange images meant to him energy in the mental world. When, in one of his later poems, the professional mystic is seeking in a supreme moment of sincerity to explain that small things may be filled with God as well as great, he uses the very same kind of image, the image of a shapeless sea-beast, to embody that noble conception :

> The Name comes close behind a stomach-cyst,
> .The simplest of creations, just a sac
> That's mouth, heart, legs, and belly at once, yet lives
> And feels, and could do neither, we conclude,
> If simplified still further one degree.
>
> ('Mr. Sludge')

These bulbous, indescribable sea-goblins are the first thing on which the eye of the poet lights in looking on a landscape, and the last in the significance of which he trusts in demonstrating the mercy of the Everlasting.

There is another and but slightly different use of the grotesque, but which is definitely valuable in Browning's poetry, and indeed in all poetry. To present a matter in a grotesque manner does certainly tend to touch the nerve of surprise and thus draw attention to the intrinsically miraculous character of the object itself. It is difficult to give examples of the proper use of grotesqueness without becoming too grotesque. But we should all agree that if St. Paul's Cathedral were suddenly presented to us upside down we should, for the moment, be more surprised at it, and look at it more than we have done all the centuries during which it has rested on its foundations. Now it is the supreme function of the philosopher of the grotesque to make the world stand on its head that people may look at it. If we say 'a man is a man' we awaken no sense of the fantastic, however much we ought to, but if we say, in the language of the old satirist, 'that man is a two-legged bird, without feathers', the phrase does, for a moment, make us look at man from the outside and gives us a thrill in his presence. When the author of the Book of Job insists upon the huge, half-witted, apparently unmeaning magnificence and might of Behemoth, the hippopotamus, he is appealing precisely to this sense of wonder provoked by the grotesque. 'Canst thou play with him as with a bird, canst thou bind him for thy maidens?' he says in an admirable passage. The notion of the hippopotamus as a household pet is curiously in the spirit of the humour of Browning.

But when it is clearly understood that Browning's love of the fantastic in style was a perfectly serious artistic love, when we understand that he enjoyed working in that style, as a Chinese potter might enjoy making dragons, or a mediæval mason making devils, there yet remains something definite which must be laid to his account as a fault. He certainly had a capacity for becoming perfectly childish in his indulgence in ingenuities that have nothing to do with poetry at all, such as puns, and rhymes, and grammatical structures that only just fit into each other like a Chinese puzzle. Probably it was only one of the marks of his singular vitality, curiosity, and interest in details. He was certainly one of those somewhat rare men who are fierily ambitious both in large things and in small. He prided himself on having written *The Ring and the Book*, and he also prided himself on knowing good wine when he tasted it. He prided himself on re-establishing optimism on a new foundation, and it is to be presumed, though it is somewhat difficult to imagine, that he prided himself on such rhymes as the following in *Pacchiarotto* :

> The wolf, fox, bear, and monkey,
> By piping advice in one key –
> That his pipe should play a prelude
> To something heaven-tinged not hell-hued,
> Something not harsh but docile,
> Man-liquid, not man-fossil.

This writing, considered as writing, can only be regarded as a kind of joke, and most probably Browning considered it so himself. It has nothing at all to do with that powerful and symbolic use of the grotesque which may be found in such admirable passages as this from 'Holy-Cross Day' :

> Give your first groan – compunction's at work;
> And soft! From a Jew you mount to a Turk.
> Lo, Micah – the self-same beard on chin
> He was four times already converted in!

This is the serious use of the grotesque. Through it passion and philosophy are as well expressed as through any other medium. But the rhyming frenzy of Browning has no particular relation even to the poems in which it occurs. It is not a dance to any measure; it can only be called the horse-play of literature. It may be noted, for example, as a rather curious fact, that the ingenious rhymes are generally only mathematical triumphs, not triumphs of any kind of assonance. 'The Pied Piper of Hamelin', a poem written for children, and bound in general to be lucid and readable, ends with a rhyme which it is physically impossible for any one to say :

> And, whether they pipe us free, fróm rats or fróm mice,
> If we've promised them aught, let us keep our promise!

This queer trait in Browning, his inability to keep a kind of demented ingenuity even out of poems in which it was quite inappropriate, is a thing which must be recognised, and recognised all the more because as a whole he was a very perfect artist, and a particularly perfect artist in the use of the grotesque. But everywhere when we go a little below the surface in Browning we find that there was something in him perverse and unusual despite all his working normality and simplicity. His mind was perfectly wholesome, but it was not made exactly like the ordinary mind. It was like a piece of strong wood with a knot in it.

The quality of what can only be called buffoonery which is under discussion is indeed one of the many things in which Browning was more of an Elizabethan than a Victorian. He was like the Elizabethans in their belief in the normal man, in their gorgeous and over-loaded language, above all in their feeling for learning as an enjoyment and almost a frivolity. But there was nothing in which he was so thoroughly Elizabethan, and even Shakespearian, as in this fact, that when he felt inclined to write a page of quite uninteresting nonsense, he immediately did so. Many great writers have contrived to be tedious, and apparently aimless, while expounding some thought which they believed to be grave and profitable; but this frivolous stupidity had not been found in any great writer since the time of Rabelais and the time of the Elizabethans. In many of the comic scenes of Shakespeare we have precisely this elephantine ingenuity, this hunting of a pun to death through three pages. In the Elizabethan dramatists and in Browning it is no doubt to a certain extent the mark of a real hilarity. People must be very happy to be so easily amused.

In the case of what is called Browning's obscurity, the question is somewhat more difficult to handle. Many people have supposed Browning to be profound because he was obscure, and many other people, hardly less mistaken, have supposed him to be obscure because he was profound. He was frequently profound, he was occasionally obscure, but as a matter of fact the two have little or nothing to do with each other. Browning's dark and elliptical mode of speech, like his love of the grotesque, was simply a characteristic of his, a trick of his temperament, and had little or nothing to do with whether what he was expressing was profound or superficial. Suppose, for example, that a person well read in English poetry but unacquainted with Browning's style were earnestly invited to consider the following verse:

> Hobbs hints blue – straight he turtle eats.
>   Nobbs prints blue – claret crowns his cup.
> Nokes outdares Stokes in azure feats –
>   Both gorge. Who fished the murex up?
> What porridge had John Keats?

The individual so confronted would say without hesitation that it must indeed be an abstruse and indescribable thought which could only be conveyed by remarks so completely disconnected. But the point of the matter is that the thought contained in this amazing verse is not abstruse or philosophical at all, but is a perfectly ordinary and straightforward comment, which any one might have made upon an obvious fact of life. The whole verse of course begins to explain itself, if we know the meaning of the word 'murex', which is the name of a sea-shell, out of which was made the celebrated blue dye of Tyre. The poet takes this blue dye as a simile for a new fashion in literature, and points out that Hobbs, Nobbs, etc., obtain fame and comfort by merely using the dye from the shell; and adds the perfectly natural comment: '. . . Who fished the murex up?/ What porridge had John Keats?' So that the verse is not subtle, and was not meant to be subtle, but is a perfectly casual piece of sentiment at the end of a light poem. Browning is not obscure because he has such deep things to say, any more than he is grotesque because he has such new things to say. He is both of these things primarily, because he likes to express himself in a particular manner. The manner is as natural to him as a man's physical voice, and it is abrupt, sketchy, allusive, and full of gaps. Here comes in the fundamental difference between Browning and such a writer as George Meredith, with whom the Philistine satirist would so often in the matter of complexity class him. The works of George Meredith are, as it were, obscure even when we know what they mean. They deal with nameless emotions, fugitive sensations, subconscious certainties and uncertainties, and it really requires a somewhat curious and unfamiliar mode of speech to indicate the presence of these. But the great part of Browning's actual sentiments, and almost all the finest and most literary of them, are perfectly plain and popular and eternal sentiments. Meredith is really a singer producing strange notes and cadences difficult to follow because of the delicate rhythm of the song he sings. Browning is simply a great demagogue, with an impediment in his speech. Or rather, to speak more strictly, Browning is a man whose excitement for the glory of the obvious is so great that his speech becomes disjointed and precipitate : he becomes eccentric through his advocacy of the ordinary, and goes mad for the love of sanity.

If Browning and George Meredith were each describing the same act, they might both be obscure, but their obscurities would be entirely different. Suppose, for instance, they were describing even so prosaic and material an act as a man being knocked downstairs by another man to whom he had given the lie, Meredith's description would refer to something which an ordinary observer would not see, or at least could not describe. It might be a sudden sense of anarchy in the brain of the assaulter, or a stupefaction and stunned serenity in that of the object of the assault. He might write, 'Wainwood's "Men vary in veracity", brought the baronet's arm up. He felt the doors of his brain burst, and Wainwood a swift rushing of himself through air accompanied with a clarity as of the annihiliated.' Meredith, in other words, would speak queerly because he was describing queer mental experiences. But Browning might simply be describing the material incident of the man being knocked downstairs, and his description would run :

> What then? 'You lie' and doormat below stairs
> Takes bump from back.

This is not subtlety, but merely a kind of insane swiftness. Browning is not like Meredith, anxious to pause and examine the sensations of the combatants, nor does he become obscure through this anxiety. He is only so anxious to get his man to the bottom of the stairs quickly that he leaves out about half the story.

Many who could understand that ruggedness might be an

artistic quality, would decisively, and in most cases rightly, deny
that obscurity could under any conceivable circumstances be an
artistic quality. But here again Browning's work requires a somewhat more cautious and sympathetic analysis. There is a certain
kind of fascination, a strictly artistic fascination, which arises
from a matter being hinted at in such a way as to leave a certain
tormenting uncertainty even at the end. It is well sometimes to
half understand a poem in the same manner that we half understand the world. One of the deepest and strangest of all human
moods is the mood which will suddenly strike us perhaps in a
garden at night, or deep in sloping meadows, the feeling that
every flower and leaf has just uttered something stupendously
direct and important, and that we have by a prodigy of imbecility
not heard or understood it. There is a certain poetic value, and
that a genuine one, in this sense of having missed the full meaning
of things. There is beauty, not only in wisdom, but in this dazed
and dramatic ignorance.

But in truth it is very difficult to keep pace with all the strange
and unclassified artistic merits of Browning. He was always trying
experiments; sometimes he failed, producing clumsy and irritating metres, top-heavy and over-concentrated thought. Far
more often he triumphed, producing a crowd of boldly designed
poems, every one of which taken separately might have founded
an artistic school. But whether successful or unsuccessful, he
never ceased from his fierce hunt after poetic novelty. He never
became a conservative. The last book he published in his lifetime, *Parleyings with Certain People of Importance in their Day*,
was a new poem, and more revolutionary than *Paracelsus*. This
is the true light in which to regard Browning as an artist. He had
determined to leave no spot of the cosmos unadorned by his
poetry which he could find it possible to adorn. An admirable
example can be found in that splendid poem ' "Childe Roland
to the Dark Tower Came" '. It is the hint of an entirely new
and curious type of poetry, the poetry of the shabby and hungry
aspect of the earth itself. Daring poets who wished to escape from
conventional gardens and orchards had long been in the habit of
celebrating the poetry of rugged and gloomy landscapes, but
Browning is not content with this. He insists upon celebrating the

poetry of mean landscapes. That sense of scrubbiness in nature, as of a man unshaved, had never been conveyed with this enthusiasm and primeval gusto before.

> If there pushed any ragged thistle-stalk
>   Above its mates, the head was chopped; the bents
>   Were jealous else. What made those holes and rents
> In the dock's harsh swarth leaves, bruised as to baulk
> All hope of greenness? 'tis a brute must walk
>   Pashing their life out, with a brute's intents.

This is a perfect realisation of that eerie sentiment which comes upon us, not so often among mountains and water-falls, as it does on some half-starved common at twilight, or in walking down some grey mean street. It is the song of the beauty of refuse; and Browning was the first to sing it. Oddly enough it has been one of the poems about which most of those pedantic and trivial questions have been asked, which are asked invariably by those who treat Browning as a science instead of a poet, 'What does the poem of "Childe Roland" mean?' The only genuine answer to this is, 'What does anything mean?' Does the earth mean nothing? Do grey skies and wastes covered with thistles mean nothing? Does an old horse turned out to graze mean nothing? If it does, there is but one further truth to be added – that everything means nothing.

SOURCE: *Robert Browning* (London, 1903) Chapter VI.

E. D. H. Johnson

AUTHORITY AND THE REBELLIOUS HEART (1952)

Browning established his eminence among Victorian poets with four volumes published over a period of twenty years in mid-century. *Dramatic Lyrics* and *Dramatic Romances and Lyrics* were followed by two additional collections of short poems: *Men and Women* (1855) and *Dramatis Personae* (1864).[1] Whether the form be the lyric, the narrative, or the monologue, the poems in these volumes, as the titles indicate, exhibit a remarkable uniformity of conception in their concentration on the dynamics of behavior. Mindful of the reproof visited on his earlier writing because of its self-conscious quality, the poet rigorously externalized his perceptions under dramatic forms. The advertisement to the original *Dramatic Lyrics* in 1842 declares: 'Such poems as the following come properly enough, I suppose, under the head of "Dramatic Pieces"; being, though for the most part Lyric in expression, always Dramatic in principle, and so many utterances of so many imaginary persons, not mine.' Henceforth Browning was to exploit all the devices of objectivity at his command in an effort to capture the attention of his age. When he was writing the poems to be gathered in *Men and Women*, he informed Milsand: 'I am writing – a first step towards popularity for me – lyrics with more music and painting than before, so as to get people to hear and see.'

Yet, a review of the four key works, *Dramatic Lyrics, Dramatic Romances and Lyrics, Men and Women,* and *Dramatis Personae,* in the light of what has already been said about his previous work, and especially *Pippa Passes,* reveals that like Sordello's reliance on the font at Goito, Browning continued to depend for inspiration on the sources which had fed his imagination from the start. The dramatic technique, as he employed it, became simply a process of sublimation equivalent in stylistic terms to Tennyson's thematic use of dream, madness, vision, and the quest. By motivating the actors in his dramas with his own ideas and impulses, Browning could speak out with greater originality and boldness than would ever have been possible in his own person. One wonders how the Victorian middle class with its worship of conformity could have failed to take exception to the poet's outspoken flouting of social conventions. It can only be supposed that approving the apparent regard for morality in his teaching, contemporary readers did not bother to look below the surface to investigate the assumptions on which that morality was founded.

By his constant advocacy of intuitive over rational knowledge, Browning took over the anti-intellectualism of the Romantics and pushed it in the direction of pure primitivism. Along with Carlyle, although much more subtly, Browning endorsed the unconscious as the true wellspring of being. Pippa is only the first of a long line of innocents, including, to name only a few, the duke's last duchess, the maligned lady of 'Count Gismond', Brother Lawrence, the Pied Piper, and the resurrected Lazarus of 'An Epistle of Karshish'. In Browning's world, the prophets and artists, the lovers and doers of great deeds are never primarily remarkable for intellectual power. Their supremacy is the result of a genius for experiencing life intuitively. They possess a phenomenal capacity for passionate emotion, combined with a childlike reliance on instinct. These qualities put them in conflict with conventionalized modes of social conduct. Whether it be Fra Lippo, or Rabbi Ben Ezra, or David in 'Saul', or the Grammarian, or Childe Roland, Browning's heroes are always the children of their intuitions.

In their capacity for instinctive action Browning's heroes are akin to Tennyson's visionaries. The moments of recognition come to both in the same mysterious and unpredictable ways. Thus, Childe Roland, reaching his journey's end, knows in a blinding flash what is expected of him. Abt Vogler and David improvise their rhapsodies in states of trance-like exaltation. More especially, true love is love at first sight. Such instantaneous perceptions of elective affinity occur, among other poems, in 'Count

M.A.W.—D

Gismond', 'Cristina', 'The Statue and the Bust', 'Evelyn Hope'.

His belief that the intuitions operate through the instrumentality of the emotions rather than the intellect led Browning to a frank celebration of man's physical nature, very foreign to Victorian reticence in such matters. Remembering the Prior's pretty niece, Fra Lippo says : 'If you get simple beauty and nought else,/ You get about the best thing God invents.'[2] Such an admission is unthinkable in Tennyson, for whom the essential philosophic problem was to league mind and spirit into effective opposition against the bodily appetites. To Browning, on the other hand, flesh and the spirit seemed natural allies against the insidious distortions of the intellect. So Fra Lippo in his defense of the street-urchin's apprenticeship to life exclaims : 'Why, soul and sense of him grow sharp alike.' Browning's constant assertion of the soul's interrelationship with the body on an instinctual plane permits him to make claims for the latter which would not otherwise have been admissible. Indeed, two of the most forthright statements that fleshly and spiritual well-being are bound up together come from the mouths of holy men. The Apostle John in 'A Death in the Desert' says :

> But see the double way wherein we are led,
> How the soul learns diversely from the flesh !
> With flesh, that hath so little time to stay,
> And yields mere basement for the soul's emprise,
> Expect prompt teaching.

And in the words of Rabbi Ben Ezra :

> Let us not always say
> 'Spite of this flesh to-day
> 'I strove, made head, gained ground upon the whole !'
> As the bird wings and sings,
> Let us cry 'All good things
> 'Are ours, nor soul helps flesh more, now, than flesh helps soul !'

The vitalism inherent in Browning's emphasis on man's intuitive as opposed to his ratioinactive faculties further explains the poet's acceptance of the real and demonstrable, and, conversely, his distrust of make-believe. The characters in his poems whom we are asked to admire are all exceptionally clear-sighted in their confrontation of actuality. They see through the false shows at which society connives, preferring to meet life on its own terms rather than to indulge in fanciful self-delusion. Although Browning's lovers are usually unhappy, there is never any question of escape into a Tennysonian dream world. In his hopeless predicament the lover of 'In a Gondola' three times falls to imagining ideal situations which would allow his mistress and himself to be together, and as often rejects the wish for the fact :

> Rescue me thou, the only real !
> And scare away this mad ideal
> That came, nor motions to depart !
> Thanks, Now, stay ever as thou art !

Finally, worldly criteria for success lose their validity in Browning's poetry. The poet's so-called philosophy of imperfection with its lesson that 'a man's reach should exceed his grasp', has anti-social implications. This belief holds that an individual's first and highest obligation is to fulfill his own being, regardless of consequences. A lifetime of devotion to settling *'Hoti's* business', properly basing *Oun*, and providing 'us the doctrine of the enclitic *De'* entitles the grammarian to a final resting-place on the heights. The lover of 'In a Gondola' makes a Romeo-like death in the fullness of his passion :

> The Three, I do not scorn
> To death, because they never lived : but I
> Have lived indeed, and so – (yet one more kiss) – can die !

And Childe Roland's ultimate intuition is that success in his quest means just to die bravely.

Once the intuitional psychology at the heart of Browning's thinking is fully understood, all the major thematic concerns in his poetry become meaningful as deriving therefrom. Among Victorian poets he is the great champion of individualism. If self-realization is the purpose of life, then it follows that any agency which thwarts that process is inimical to the best interests of

human nature. And since formalized systems of thought operating
through social institutions have always tended to repress freedom
of belief and action, Browning's most characteristic poems have
to do with the conflict between the individual and his environment. There is a wisdom of the mind and a wisdom of the heart;
and the two are always at odds, since the one teaches compliance
with the ways of the world while the other inculcates non-con-
formity. Thus, where his political and religious convictions or his
beliefs about love and art are concerned, each man must make a
choice between intellectual subservience to customary values and
emancipation from all such restrictions.

In insisting on the integrity of the individual soul, Browning
allies himself on one side with the Romantic poets, and on the
other with the Pre-Raphaelites. He differs from both, however,
in his concept of the artist's responsibilities. Whereas Byron
delivered frontal assaults on contemporary manners and morals
and Rossetti inclined to ignore his milieu, Browning adopted an
oblique approach to his age. By dramatizing individual case
histories, he stepped before his readers in such a variety of poetic
guises that it was impossible to identify him with any single rôle.
Furthermore, since he made his attacks piecemeal through ana-
tomizing characters each of whom embodied but a single aspect
of contemporary thought, he could be sure of enlisting on his
side all those who did not share this particular foible, and so of
forestalling unified opposition. It is only when the widely diversified types in Browning's catalogue are grouped according to
family resemblance that one begins to comprehend the scope and
consistency of the poet's opposition to existing values, and hence
the extent of his alienation from Victorian society.

One such grouping, it has been suggested, would include all
those characters whose ways of life are conditioned by some
clearly defined set of conventions. Superficially dissimilar
though they are, 'My Last Duchess' and 'Soliloquy of the Spanish
Cloister' present versions of a single conflict. Just as the duke in
the former is motivated in all he does by punctilious pride of
rank, so the hypocritical friar who soliloquizes in the second
poem appeals to the minutiae of religious observance. And just
as the dead duchess in her childlike response to all innocent

pleasures unknowingly made a mockery of her husband's cere-
moniousness, so Brother Lawrence's every spontaneous action
criticizes religious formalism. In both poems the central irony
grows out of the fact that the speaker damns himself in endeavor-
ing to cast discredit on his unsuspecting adversary.

So, in poem after poem representing every kind of career, the
protagonist must make his decision between the practical induce-
ments to worldly success and lonely integrity of spirit. The Lost
Leader, who sold out 'just for a handful of silver . . . just for
a riband to stick in his coat', stands in telling contrast to the
Italian in England who, even in exile, remains loyal to the
patriot's dream. For the grammarian, gifted above his fellows,
the search for knowledge means sacrifice of all that would otherwise have been his due :

> He knew the signal, and stepped on with pride
>   Over men's pity;
> Left play for work, and grappled with the world
>   Bent on escaping . . .

Childe Roland's thoughts are saddened by memories of his lost
companions, Cuthbert and Giles, who, presumably unable to sus-
tain the rigors of the quest, fell away, seduced by the world's
allurements. All the grotesque properties of this poem – the 'hateful cripple', the 'stiff blind horse, his every bone astare', the
engine of torture, the 'great black bird, Apollyon's bosom-friend'
– are marshalled as if to epitomize the malice of society against
the dedicated ones who step aside from the trodden path.

Browning's most forcible condemnations of rationalism, however, come in those poems which deal with the problems of
religious belief. In *Christmas-Eve and Easter-Day*, published in
the same year as *In Memoriam*, the poet had worked out the
grounds of his own highly individualistic faith. It sprang from a
purely intuitive conviction of the necessity for a loving God. 'Saul'
and 'Rabbi Ben Ezra' give full expression to this religious optimism; but the modern reader may well take greater interest in
those works which dramatize alternative positions and show the
poet dealing with the sceptical tendencies in contemporary

thought. Among the best things to be found in *Men and Women* and *Dramatis Personae* is a series of monologues surveying the principal intellectual traditions which have militated against the Christian revelation.

A uniform tone of nostalgia pervades 'An Epistle, Containing the Strange Medical Experience of Karshish, the Arab Physician'; 'Cleon'; and 'Caliban upon Setebos; or Natural Theology in the Island'. The speaker in each poem, instinctively realizing the spiritual limitations of the system of thought to which he is committed, is driven against his will to postulate a Christian deity. Yet wistful longing never actualizes itself in terms of faith, because it is smothered under the weight of inherited prejudice. Karshish stands for the scientific mentality wholly at a loss to cope with the mystery of Lazarus' resurrection. Cleon, living in the end of the Hellenistic era, finds such meager consolation as he can in the synthesizing temper of a decadent culture. In the superficial view Caliban appears to belong among Browning's primitives; actually he is man materialized to the point where he can only construct God in his own capricious and spiteful image. The historical or literary guise under which these issues are presented suggests the devious operation of Browning's critical intent. The poet was not really interested in the historical process, as Carlyle or Ruskin tried to be; nor did he have Tennyson's genius for reanimating myth. Karshish, Cleon and Caliban are representative Victorians in fancy dress. As time passed, Browning inclined more and more to put aside the cloak of historical remoteness and to address himself to the psychoanalysis of contemporary types. 'Bishop Blougram's Apology' and 'Mr. Sludge, "The Medium" ', for example, bring the charge of spiritual sterility directly home to Victorian society.

'Bishop Blougram's Apology' is an early example of the special pleading, the skillful conduct of casuistic argument, which bewildered so many of Browning's readers. The difficulty, of course, is that Blougram is a sort of devil's advocate who appropriates typical Browningesque doctrines and converts them to his own ends. In the words of his creator : 'He said true things, but called them by wrong names.' The whole tenor of the Bishop's plea points to the conclusion that worldly self-interest is identical with spiritual well-being. In demonstrating this line of reasoning, Blougram boldly enlists theories which have a diametrically opposed significance in Browning's own thinking. Thus, he says : 'My business is not to remake myself,/ But to make the absolute best of what God made'; and again :

> Let us concede (gratuitously though)
> Next life relieves the soul of body, yields
> Pure spiritual enjoyment : well, my friend,
> Why lose this life i' the meantime, since its use
> May be to make the next life more intense?

Only gradually do we recognize the extent of the clever Bishop's compromise with the existing order. In making choice of a way of life, he has consulted only his physical comfort, out of regard for which he has become the servant of institutionalized religion. He has, in other words, allowed himself to be corrupted by the self-deluding operations of his own intellect. The key to Browning's meaning in the more abstruse dramatic monologues may nearly always be discovered in the culminating action. In this case Gigadibs instinctively revolts against Blougram's intellectual gymnastics, and turning his back on England, takes up a Car-lylean life of unthinking action as a colonist.

'Mr. Sludge, "The Medium" ' follows a similar pattern. Browning, of course, had no use for mediums, seeing in their vogue clear evidence of the frivolous sensation-seeking of a society that had lost its spiritual bearings. Nevertheless, until the last extraordinary diatribe which reveals Sludge as the unregenerate charlatan he is, the poet allows his protagonist to make out the best possible case for himself. Ironically, despite the fact that Sludge has been caught red-handed at his sham practices, he has relied on trickery for so long that he is partially self-duped :

> I tell you, sir, in one sense, I believe
> Nothing at all, – that everybody can,
> Will, and does cheat : but in another sense
> I'm ready to believe my very self –
> That every cheat's inspired, and every lie
> Quick with a germ of truth.

More damaging, however, as a concealed expression of Browning's own sense of the price which society pays for trifling with its genuine spiritual impulses, is Sludge's mocking vindication of himself. In a world where the prizes go to those who live by their wits, Sludgehood is a normal phenomenon:

> Or, finally,
> Why should I set so fine a gloss on things?
> What need I care? I cheat in self-defence,
> And there's my answer to a world of cheats!
> Cheat? To be sure, sir! What's the world worth else?

Browning's intuitionism announces itself most ardently when he writes about love, this being a subject which he handles with greater candor and penetration than any other poet of the early and mid-Victorian periods. It is not hard to understand why he should have thought the experience of love so important. Through the emotions which it releases man reaches heights of intensity, both physical and spiritual, such as are achievable in no other way. Romantic love, however, is little subject to discipline; and the Victorians in their regard for social stability endeavored to safeguard themselves against its disruptive power behind an elaborate system of conventions. A double standard of conduct was in force for the sexes, and the family stood as the central support of the entire social fabric. To the authority of these ideals Tennyson's poetry bears constant testimony. Browning, on the other hand, challenges the sexual morality of the Victorians at nearly every point. His interest is in the fulfillment of passion, rather than in the preservation of domestic proprieties. In no way are his convictions less conformable to accepted theories than in his refusal to recognize any basis for social inequality between men and women. His adoration of Elizabeth Barrett no doubt explains a good deal in this connection; but while Browning yielded to no other Victorian in his idealization of womanhood, his thinking had very little in common with the contemporary concept of the womanly woman. Only Meredith's heroines challenge Browning's in the qualities of fortitude, loyalty, idealism, intelligence, and insight. The Euripides of 'The Last Adventure of Balaustion' is speaking for his creator when he says: 'Mere puppets once, I now make womankind,/ For thinking, saying, doing, match the male.' Browning, like Meredith, finds that the woman is usually right. With a few exceptions, his love lyrics fall into two classes. In the first the speaker is a man who has been rejected and who humbly accepts responsibility for failure, attributing it to some inadequacy in his own nature. In the second it is the woman who has been cast off. She too is humble; but we are made to feel that she suffers not because of any innate unworthiness, but rather because of some flaw in her lover.

The central problem in Browning's love poetry is invariably one of communication between the sexes. The intangible influences which encourage or destroy intimacy between men and women elicit all his skill in psychological analysis; for love exists in and through human intuitions. Reference has already been made to the poet's belief that destined lovers recognize each other on first sight. But these moments of full and perfect communion are precarious; and, save for the most exceptional cases, the initial harmony does not survive social pressures or the importunities of individual temperament. It is rare in Browning's work to find such a poem as 'By the Fire-Side', in which the lovers have so come to exist in each other that one of them can say:

> When, if I think but deep enough,
>   You are wont to answer, prompt as rhyme;
> And you, too, find without rebuff
>   Response your soul seeks many a time
> Piercing its fine flesh-stuff.

More commonly the good moment passes, as in 'Two in the Campagna', where we watch it slip away despite the lovers' longing to prolong their felicity; or 'The Last Ride Together', in which the speaker strives desperately to eternalize his fleeting togetherness with the woman he loves.

Ideal love is for Browning the consummation of an intuitive process by which the lovers transcend the barriers of their separate individualities and achieve spiritual union. Whenever this happens, there results the most exquisite and productive form of

communication possible between human beings. The very possibility of a love like this excites the heroine of 'The Flight of the
Duchess' to say :

> If any two creatures grew into one,
> They would do more than the world has done :
> Though each apart were never so weak,
> Ye vainly through the world should seek
> For the knowledge and the might
> Which in such union grew their right . . .

Browning's men and women, then, are always seeking to pierce
the barrier which, in his favorite metaphor, separates two isolated souls reaching towards each other. The lover of 'In a Gondola' pleads with his mistress :

> Do, break down the partition-wall
> 'Twixt us, the daylight world beholds
> Curtained in dusk and splendid folds !
> What's left but – all of me to take?

And in 'By the Fire-Side' Browning, speaking for once in his own
person, describes the loss of personal identity under love's
mysterious spell :

> If two lives join, there is oft a scar,
>   They are one and one, with a shadowy third ;
> One near one is too far.
>
> A moment after, and hands unseen
>   Were hanging night around us fast ;
> But we knew that a bar was broken between
>   Life and life : we were mixed at last
> In spite of the mortal screen.

As one would expect from what has already been said, Browning holds that undue reliance on the intellect with its ulterior
motivations makes for failure in affairs of the heart. The femi-
nine nature is wiser than the masculine in its instinctive response
to emotional impulse. In a number of poems love is destroyed

through the man's determination to establish his mental superiority over the woman. This is the theme of 'Mesmerism', for example, as well as of 'A Woman's Last Word' in which the woman soliloquizes:

> What so false as truth is,
>   False to thee?
> Where the serpent's tooth is
>   Shun the tree –

Since in the poet's thinking the intellectual faculties are self-corrupting and prone to infection by the uses of the world, another group of poems, written from the female point of view, lays blame for the man's infidelity on the temptations held out by society. Examples in this vein are 'Any Wife to Any Husband', and the group of highly sophisticated lyrics, 'James Lee's Wife'. The comparatively early 'Cristina' departs from the usual pattern of Browning's love poems after he had come to know Elizabeth Barrett. For here it is the woman who is found wanting to the moment of recognition when 'mine and her souls rushed together':

> Oh, observe! Of course, next moment,
>   The world's honours, in derision,
> Trampled out the light for ever:
>   Never fear but there's provision
> Of the devil's to quench knowledge
>   Lest we walk the earth in rapture!
> – Making those who catch God's secret
>   Just so much more prize their capture!

Browning's conviction that the passionate intensity of romantic love is incompatible with conventionalized social morality leads him to glorify the one at the expense of the other. That perennial theme, the world well lost for love, is so appealing that Victorian readers in their sentimentality were apparently willing to overlook its frequent anti-social corollary in Browning's poetry, where the decision to give all for love more often than not involves some course of action at variance with established codes of conduct. Too extreme, perhaps, is the example of 'Porphyria's Lover' where

the demented narrator has committed murder and in this way
made the final choice for a mistress

> Too weak, for all her heart's endeavour,
> To set its struggling passion free
> From pride, and vainer ties dissever,
> And give herself to me for ever.

In 'The Flight of the Duchess', however, we are compelled to
sympathize with the duchess in her flight from the staidly for-
malistic home of her husband to join the gypsies; and the pre-
varicating speaker in 'Too Late' seems most manly when he
reconstructs the lost opportunity to take his beloved away from
her husband, by force if necessary. 'In a Gondola' presents a more
fatal but equally persuasive picture of adultery as the solution to
loveless marriage. And the inescapable implication of 'Respectability' is that the illicit affair there described has gained its intensity and seriousness from being carried on outside the pale of
social conventions :

> Dear, had the world in its caprice
> Deigned to proclaim 'I know you both,
> Have recognized your plighted troth,
> Am sponsor for you : live in peace !' –
> How many precious months and years
> Of youth had passed, that speed so fast,
> Before we found it out at last,
> The world, and what it fears?
>
> How much of priceless life were spent
> With men that every virtue decks,
> And women models of their sex,
> Society's true ornament, –
> Ere we dared wander, nights like this,
> Thro' wind and rain, and watch the Seine,
> And feel the Boulevard break again
> To warmth and light and bliss?
>
> I know ! the world proscribes not love;
> Allows my finger to caress
> Your lips' contour and downiness,
> Provided it supply a glove.
> The world's good word !

'In a Balcony' and 'The Glove' present in unequivocal terms the conflict between the wisdom of the intuitions and the usages of society. The theme of 'In a Balcony' is conveyed in Norbert's reference to the 'instincts of the heart that teach the head'. The Queen, a marble figure of authority, comes, through passion for her minister of state, to recognize the hollowness of worldly power. Of the reality of love, on the contrary, she learns:

> 'T is as different from dreams,
> From the mind's cold calm estimate of bliss,
> As these stone statues from the flesh and blood.

Meanwhile, Constance, the Queen's protégée, who resembles the speaker in 'Respectability' in her fear of the world's callous incomprehension, would prefer that her liaison with Norbert remain clandestine. In effect, she is matching wits against society out of a desire to secure her lover to herself. When Norbert wants to make an open declaration of their attachment, she replies:

> A year of this compression's ecstasy
> All goes for nothing! You would give this up
> For the old way, the open way, the world's,
> His way who beats, and his who sells his wife!
> What tempts you? – their notorious happiness
> Makes you ashamed of ours?

In the end Constance prevails on Norbert to make his request in a manner so ambiguous that the Queen misunderstands his intention and believes that her own love is returned. Only when Constance's subterfuges have ruined her hopes does she learn the error of playing the world's game in the world's way. Then finally she lets her heart speak out without restraint. She is willing to sacrifice her happiness to Norbert's career, but at the same time she will stop treating love as though it were a marketable commodity:

> I know the thriftier way
> Of giving – haply, 't is the wiser way.
> Meaning to give a treasure, I might dole

Coin after coin out (each, as that were all,
With a new largess still at each despair)
And force you keep in sight the deed, preserve
Exhaustless till the end my part and yours,
My giving and your taking; both our joys
Dying together. Is it the wiser way?
I choose the simpler; I give all at once.
Know what you have to trust to, trade upon!
Use it, abuse it, – anything but think
Hereafter, 'Had I known she loved me so,
And what my means, I might have thriven with it.'
This is your means. I give you all myself.

The social satire in 'The Glove' results from a seeming paradox
in the lady's behavior. Her motive for casting the glove into the
lion-pit seems purely capricious; and the reader's first inclination
is to side with King Francis' court in its condemnation of the
lady and approval of De Lorge when he flings the glove back in
her face after its retrieval. On reconsideration, however, we perceive that our initial judgment was conditioned by a code of
etiquette, rather than by any real concern for the heroine's
situation. By trifling with convention in an apparently irresponsible way, she has shown up the ingrained conventionality of her
admirer whose bravery, like his subsequent rudeness, was displayed not for the lady's sake, but solely to win popular approval.
The dénouement reveals the poet's meaning. The lady, followed
by the youth who alone comprehends her action, departs from
the artificial life of the court, while De Lorge remains to marry
a lady-in-waiting and to see her become the king's mistress, while
he is relegated to the position of glove-bearer.

If, for Browning, true love necessitates total disregard of the
ways of the world, then it follows that self-interest is love's
greatest enemy. A long succession of poems, concerned with individuals for whom the voice of society drowns out that of passion,
dramatizes, on the negative side, the poet's sense that no worldly
gain is ever achieved without spiritual loss. The disillusioned lover
of 'Dîs Aliter Visum; or, Le Byron de nos Jours' recalls in bitterness of heart how he let opportunity slip through his fingers from
cynical disbelief that the good moment could be prolonged:

> She might take me as I take her.
>   Perfect the hour would pass, alas!
> Climb high, love high, what matter? Still,
>   Feet, feelings, must descend the hill:
> An hour's perfection can't recur.

So, instead, he has elected the tamer consolation of a career:

> What? All I am, was, and might be,
>   All, books taught, art brought, life's whole strife,
> Painful results since precious, just
>   Were fitly exchanged, in wise disgust,
> For two cheeks freshened by youth and sea?

But the moment, once gone past, does not return; and in the resolution we learn that each has made a wretched marriage, he with a young ballet-dancer, she with a too-old whist-player. Artistic ambition is the force which keeps the lovers of 'Youth and Art' apart; but through their failure to perceive the all-important connection between art and life, the former has betrayed them to triviality. The girl, who would surpass Grisi, is now queen at *bals-paré*; and the sculptor, aspiring to replace Gibson, has had to be content with the dubious distinction of membership in the Royal Academy.

Browning's most provocative examination of failure in love as the penalty of faint-hearted conformity to social conventions occurs in 'The Statue and the Bust'. The duke first beheld the lady on the day of her wedding to another man, and at once their souls 'rushed together'. Neither is restrained by moral scruples; yet they postpone the consummation of their love. Each is content with the daily encounter when the duke rides under the window where his beloved sits like another Lady of Shalott, but more remote from reality in her too-patient waiting. So the passing of time and the inconsequential demands of everyday existence imperceptibly dull the edge of resolve, although the lovers continue to delude themselves with the belief that such steadfastness as theirs must eventually be rewarded. Meanwhile, it is better not to provoke a scandal:

And still, as love's brief morning wore,
With a gentle start, half smile, half sigh,
They found love not as it seemed before.

They thought it would work infallibly,
But not in despite of heaven and earth :
The rose would blow when the storm passed by.

Meantime they could profit in winter's dearth
By store of fruits that supplant the rose :
The world and its ways have a certain worth :

And to press a point while these oppose
Were a simple policy; better wait :
We lose no friends and we gain no foes.

When it is too late, they awaken to the realization that they have
wasted their lives in make-believe :

And both perceived they had dreamed a dream;

Which hovered as dreams do, still above :
But who can take a dream for a truth?
Oh, hide our eyes from the next remove!

In the end the lovers call in art to eternalize their devotion; but
the statue and the bust mock rather than glorify the impulse
which brings them into being. Fixed in their apartness, they are
as futile and as static as the couple they commemorate. Art has
been made a substitute for, not a confirmation of life. That there
might be no mistaking his meaning, Browning attached a coda to
the poem. In Hamlet's phrase, 'The readiness is all'. Virtue is not
in the goal, but in the passionate intensity of striving :

Do your best, whether winning or losing it,

If you choose to play ! – is my principle.
Let a man contend to the uttermost
For his life's set prize, be it what it will !

The counter our lovers staked was lost
As surely as if it were lawful coin :
And the sin I impute to each frustrate ghost

Is – the unlit lamp and the ungirt loin,
Though the end in sight was a vice, I say.

If we turn now to Browning's aesthetics, it is immediately apparent from such poems as 'Youth and Art' and 'The Statue and the Bust' that for this poet art could never supplant life. No position is more consistently maintained throughout his writing than the one deriving from the assumption that all enduring artistic expression is incidental to the experience which inspires it. Poems otherwise so different as 'The Last Ride Together', 'In a Balcony', 'Cleon', 'Old Pictures in Florence', 'Transcendentalism : A Poem in Twelve Books', 'James Lee's Wife', and 'One Word More' reiterate the author's vitalism. Art exists simply as one form of creative endeavor to educe life's meaning. The test of an artist's genius lies in his ability to move his audience to action. The Pied Piper, Fra Lippo Lippi, and the David of 'Saul' have this faculty in common. The rats and children of Hamelin Town jubilantly follow wherever the piper's music leads. Fra Lippo is going to have to repaint his fresco of St. Laurence at Prato since the faithful are obliterating its details in their devout rage. The mounting ecstasy of David's songs lifts from Saul's spirit the gloom which has incapacitated him.

On first glance, Browning's artistic theories seem to accord fully with his age in its endorsement of the Ruskinian arguments that the highest art results from the perception of moral truth and promotes virtuous conduct. The poet's application of these propositions, however, is again suggestive of a double awareness. Just as the religious or political man must take a stand with regard to institutionalism and the lover with regard to conventional morality, so the artist is threatened by the tyranny of tradition. As it impinges on the life of the imagination, traditionalism has a dual authority. Its influence may be largely intellectual, regimenting instinct to a lifeless formalism. This way leads to art for art's sake. Or, in its more popular aspect, tradition may inform the artist's desire to communicate and so make of him a virtuoso.

Whether he inhabit an ivory tower or the market place, the artist who subordinates his native talent to traditional modes has, in Browning's opinion, betrayed his birthright.

The nameless painter of 'Pictor Ignotus', like Aprile and Eglamor, has sought refuge from the harsh importunities of the world in the recesses of his inner being. As one naturally

> inquisitive, to scan
> The licence and the limit, space and bound,
> Allowed to truth made visible in man,

he is all too conscious of the loss in vitality to his painting consequent on denial of the sensory world. He looks outward and sadly asks: 'O human faces, hath it spilt, my cup?' Self-withdrawal, we learn, has not taken place out of temperamental inability to respond to external stimuli, but rather because the painter shrinks from the callously imperceptive way that would-be connoisseurs deal with artists and their work. Yet within the privacy of his individual consciousness he discovers no impulse towards original creation, but only the pale inspiration of inherited tradition. The sole consolation left him after producing unending variations on stock religious themes is that he has at least dictated the terms of his defeat:

> If at whiles
> My heart sinks, as monotonous I paint
> These endless cloisters and eternal aisles
> With the same series, Virgin, Babe and Saint,
> With the same cold calm beautiful regard, –
> At least no merchant traffics in my heart;
> The sanctuary's gloom at least shall ward
> Vain tongues from where my pictures stand apart:
> Only prayer breaks the silence of the shrine
> While, blackening in the daily candle-smoke,
> They moulder on the damp wall's travertine,
> 'Mid echoes the light footstep never woke.
> So, die my pictures! surely, gently die!
> O youth, men praise so, – holds their praise its worth?
> Blown harshly, keeps the trump its golden cry?
> Tastes sweet the water with such specks of earth?

The reasons for the failure of Andrea del Sarto are at once more complex and more symptomatic of the iconoclastic bias which carries over into Browning's aesthetic thinking. Where the speaker in 'Pictor Ignotus' is frightened of the world's rough handling, Andrea has shamelessly courted popularity. The unknown painter's talent is exercised for purely private ends; Andrea paints to make money, allowing his choice of subjects to be determined by the market. He panders to the type of material-minded collector that Browning describes in 'My Last Duchess' and 'The Bishop Orders his Tomb at St. Praxed's Church'. The Pictor Ignotus follows in the tradition of the Primitives who stressed soul at the expense of body; Andrea is no less slave to a realistic tradition which ignores spiritual overtones in its care for anatomic fidelity. Reluctant to acknowledge where he has gone wrong, Andrea, like the unknown painter, hypocritically pretends to exist in the realm of his imaginings:

> I, painting from myself to myself,
> Know what I do, am unmoved by men's blame
> Or their praise either.

Later on he declares: 'Beside, incentives come from the soul's self;/ The rest avail not.' But the hypocrisy of this statement, when applied to his own work, is evident even to Andrea. The error lies not in his hand with its matchless skill, but in the soul which directs that hand. Preferring any compromise to the loss of his worthless wife, the painter has silenced the admonitions of his spiritual nature. Thinking of the gigantic, though flawed genius of Michelangelo and Leonardo and Raphael, he ejaculates: 'The sudden blood of these men!' The recognition that he can put over against their achievements only a certain cold proficiency wrings from him the lament: 'But all the play, the insight and the stretch – / Out of me, out of me!' No sooner does he undertake to correct a clumsy line in a drawing by Raphael than the chalk falls from his fingers: 'Ay! but the soul! he's Rafael! rub it out!' Andrea's virtuosity, we see, is simply a skill acquired through patient mastery of others' techniques, handed down in the schools and now corrupted for venal ends. It is his

unforgivable fault to be faultless : 'Well, less is more, Lucrezia :
I am judged.'

In 'An Essay on Shelley', written in 1852 to preface a spurious
collection of that poet's letters, Browning distinguished between
two kinds of objective poet or 'fashioner'. Concerning the creative
impulse of the first kind, the question to be asked is : 'Did a
soul's delight in its own extended sphere of vision set it, for the
gratification of an insuppressible power, on labor, as other men
are set on rest?' For the second class, the question is rephrased
as follows : 'Or did a sense of duty or of love lead it to communicate its own sensations to mankind? Did an irresistible sympathy
with men compel it to bring down and suit its own provision of
knowledge and beauty to their narrow scope?' 'Pictor Ignotus'
and 'Andrea del Sarto' seem to exemplify the corrupt extremes
of these two types. The unknown painter has become the morbidly
self-conscious victim of his 'soul's delight in its own extended
sphere of vision', while Andrea in his desire to communicate has
sacrificed originality and compelled his talent 'to bring down and
suit its own provision of knowledge and beauty' to the 'narrow
scope' of a vulgar audience. 'An Essay on Shelley', however, goes
on to propose another kind of poet whose response to experience
is primarily subjective. This is the seer, described by Browning as
follows :

He, gifted like the objective poet with the fuller perception of nature
and man, is impelled to embody the thing he perceives not so much
with reference to the many below as to the one above him, the
supreme Intelligence which apprehends all things in their absolute
truth, – an ultimate view ever aspired to, if but partially attained,
by the poet's own soul. . . . Not with the combination of humanity
in action, but with the primal elements of humanity, he has to do;
and he digs where he stands, – preferring to seek them in his own
soul as the nearest reflex of the absolute Mind, according to the
intuitions of which he desires to perceive and speak. . . . He is
rather a seer, accordingly, than a fashioner, and what he produces
will be less a work than an effluence.

Although in his Shelley essay Browning declined to favor either
the objective or the subjective artist at the expense of the other,

the general tone of his remarks strongly suggests that in his concept of the seer he was proposing a higher orientation for the poetic impulse than would result from conforming to the demands either of the individual ego or of society at large. And certainly in Browning's own poetry devoted to the arts and their practice it is the seer who emerges as the supreme type of artist, embodying in transmuted form the two aspects of the fashioner and merging them under the authority of a transcendent vision adequate to the opposing impulses which inhere in a double awareness.

Although *Christmas-Eve and Easter-Day* is largely a defense of Browning's particular brand of Christianity, the philosophic implications of religion and art were so closely allied in his thinking that the poem is also a declaration of his aesthetic creed. *Christmas-Eve* considers among other things the discrepancy between the ideal and the actual in this life – all that is signified by Abt Vogler's statement : 'On the earth the broken arcs; in the heaven, a perfect round.' The ideal, as it exists in God, in unattainable on earth; but this knowledge does not exonerate humanity from attempting the impossible; for in the effort lies the hope of spiritual salvation. Hence Andrea del Sarto's saddened perception : 'Ah, but a man's reach should exceed his grasp,/ Or what's a heaven for?' The artist, endowed with special intuitions, is better equipped than other men to apprehend the spirit world. His senses are more keenly responsive to beauty and his mind probes deeper into the laws of cause and effect; but the faculty on which before all others he relies is imaginative insight. Possession of this attribute to an unequalled degree made Shakespeare a poet apart. But, as Browning proceeds to expound in *Easter-Day*, the artist's unique gifts impose on him the highest possible responsibility. Perceiving the divine plan, he must place his genius at God's disposal. Thus, although the creative impulse has its source within the individual consciousness, its operation must not be expended on self-expression, but rather on elucidation of the heavenly will. It is on these grounds that Browning takes issue with art for art's sake. Whereas the deluded devotee of this doctrine endeavors to meet self-imposed standards of perfection, the true artist hears a more imperious voice speaking through his intuitions. While humbly aware that the human imagination is at

best a distorting medium, he nevertheless tries, as much as possible, to keep his message uncontaminated by the vanity of artifice. So the apocalyptic presence in *Easter-Day* admonishes the
desperate poet who places reliance in his own earth-bound
powers :

> 'And so much worse thy latter quest,'
> (Added the voice,) 'that even on earth –
> Whenever, in man's soul, had birth
> Those intuitions, grasps of guess,
> Which pull the more into the less,
> Making the finite comprehend
> Infinity, – the bard would spend
> Such praise alone, upon his craft,
> As, when wind-lyres obey the waft,
> Goes to the craftsman who arranged
> The seven strings, changed them and rechanged –
> Knowing it was the South that harped.
> He felt his song, in singing, warped ;
> Distinguished his and God's part : whence
> A world of spirit as of sense
> Was plain to him, yet not too plain,
> Which he could traverse, not remain
> A guest in : – else were permanent
> Heaven on earth its gleams were meant
> To sting with hunger for full light, –
> Made visible in verse, despite
> The veiling weakness, – truth by means
> Of fable, showing while it screens, –
> Since highest truth, man e'er supplied,
> Was ever fable on outside.
> Such gleams made bright the earth an age ;
> Now the whole sun 's his heritage !
> Take up thy world, it is allowed,
> Thou who hast entered in the cloud !'

Browning's belief that the creative instinct can only function
at its highest potential under divine inspiration is the counterpart
of Tennyson's reliance on vision. It follows, then, that the poet-
seer must acknowledge the sanction under which he fulfills his

mission, and that, in Browning's own words, he will be 'impelled to embody the thing he perceives not so much with reference to the many below, as to the one above him, the supreme Intelligence which apprehends all things in their absolute truth'. 'How It Strikes a Contemporary' exemplifies this concept of the artist in his capacity as God's 'recording chief-inquisitor'. The protagonist of the poem is a solitary figure, alert to every incident in the life around him, yet mysteriously alien to his environment, his whole loyalty absorbed by the 'King' to whom he writes his nightly missive. Of the poet-seer Browning also says that his writing will 'be less a work than an effluence'. 'Saul' and 'Abt Vogler' illustrate the true nature of artistic inspiration. David in the former poem, at the approach of the final ecstatic vision of Christ, flings away the harp which has formalized his earlier utterances : 'Then truth came upon me. No harp more – no song more!' And in contrast to the musician who labors over the mannered fugues of Hugues of Saxe-Gotha, Abt Vogler is a master of extemporization. Vogler, furthermore, is playing in an empty church solely for his own pleasure when the inspiration descends. His mystic communion with God is thus achieved as a private revelation. And although his improvisations can never be recaptured on earth, he is consoled by the knowledge that they have reached the One to whom they were addressed :

> All we have willed or hoped or dreamed of good shall exist;
>   Not its semblance, but itself; no beauty, nor good, nor power
> Whose voice has gone forth, but each survives for the melodist
>   When eternity affirms the conception of an hour.
> The high that proved too high, the heroic for earth too hard,
>   The passion that left the ground to lose itself in the sky,
> Are music sent up to God by the lover and the bard;
>   Enough that he heard it once : we shall hear it by-and-by.

But Abt Vogler remains something of an exception in Browning's gallery of artists. Even the seer's field of activity is this world and the life which he shares with other men. God is manifest through his handiwork, and all that mortals can know of his being comes in rightly interpreting the phenomena which condition earthly existence. It is on these phenomena that the imagination must exercise itself, avoiding all willful delusions prompted by the intellect. Any work of the imagination which fails to take cognizance of the facts of human experience is necessarily for Browning either false or imperfect. Thus in 'Old Pictures in Florence' he chooses Christian in preference to Greek art because of the classic artist's unrealistic refusal to 'paint man man'. Similarly, the speaker in the eighth lyric of 'James Lee's Wife' has learned from Leonardo that there is more true beauty in the work-worn hand of a peasant than in any academic dream of perfection that 'lived long ago or was never born'. And in 'Transcendentalism : A Poem in Twelve Books' the youthful poet gets severely scolded for letting his vision of actuality become obscured by metaphysical theories: 'So come, the harp back to your heart again ! / You are a poem, though your poem's naught.'

The greatest artists are those whose sense and intuitions work together in harmonious unison. The great enemy of man's intuitional nature, as we have seen, is the intellect; and in artistic enterprises the intellect's weapon of attack against the freshness and immediacy of sensory impressions is tradition. Therefore, the artists whom Browning holds up for admiration are, like his lovers and men of action, non-conformists, rebels and individualists on instinct. The fullest expression of the poet's aesthetic philosophy is to be found in 'Fra Lippo Lippi'. The circumstances under which we encounter Fra Lippo are significant in themselves; for he has just been apprehended as a potential lawbreaker. We learn that he has fled the confinement of his patron's house because it is carnival time and he is unable to resist the lure of the streets. The irrepressible gaiety of life is implicit in the jigging refrain that keeps running through the painter's mind :

> Flower o' the broom,
> Take away love, and our earth is a tomb!

With this preparation, it is not surprising to find that Fra Lippo has rejected the institutional repression of the Church, and especially that he has thrown over traditional forms of ecclesiastical art as exemplified in the work of such artists as Fra Angelico and Lorenzo Monaco. Fra Lippo is one of Browning's incorruptible innocents. He paints by instinct; and what he paints is the world of his perceptions, not an intellectualized abstraction of it: 'The world and life's too big to pass for a dream.' But underlying the intensity of his response to human experience is the innate perception of a higher reality made manifest, if at all, through the appearances of this world. The artist cannot do better than reproduce with as great fidelity as possible his individual sense of the observed fact; in so doing he records his own gratitude for the privilege of living, and in the process opens the eyes of others to the meaning of life :

> However, you're my man, you've seen the world
> – The beauty and the wonder and the power,
> The shapes of things, their colours, lights and shades,
> Changes, surprises – and God made it all !
> – For what? Do you feel thankful, ay or no,
> For this fair town's face, yonder river's line,
> The mountain round it and the sky above,
> Much more the figures of man, woman, child,
> These are the frame to? What's it all about?
> To be passed over, despised? or dwelt upon,
> Wondered at? oh, this last of course ! – you say.
> But why not do as well as say, – paint these
> Just as they are, careless what comes of it?
> God's works – paint any one, and count it crime
> To let a truth slip. Don't object, 'His works
> 'Are here already; nature is complete :
> 'Suppose you reproduce her – (which you can't)
> 'There's no advantage ! you must beat her, then.'
> For, don't you mark? we're made so that we love
> First when we see them painted, things we have passed
> Perhaps a hundred times nor cared to see;
> And so they are better, painted – better to us,
> Which is the same thing. Art was given for that;
> God uses us to help each other so,
> Lending our minds out. Have you noticed, now,
> Your cullion's hanging face? A bit of chalk,
> And trust me but you should, though ! How much more,
> If I drew higher things with the same truth !
> That were to take the Prior's pulpit-place,

Interpret God to all of you ! Oh, oh,
It makes me mad to see what men shall do
And we in our graves ! This world's no blot for us,
Nor blank; it means intensely, and means good :
To find its meaning is my meat and drink.

In the appeal which his paintings make to the emotions of an unsophisticated populace Fra Lippo finds the ultimate vindication of his artistic theories. But while Browning believed that great art would always communicate so long as the sensibilities of its audience had not been deadened by tradition or materialized by social pressures, the half-hearted reception of his own early work inclined him to emphasize the creator's individual integrity rather than his influence. After *Sordello*, worldly prestige is never invoked as a consideration relevant to artistic success. Almost invariably, the artists in his poetry are somewhat alien figures, either neglected or misprized by the society in which they live. Even Fra Lippo shows a defensive attitude in challenging the tradition-ridden prejudices of his age. In 'A Toccata of Galuppi's' the composer plays his premonitory compositions to an unheeding audience. 'Memorabilia' and 'Popularity' have a like theme in the disheartening failure of Shelley and Keats to make an impression on their generation. And in 'One Word More' Browning, speaking out of his own experience, refers to the intolerable burden of misunderstanding to which the modern poet is subject when once he has assumed the prophet's rôle :

Wherefore? Heaven's gift takes earth's abatement !
He who smites the rock and spreads the water,
Bidding drink and live a crowd beneath him,
Even he, the minute makes immortal,
Proves, perchance, but mortal in the minute,
Desecrates, belike, the deed in doing.
While he smites, how can he but remember,
So he smote before, in such a peril,
When they stood and mocked – 'Shall smiting help us?'
When they drank and sneered – 'A stroke is easy !'
When they wiped their mouths and went their journey,
Throwing him for thanks – 'But drought was pleasant.'

Thus old memories mar the actual triumph;
Thus the doing savours of disrelish;
Thus achievement lacks a gracious somewhat;
O'er-importuned brows becloud the mandate,
Carelessness or consciousness, the gesture.
For he bears an ancient wrong about him,
Sees and knows again those phalanxed faces,
Hears, yet one time more, the 'customed prelude –
'How shouldst thou, of all men, smite and save us?'
Guesses what is like to prove the sequel –
'Egypt's flesh-pots – nay, the drought was better.'

Oh, the crowd must have emphatic warrant!
Theirs, the Sinai-forehead's cloven brilliance,
Right-arm's rod-sweep, tongue's imperial fiat.
Never dares the man put off the prophet.

SOURCE : *The Alien Vision of Victorian Poetry* (Princeton, N.J., 1952) pp. 91–119.

NOTES

1. In the ensuing discussion no attempt is made to adhere to the chronological order of these four collections. The fact that for the edition of his poems in 1863 Browning retained the original titles of his first three volumes of short pieces, but completely redistributed their contents, is evidence enough that he did not attach any significance to dates of composition within this body of work.

2. See Browning's defense of the nude art in the Parleying *With Francis Furini.*

Robert Langbaum

THE DRAMATIC MONOLOGUE: SYMPATHY VERSUS JUDGMENT (1957)

Writers on the dramatic monologue never fail to remark how little has been written on the subject – and I shall be no exception. The reason for the neglect is, I think, that no one has quite known what to do with the dramatic monologue except to classify it, to distinguish kinds of dramatic monologues and to distinguish the dramatic monologue from both the lyrical and the dramatic or narrative genres. Such classifications are all too easily made and have a way of killing off further interest in the subject. For they too often mean little beyond themselves, they close doors where they ought to open them.

The usual procedure in discussing the dramatic monologue is to find precedents for the form in the poetry of all periods, and then to establish, on the model of a handful of poems by Browning and Tennyson, objective criteria by which the form is henceforth to be recognized and judged. The procedure combines, I think, opposite mistakes; it is at once too restrictive and not restrictive enough, and in either case tells us too little. For once we decide to treat the dramatic monologue as a traditional genre, then every lyric in which the speaker seems to be someone other than the poet, almost all love songs and laments in fact (*Lycidas*, *The Song of Songs*, *Polyphemus' Complaint* by Theocritus, the Anglo-Saxon *Banished Wife's Complaint*) become dramatic monologues; as do all imaginary epistles and orations and all kinds of excerpts from plays and narratives – e.g. all long speeches and soliloquies, those portions of epics in which the hero recounts the events that occurred before the opening of the poem, Chaucer's prologues to the *Canterbury Tales* and the tales themselves since they are told by fictitious persons: almost all first person narratives, in fact, become dramatic monologues. While such a classification is *true* enough, what does it accomplish except to identify a certain mechanical resemblance? – since the poems retain more affinity to the lyric, the drama, the narrative than to each other.

But if we are, on the other hand, too restrictive, we do little more than describe the handful of Browning and Tennyson poems we are using as models. We come out with the idea that dramatic monologues are more or less like Browning's 'My Last Duchess', and that most dramatic monologues being rather less like it are not nearly so good. We are told, for example, that the dramatic monologue must have not only a speaker other than the poet but also a listener, an occasion, and some interplay between speaker and listener. But since a classification of this sort does not even cover all the dramatic monologues of Browning and Tennyson, let alone those of other poets, it inevitably leads to quarrels about which poems are to be admitted into the canon; and worse, it leads to sub-classifications, to a distinction between what one writer calls 'formal' dramatic monologues, which have only three of the necessary criteria, and 'typical' dramatic monologues, which have all four. As for poems with only the dramatized speaker and perhaps the occasion – poems like Tennyson's 'St Simeon Stylites' and Browning's 'Childe Roland' and 'Caliban', which are among the best and most famous of all dramatic monologues – this writer, in order to salvage her classification, calls them 'approximations'.[1]

The trouble with so narrow a criterion is that is suggests a decline of the dramatic monologue since Browning's time. It blinds us to the developing life of the form, to the importance of dramatic monologues in the work of such twentieth-century poets as Yeats, Eliot, Pound, Frost, Masters, Robinson and both Lowells, Amy and Robert (the form is particularly favoured by American poets). Robert Lowell's latest volume (*The Mills of the Kavanaughs*, 1951) consists entirely of dramatic monologues; while Pound, who in many places acknowledges his debt to Browning, has said of the dramatic monologues of Browning's *Men and Women* that 'the form of these poems is the most vital form of that period',[2] and has called a volume of his own *Personae*.

Although Eliot has little to say in favour of Browning, the dramatic monologue has been the main form in his work until he assumed what appears to be a personal voice in the series of religious meditations beginning with *Ash Wednesday*. The dramatic monologue is proportionately as important in Eliot's work as in Browning's, Eliot having contributed more to the development of the form than any poet since Browning.[3] Certainly *Prufrock, Portrait of a Lady, Gerontion, Journey of the Magi, A Song for Simeon* and *Marina* do as much credit to the dramatic monologue as anything of Browning's; while in *The Waste Land* Eliot has opened new possibilities for the form by constructing with a *collage* of voices the dramatic monologue of a modern consciousness that is also a cultural memory.[4]

To understand the continuing life of the dramatic monologue, we must abandon the exclusive concern with objective criteria by which poems are either combined when they lack any effect in common, or else are separated when they have a common effect but lack the necessary mechanical resemblance. It is when we look inside the dramatic monologue, when we consider its effect, its *way* of meaning, that we see its connection with the poetry that precedes and follows Browning. We see, on the one hand, that the dramatic monologue is unprecedented in its effect, that its effect distinguishes it, in spite of mechanical resemblance, from the monologues of traditional poetry; and on the other hand, we welcome as particularly illuminating just those 'approximations' that distress the classifiers. We welcome them because, having without the mechanical resemblance the same effect as the so-called 'typical' dramatic monologues, they show us what the form is essentially doing.

One writer on the dramatic monologue has managed to suggest what it is essentially doing; and he has done this at just the point where he abandons objective criteria to make an intuitive leap inside the form. In a Warton Lecture of 1925 which remains the best study of the dramatic monologue, M. W. MacCallum sees sympathy as its way of meaning:

But in every instance . . . the object [of the dramatic monologue] is to give facts from within. A certain dramatic understanding of the person speaking, which implies a certain dramatic sympathy with him, is not only the essential condition, but the final cause of the whole species.[5]

Unfortunately, MacCallum does not pursue the implications of this insight. If he had, he would not be so disposed to isolate the dramatic monologue within the Victorian period, and he would not confine his consideration to its quality as a monologue. Although the fact that a poem is a monologue helps to determine our sympathy for the speaker, since we must adopt his viewpoint as our entry into the poem, the monologue quality remains nevertheless a means, and not the only means, to the end – the end being to establish the reader's sympathetic relation to the poem, to give him 'facts from within'.

The distinction may seem niggling unless we see that, by subordinating the dramatic monologue's quality as a monologue to the larger question of the reader's relation to it, we are able to understand the wider connections of the form. For to give facts from within, to derive meaning that is from the poetic material itself rather than from an external standard of judgment, is the specifically romantic contribution to literature; while sympathy or projectiveness, what the Germans call *Einfühlung*, is the specifically romantic way of knowing. Once we consider the dramatic monologue as a poetry of sympathy, we are in a position to see the connection not only between the dramatic monologues of the nineteenth and twentieth centuries but between the dramatic monologue and all that is unprecedented in poetry since the later eighteenth century. We can see in the differences between the dramatic monologue on the one hand, and the dramatic lyric and lyrical drama of the romanticists on the other, the articulation of a form potential in romantic poetry from the start.

The standard account of the dramatic monologue is that Browning and Tennyson conceived it as a reaction against the romantic confessional style. This is probably true. Both poets had been stung by unfriendly criticism of certain early poems in which they had too much revealed themselves; and both poets published, in 1842, volumes which were a new departure in their careers and which contained dramatic monologues. The personal sting was probably responsible for Tennyson's decade of silence before 1842; it was almost certainly responsible for the disclaimer attached by Browning to his 1842 *Dramatic Lyrics*: 'so many utterances of so many imaginary persons, not mine'. Yet the reserve of the two poets cannot explain the coincidence that, working independently, they both arrived at the same form and produced at first try dramatic monologues so perfect (Browning's 'My Last Duchess' and Tennyson's 'Ulysses' and 'St Simeon Stylites') that they were never themselves to surpass them. We must look for precedents; we must suspect that they inherited a form which required only one more step in its development to achieve the objectivity they desired.

Browning's poetry before 1842 suggests by the manner of its failure the kind of precedent that lay behind the dramatic monologue, and the kind of problem that remained for the dramatic monologue to solve. His first published work, *Pauline* (1833), is the poem in which he too much revealed himself. It is transparently autobiographical (although the fictitious identity of the lady addressed provides a disguise of a sort), tracing the poet's intellectual development up to the age of twenty, the time of writing. It was of *Pauline* that John Stuart Mill said: 'The writer seems to me possessed with a more intense and morbid self-consciousness than I ever knew in any sane human being' – a criticism Browning took so to heart that he would not allow *Pauline* to be published again until 1867; and then with an apologetic preface which repeats the disclaimer of 1842: 'The thing was my earliest attempt at "poetry always dramatic in principle, and so many utterances of so many imaginary persons, not mine."' In spite of which disclaimer, he is reported to have said in his old age that 'his early poems were so transparent in their meaning as to draw down upon him the ridicule of the critics, and that, boy as he was, this ridicule and censure stung him into quite another style of writing'.[6]

We can follow his attempts at 'another style' in *Paracelsus* (1835), a dramatic poem, and *Sordello* (1833–40), an historical narrative. There is, however, little enough drama in *Paracelsus*, and the narrative line is at best intermittent in *Sordello*; in both poems the style that takes over is the introspective, transparently autobiographical history of a soul in the manner of *Pauline* – the soul being in all three recognizable as the same passionately idealistic and endlessly ambitious, endlessly self-absorbed disciple of Shelley. In the preface to the first edition of *Paracelsus*, Browning says that he has reversed the usual method of drama:

> Instead of having recourse to an external machinery of incidents to create and evolve the crisis I desire to produce, I have ventured to display somewhat minutely the mood itself in its rise and progress, and have suffered the agency by which it is influenced and determined to be generally discernible in its effects alone, and subordinate throughout, if not altogether excluded.

And reflecting in 1863 on the failure of *Sordello*, he says in the preface dedicating the new edition of the poem to his friend, the French critic Milsand: 'My stress lay on the incidents in the development of a soul: little else is worth study. I, at least, always thought so – you, with many known and unknown to me, think so – others may one day think so.'

Did Browning forget that the romantic poets had thought so, that even Arnold, who disagreed, could hardly help but write poetry as though he too thought so, and that the enormous popularity of the 'spasmodic' poets gave evidence that by mid-century almost everyone thought so? The question is perhaps answered by Milsand, who, in reviewing *Men and Women* for the *Revue Contemporaine* of September 1856, describes Browning's dramatic monologues in terms applicable to the whole of what I have been calling the poetry of experience. 'What Mr Browning has attempted,' says Milsand, 'is the fusion of two kinds of poetry into one.' And after citing Browning's remarks in the 'Essay on Shelley' on the distinction between subjective and objective poetry:

> This alone indicates that he sympathizes equally with both kinds of inspiration, and I am inclined to think that from the beginning, and partly without his knowing it, his constant effort has been to reconcile and combine them, in order to find a way of being, not in turn but simultaneously, lyric and dramatic, subjective and pictorial. . . . [His poetry] would have us conceive the inner significance of things by making us see their exteriors.[7]

M.A.W.—E

Compare these remarks of Milsand and Browning with Wordsworth's : 'the feeling therein developed gives importance to the
action and situation, and not the action and situation to the
feeling', and with Pound's description of his own poetry :

To me the short so-called dramatic lyric – at any rate the sort of
thing I do – is the poetic part of a drama the rest of which (to
me the prose part) is left to the reader's imagination or implied or
set in a short note. I catch the character I happen to be interested
in at the moment he interests me, usually a moment of song, self-
analysis, or sudden understanding or revelation. And the rest of
the play would bore me and presumably the reader.[8]

Add to the comparison Pound's idea that drama is less poetic
than other kinds of poetry because 'the maximum charge of
verbal meaning cannot be used on the stage',[9] and Virginia
Woolf's aim 'to saturate' in her novels 'every atom' :

I mean to eliminate all waste, deadness, superfluity : to give the
moment whole; whatever it includes. . . . Waste, deadness, come
from the inclusion of things that don't belong to the moment; this
appalling narrative business of the realist : getting on from lunch
to dinner : it is false, unreal, merely conventional. Why admit anything to literature that is not poetry – by which I mean saturated?[10]

And we see Browning's innovations as part of a general change of
sensibility – a demand that all literature yield much the same
effect, an effect of lyrical intensity.

When we have said all the objective things about Browning's 'My
Last Duchess', we will not have arrived at the meaning until we
point out what can only be substantiated by an appeal to effect –
that moral judgment does not figure importantly in our response
to the duke, that we even identify ourselves with him. But how
is such an effect produced in a poem about a cruel Italian duke
of the Renaissance who out of unreasonable jealousy has had his
last duchess put to death, and is now about to contract a second
marriage for the sake of dowry? Certainly, no summary or para-
phrase would indicate that condemnation is not our principal

response. The difference must be laid to form, to that extra quantity which makes the difference in artistic discourse between content and meaning.

The objective fact that the poem is made up entirely of the duke's utterance has of course much to do with the final meaning, and it is important to say that the poem is in form a monologue. But much more remains to be said about the way in which the content is laid out, before we can come near accounting for the whole meaning. It is important that the duke tells the story of his kind and generous last duchess to, of all people, the envoy from his prospective duchess. It is important that he tells his story while showing off to the envoy the artistic merits of a portrait of the last duchess. It is above all important that the duke carries off his outrageous indiscretion, proceeding triumphantly in the end downstairs to conclude arrangements for the dowry. All this is important not only as content but also as form, because it establishes a relation between the duke on the one hand, and the portrait and the envoy on the other, which determines the reader's relation to the duke and therefore to the poem – which determines, in other words, the poem's meaning.

The utter outrageousness of the duke's behaviour makes condemnation the least interesting response, certainly not the response that can account for the poem's success. What interests us more than the duke's wickedness is his immense attractiveness. His conviction of matchless superiority, his intelligence and bland amorality, his poise, his taste for art, his manners – high-handed aristocratic manners that break the ordinary rules and assert the duke's superiority when he is being most solicitous of the envoy, waiving their difference of rank ('Nay, we'll gò/ Together down, sir'); these qualities overwhelm the envoy, causing him apparently to suspend judgment of the duke, for he raises no demur. The reader is no less overwhelmed. We suspend moral judgment because we prefer to participate in the duke's power and freedom, in his hard core of character fiercely loyal to itself. Moral judgment is in fact important as the thing to be suspended, as a measure of the price we pay for the privilege of appreciating to the full this extraordinary man.

It is because the duke determines the arrangement and relative

subordination of the parts that the poem means what it does. The
duchess's goodness shines through the duke's utterance; he makes
no attempt to conceal it, so preoccupied is he with his own
standard of judgment and so oblivious of the world's. Thus the
duchess's case is subordinated to the duke's, the novelty and complexity of which engages our attention. We are busy trying to
understand the man who can combine the connoisseur's pride in
the lady's beauty with a pride that caused him to murder the
lady rather than tell her in what way she displeased him, for in
that 'would be some stooping; and I choose/ Never to stoop.'
The duke's paradoxical nature is fully revealed when, having
boasted how at his command the duchess's life was extinguished,
he turns back to the portrait to admire of all things its lifelikeness : 'There she stands/ As if alive.'

     This occurs ten lines from the end, and we might suppose we
have by now taken the duke's measure. But the next ten lines
produce a series of shocks that outstrip each time our understanding of the duke, and keep us panting after revelation with no
opportunity to consolidate our impression of him for moral
judgment. For it is at this point that we learn to whom he has
been talking; and he goes on to talk about dowry, even allowing
himself to murmur the hypocritical assurance that the new bride's
self and not the dowry is of course his object. It seems to me that
one side of the duke's nature is here stretched as far as it will go;
the dazzling figure threatens to decline into paltriness admitting
moral judgment, when Browning retrieves it with two brilliant
strokes. First, there is the lordly waiving of rank's privilege as
the duke and the envoy are about to proceed downstairs, and
then there is the perfect all-revealing gesture of the last two and a
half lines when the duke stops to show off yet another object in
his collection :

<blockquote>
Notice Neptune, though,
Taming a sea-horse, thought a rarity,
Which Claus of Innsbruck cast in bronze for me !
</blockquote>

     The lines bring all the parts of the poem into final combination,
with just the relative values that constitute the poem's meaning.

The nobleman does not hurry on his way to business, the connoisseur cannot resist showing off yet another precious object, the possessive egotist counts up his possessions even as he moves toward the acquirement of a new possession, a well-dowered bride; and most important, the last duchess is seen in final perspective. She takes her place as one of a line of objects in an art collection; her sad story becomes the *cicerone's* anecdote lending piquancy to the portrait. The duke has taken from her what he wants, her beauty, and thrown the life away; and we watch with awe as he proceeds to take what he wants from the envoy and by implication from the new duchess. He carries all before him by sheer force of will so undeflected by ordinary compunctions as even, I think, to call into question – the question rushes into place behind the startling illumination of the last lines, and lingers as the poem's haunting afternote – the duke's sanity.

The duke reveals all this about himself, grows to his full stature, because we allow him to have his way with us; we subordinate all other considerations to the business of understanding him. If we allowed indignation, or pity for the duchess, to take over when the duke moves from his account of the murder to admire the lifelikeness of the portrait, the poem could hold no further surprises for us; it could not even go on to reinforce our judgment as to the duke's wickedness, since the duke does not grow in wickedness after the account of the murder. He grows in strength of character, and in the arrogance and poise which enable him to continue command of the situation after his confession of murder has threatened to turn it against him. To take the full measure of the duke's distinction we must be less concerned to condemn than to appreciate the triumphant transition by which he ignores clean out of existence any judgment of his story that the envoy might have presumed to invent. We must be concerned to appreciate the exquisite timing of the duke's delay over Neptune, to appreciate its fidelity to the duke's own inner rhythm as he tries once more the envoy's already sorely tried patience, and as he teases the reader too by delaying for a lordly whim the poem's conclusion. This willingness of the reader to understand the duke, even to sympathize with him as a necessary condition of reading the poem, is the key to the poem's form. It alone is responsible for a meaning not inherent in the content itself but determined peculiarly by the treatment.

I have chosen 'My Last Duchess' to illustrate the working of sympathy, just because the duke's egregious villainy makes especially apparent the split between moral judgment and our actual feeling for him. The poem carries to the limit an effect peculiarly the genius of the dramatic monologue – I mean the effect created by the tension between sympathy and moral judgment. Although we seldom meet again such an unmitigated villain as the duke, it is safe to say that most successful dramatic monologues deal with speakers who are in some way reprehensible.

Browning delighted in making a case for the apparently immoral position; and the dramatic monologue, since it requires sympathy for the speaker as a condition of reading the poem, is an excellent vehicle for the 'impossible' case. Mr Sludge and Bishop Blougram in matters of the spirit, Prince Hohenstiel-Schwangau in politics, and in love Don Juan of *Fifine*, are all Machiavellians who defend themselves by an amoral casuistry. The combination of villain and aesthete creates an especially strong tension, and Browning exploits the combination not only in 'My Last Duchess' but again in 'The Bishop Orders his Tomb', where the dying Renaissance bishop reveals his venality and shocking perversion of Christianity together with his undeniable taste for magnificence :

> Some lump, ah God, of *lapis lazuli*,
> Big as a Jew's head cut off at the nape,
> Blue as a vein o'er the Madonna's breast . . .

and again in 'The Laboratory' where the Rococo court lady is much concerned with the colour of the poison she buys and would like

> To carry pure death in an earring, a casket,
> A signet, a fan-mount, a filigree basket !

To the extent that these poems are successful, we admire the speaker for his power of intellect (as in 'Blougram') or for his aesthetic passion and sheer passion for living (as in 'The Bishop Orders his Tomb'). 'Hohenstiel-Schwangau' and *Fifine* are not successful because no outline of character emerges from the intricacy of the argument, there is no one to sympathize with and we are therefore not convinced even though the arguments are every bit as good as in the successful poems. Arguments cannot make the case in the dramatic monologue but only passion, power, strength of will and intellect, just those existential virtues which are independent of logical and moral correctness and are therefore best made out through sympathy and when clearly separated from, even opposed to, the other virtues. Browning's contemporaries accused him of 'perversity' because they found it necessary to sympathize with his reprehensible characters.

But Browning's perversity is intellectual and moral in the sense that most of his characters have taken up their extraordinary positions through a perfectly normal act of will. Tennyson, on the other hand, although less interested in novel moral positions, goes much farther than Browning in dealing in his successful dramatic monologues with an emotional perversity that verges on the pathological. Morally, Tennyson's 'St Simeon Stylites' is a conventional liberal Protestant attack upon asceticism. But the poem is unusual because the saint's passion for a heavenly crown is shown as essentially demonic; his hallucinations, self-loathing and insatiable lust for self-punishment suggest a psyche as diseased (we should nowadays call it sado-masochistic) as the ulcerous flesh he boasts of. St Simeon conceives himself in both body and soul as one disgusting sore:

> Altho' I be the basest of mankind,
> From scalp to sole one slough and crust of sin,

and there is in his advice to his disciples a certain obscene zest:

> Mortify
> Your flesh, like me, with scourges and with thorns;
> Smite, shrink not, spare not.

Browning would have complicated the case against asceticism, he might have emphasized the moral ambiguity presented by the saintly ambition which does not differ in quality from the ambition for money or empire; or if he did simplify, it would be to present the case against ascetic ritualism satirically as in 'The Spanish Cloister'. Tennyson, however, is more interested in the psychological ambiguity, pursuing the saint's passion to its obscurely sexual recesses.

Treating a similar example of religious buccaneering, Browning has written in 'Johannes Agricola in Meditation' a dramatic monologue of sheer lyric exultation. Johannes is, like St Simeon, on a rampage for salvation and confident of attaining it. But compare with St Simeon's the beauty of Johannes' conception of his own spiritual position :

> There's heaven above, and night by night
>   I look right through its gorgeous roof;
> No suns and moons though e'er so bright
>   Avail to stop me; splendour-proof
>   I keep the broods of stars aloof :
> For I intend to get to God,
>   For 'tis to God I speed so fast,
> For in God's breast, my own abode,
>   Those shoals of dazzling glory passed,
>   I lay my spirit down at last.

Although Browning clearly intends us to disapprove of Johannes' Antinomianism, he complicates the issue by showing the lofty passion that can proceed from the immoral doctrine. Nevertheless, the passion is rationally accounted for by the doctrine; Johannes is a fanatic, one who has gone to a philosophical extreme. A moral and philosophical term like *fanatic* will not suffice, however, to characterize St Simeon; we need also a term out of abnormal psychology. It is interesting to note in this connection that 'Johannes Agricola' originally appeared together with 'Porphyria's Lover' under the common heading of 'Madhouse Cells', but the poems were later seperated and the heading abandoned. Without the heading, there is nothing in 'Johannes Agricola' to make us suppose that the speaker is mad, that he is anything more than fanatically devoted to his Antinomian principles. That is because Browning does not, like Tennyson in

'St Simeon', pursue the passion downward to those subrational depths where lurk unsuspected motives.

In 'Porphyria's Lover', the speaker is undoubtedly mad. He strangles Porphyria with her own hair, as a culminating expression of his love and in order to preserve unchanged the perfect moment of her surrender to him. But even here, Browning is relying upon an extraordinary complication of what still remains a rationally understandable motive. The motive and action are no more unreasonable than in 'A Forgiveness', where we do not consider the speaker or his wife mad. She is unfaithful because of her great love for him, and he eventually forgives her by awarding her hate instead of contempt; she allows the life blood to flow out of her to help his hate pass away in vengeance. The motives in both poems are likely to demonstrate for us rather more ingenuity than madness; and it is generally true that extraordinary motives in Browning come not from disordered subconscious urges but, as in Henry James, from the highest moral and intellectual refinement. . . .

* * * * *

Certainly the Italian Renaissance setting of 'My Last Duchess' helps us to suspend moral judgment of the duke, since we partly at least take an historical view; we accept the combination of villainy with taste and manners as a phenomenon of the Renaissance and of the old aristocratic order generally. The extraordinary combination pleases us the way it would the historian, since it impresses upon us the difference of the past from the present. We cannot, however, entirely historicize our moral judgment in this poem, because the duke's crime is too egregious to support historical generalization. More important, therefore, for the suspension of moral judgment is our psychologizing attitude – our willingness to take up the duke's view of events purely for the sake of understanding him, the more outrageous his view the more illuminating for us the psychological revelation.

In 'The Bishop Orders his Tomb', however, our judgment is mainly historicized because the bishop's sins are not extraordinary but the universally human venalities couched, significantly for the historian, in the predilections of the Italian Renaissance. Thus, the bishop gives vent to materialism and snobbery by planning a bigger and better tomb than his clerical rival's. This poem can be read as a portrait of the age, our moral judgment of the bishop depending upon our moral judgment of the age. Ruskin praised the poem for its historical validity: 'It is nearly all that I said of the Central Renaissance in thirty pages of *The Stones of Venice* put into as many lines'; but being no friend of the Renaissance, this is the spirit of the age he conceived Browning to have caught: 'its worldliness, inconsistency, pride, hypocrisy, ignorance of itself, love of art, of luxury, and of good Latin.'[11] Browning, who admired the Renaissance, would have admitted all this but he would have insisted, too, upon the enterprise and robust aliveness of the age. What matters, however, is that Browning has presented an historical image the validity of which we can all agree upon, even if our moral judgments differ as they do about the past itself.

In the same way, our understanding of the duke in 'My Last Duchess' has a primary validity which is not disturbed by our differing moral judgments after we have finished reading the poem – it being characteristically the style of the dramatic monologue to present its material empirically, as a fact existing before and apart from moral judgment which remains always secondary and problematical. Even where the speaker is specifically concerned with a moral question, he arrives at his answer empirically, as a necessary outcome of conditions within the poem and not through appeal to an outside moral code. Since these conditions are always psychological and sometimes historical as well – since the answer is determined, in other words, by the speaker's nature and the time he inhabits – the moral meaning is of limited application but enjoys within the limiting conditions of the poem a validity which no subsequent differences in judgment can disturb.

Take as an example Browning's dramatic monologues in defence of Christianity. Although the poet has undoubtedly an axe to grind, he maintains a distinction between the undeniable fact of the speaker's response to the conditions of the poem and the general Christian formulation which the reader may or may not draw for himself. The speaker starts with a blank slate as regards Christianity, and is brought by the conditions of the poem to a perception of need for the kind of answer provided by Christianity. Nevertheless, the perception is not expressed in the vocabulary of Christian dogma and the speaker does not himself arrive at a Christian formulation.

The speakers of the two epistolary monologues, 'Karshish' and 'Cleon', are first-century pagans brought by the historical moment and their own psychological requirements to perceive the need for a God of Love ('Karshish') and a promise of personal immortality ('Cleon'). But they arrive at the perception through secular concepts, and are prevented by these same concepts from embracing the Christian answer that lies before them. Karshish is an Arab physician travelling in Judea who reports the case of the risen Lazarus as a medical curiosity, regarding Jesus as some master physician with the cure for a disease that simulates death. He is ashamed, writing to his medical teacher, of the story's mystical suggestions and purposely mixes it up with, and even tries to subordinate it to, reports of cures and medicinal herbs. Yet it is clear throughout that the story haunts him, and he has already apologized for taking up so much space with it when he interrupts himself in a magnificent final outburst that reveals the story's impact upon his deepest feelings:

> The very God! think, Abib; dost thou think?
> So, the All-great, were the All-Loving too – .

Nevertheless, he returns in the last line to the scientific judgment, calling Lazarus a madman and using to characterize the story the same words he has used to characterize other medical curiosities: 'it is strange.'

Cleon is a Greek of the last period; master of poetry, painting, sculpture, music, philosophy, he sums up within himself the whole Greek cultural accomplishment. Yet writing to a Greek Tyrant who possesses all that Greek material culture can afford, he encourages the Tyrant's despair by describing his own. The fruits of culture – self-consciousness and the increased capacity for joy – are curses, he says, since they only heighten our aware-

ness that we must die without ever having tasted the joy our refinement has taught us to conceive. He demonstrates conclusively,
in the manner of the Greek dialectic, that life without hope of
immortality is unbearable. 'It is so horrible,' he says,

> I dare at times imagine to my need
> Some future state revealed to us by Zeus,
> Unlimited in capability
> For joy, as this is in desire for joy,
> – To seek which, the joy-hunger forces us.

He despairs because Zeus has not revealed this. Nevertheless, he
dismisses in a hasty postscript the pretentions of 'one called
Paulus', 'a mere barbarian Jew', to have 'access to a secret shut
from us'.

The need for Christianity stands as empiric fact in these poems,
just because it appears in spite of intellectual and cultural objections. In 'Saul' there are no objections, but the need is still
empiric in that it appears before the Christian formulation of it.
The young David sings to Saul of God's love, of His sacrifice for
man, and His gift of eternal life, because he needs to sing of the
highest conceivable joy, his songs about lesser joys having failed
to dispel Saul's depression. David 'induces' God's love for Saul
from his own, God's willingness to suffer for Saul from his own
willingness, and God's gift of eternal life from his own desire to
offer Saul the most precious gift possible.

> 'O Saul,
>   it shall be
> A face like my face that receives thee; a Man like to me,
> Thou shalt love and be loved by, for ever :
>   a Hand like this hand
> Shall throw open the gates of new life to thee !
>   See the Christ stand !'

The speaker of 'A Death in the Desert' is a Christian – St John,
the beloved disciple and author of the Fourth Gospel, conceived
as speaking his last words before dying at a very old age. He has
outlived the generation that witnessed the miracles of Christ and
the apostles, and has lived to see a generation that questions the
promise of Christ's coming and even His existence. As the last

living eye-witness, John has been able to reassure this generation; but dying, he leaves a kind of Fifth Gospel for the skeptical generations to follow, generations that will question the existence of John himself. It is an empiricist gospel. 'I say, to test man, the proofs shift,' says John. But this is well, since belief in God would have no moral effect were it as inevitable as belief in the facts of nature. Myth, man's apprehension of truth, changes; but the Truth remains for each generation to rediscover for itself. The later generations will have sufficiently profited from the moral effect of Christianity, so as not to require proof by miracle or direct revelation. They will be able to 'induce' God's love from their own and from their need to conceive a love higher than theirs. Thus, Browning invests with dogmatic authority his own anti-dogmatic line of Christian apologetics.

In 'Bishop Blougram's Apology', the case is complicated by the inappropriateness of the speaker and his argument to the Christian principles being defended. Blougram, we are told in an epilogue, 'said true things, but called them by wrong names'. A Roman Catholic bishop, he has achieved by way of the Church the good things of this world and he points to his success as a sign that he has made the right choice. For his relatively unsuccessful opponent, the agnostic literary man, Gigadibs, the bishop is guilty of hypocrisy, a vice Gigadibs cannot be accused of since he has made no commitments. Since the bishop admits to religious doubt (Gigadibs lives 'a life of doubt diversified by faith', the bishop 'one of faith diversified by doubt'), Gigadibs can even take pride in a superior respect for religion, he for one not having compromised with belief. Thus, we have the paradox of the compromising worldly Christian against the uncompromising unworldly infidel – a conception demonstrating again Browning's idea that the proofs do not much matter, that there are many proofs better and worse for the same Truth. For if Blougram is right with the wrong reasons, Gigadibs with admirable reasons or at least sentiments is quite wrong.

The point of the poem is that Blougram makes his case, even if on inappropriate grounds. He knows his argument is not the best ('he believed,' according to the epilogue, 'say, half he spoke'), for the grounds are his opponent's; it is Blougram's achievement

that he makes Gigadibs see what the agnostic's proper grounds
are. He is doing what Browning does in all the dramatic monologues on religion – making the empiricist argument, starting
without any assumptions as to faith and transcendental values.
Granting that belief and unbelief are equally problematical,
Blougram proceeds to show that even in terms of this world only
belief bears fruit while unbelief does not. This is indicated by
Blougram's material success, but also by the fact that his moral
behaviour, however imperfect, is at least in the direction of his
professed principles; whereas Gigadibs' equally moral behaviour
is inconsistent with his principles. Who, then, is the hypocrite? 'I
live my life here;' says Blougram, 'yours you dare not live.'

But the fact remains – and this is the dramatic ambiguity
matching the intellectual – that the bishop is no better than his
argument, though he can conceive a better argument and a better
kind of person. He cannot convert Gigadibs because his argument,
for all its suggestion of a Truth higher than itself, must be understood dramatically as rationalizing a selfish wordly existence.
What Gigadibs apparently does learn is that he is no better than
the bishop, that he has been the same kind of person after the
same kind of rewards only not succeeding so well, and that he
has been as intellectually and morally dishonest with his senti-
mental liberalism as the bishop with his casuistry. All this is suggested indirectly by the last few lines of the epilogue, where we
are told that Gigadibs has gone off as a settler to Australia. Rid
of false intellectual baggage (the bishop's as well as his own), he
will presumably start again from the beginning, 'inducing' the
Truth for himself. 'I hope,' says Browning,

> By this time he has tested his first plough,
> And studied his last chapter of St John.

St John, note, who makes the empiricist argument in 'A Death
in the Desert', and whose Gospel concludes with the risen Jesus
feeding the disciples and bidding them 'Feed my sheep'.

Although 'Blougram' and 'A Death in the Desert' are too dis-
cursive to communicate their religious perceptions in the manner
of 'Karshish', 'Cleon' and 'Saul', as the speaker's immediate

experience, they make their case empirically because in non-Christian terms. They might be considered as setting forth the rhetorical method of the more dramatic poems, a method for being taken seriously as intelligent and modern when broaching religion to the skeptical post-Enlightenment mind. The reader is assumed to be Gigadibs (it is because the bishop is so intelligent that Gigadibs finds it difficult to understand how he can believe), and the poet makes for his benefit a kind of 'minimum argument', taking off from his grounds and obtruding no dogmatic assertions.

Eliot addresses his religious poetry to the same kind of reader, communicating his religious perceptions in terms that fall short of Christian dogma. This is especially interesting in Eliot since his concern has been with dogmatic religion, whereas Browning was always anti-dogmatic. Of course, the method is in both poets not merely a deliberate rhetorical device but the necessary outcome of their own religious uncertainties, and a sign that they share like Blougram the post-Enlightenment mind. This is again especially apparent in Eliot, who has dramatized in his poetry his movement from skepticism to orthodoxy, whereas Browning's poetry shows no significant religious *development*. Nevertheless, there is something of the obtuseness of Karshish and Cleon in those speakers of Eliot's dramatic monologues whose religious perceptions fall short of the Christian truth – and with the same effect as in Browning, that the reader can give assent to the speaker's experience without having to agree on doctrine.

In *Journey of the Magi*, one of the Magi describes with great clarity and detail the hardships of the journey to Bethlehem, but cannot say for certain what he saw there or what it meant. The Magi returned to their Kingdoms, like Karshish and Cleon 'no longer at ease here, in the old dispensation', but still without light. The old Jew Simeon, in *A Song for Simeon*, is somewhat in the position of Browning's David in 'Saul'; he sees clearly the glory of Christianity, but is too old to embrace it – not for him 'the ultimate vision', the new dispensation is ahead of his time. In *Marina*, the speaker apparently finds the ultimate vision in the face of his newly recovered daughter and in the woodthrush song through the fog, but the vision is still not intelligible, not translated into Christian terms.

In the earlier skeptical poems, the fog is even thicker and no song of revelation comes through it. But Eliot uses idolatrous or 'minimum' analogues to the Christian myth to indicate the groping for meaning, his own groping and that of the characters within the poem. The characters in 'Gerontion' and *The Waste Land* practise idolatries, aesthetic and occultist. 'Gerontion' ends with an occultist vision of the modern, cosmopolitan, unbelieving dead whirled around the universe on a meaningless wind:

> De Bailhache, Fresca, Mrs Cammel, whirled
> Beyond the circuit of the shuddering Bear
> In fractured atoms.

Yet seen in the subsequent lines as a natural phenomenon, the wind has a certain meaning in that it unites the parts of nature, north and south, into a single living whole:

> Gull against the wind, in the windy straits
> Of Belle Isle, or running on the Horn,
> White feathers in the snow, the Gulf claims,

and there is, I think, the suggestion that the wind may be a cleansing wind, one which may bring the rain the aged speaker has been waiting for. The same wind that carries off the dead may bring renewal to the depleted living; that is as much meaning and as much hope as the speaker can achieve.

It is as much meaning as our pagan ancestors achieved in the primitive vegetation myths of death and renewal, and Eliot uses the analogy of these myths to give at least that much meaning to the jumbled fragments of *The Waste Land*. Just as the vegetation gods were slain so they might rise renewed and restore the fertility of the land; so the longing for death, which pervades the modern waste land, is a longing for renewal and, if the reader wants to carry the analogy a step farther, a longing for redemption through the blood of Christ, the slain God.

The analogy with the vegetation myths is maintained even in the *Four Quartets*, which are written from a solidly orthodox position. The religious perceptions of these poems are couched less in

Christian terms than in terms of that mystical fusion of anthropology and psychology, of myth and the unconscious, that Jung effected.[12] One wonders if the *Four Quartets* are not, for all their orthodoxy, more satisfying to the skeptical than to the orthodox, since the latter might well prefer an articulation of religious truth no less explicit than their own convictions. Post-Enlightenment minds, on the other hand, are particularly fascinated by the mystique of myth and the unconscious as a way back, I think, to a kind of religious speculation which commits them to nothing while preserving intact their status as intelligent, scientific and modern. Myth and the unconscious are contemporary equivalents of Browning's pragmatism in making the 'minimum' argument for Christianity.

Although not the only way to talk religion empirically, the dramatic monologue offers certain advantages to the poet who is not committed to a religious position, or who is addressing readers not committed and not wanting to be. The use of the speaker enables him to dramatize a position the possibilities of which he may want to explore as Browning explores the 'impossible' case. The speaker also enables him to dramatize an emotional apprehension in advance of or in conflict with his intellectual convictions – a disequilibrium perhaps inevitable to that mind which I have been calling post-Enlightenment or romantic because, having been intellectually through the Enlightenment, it tries to re-establish some spiritual possibility. Browning's St John, in 'A Death in the Desert', defends religious myth as the expression of just this disequilibrium, of the emotional apprehension that exceeds formulated knowledge:

> 'man knows partly but conceives beside,
> Creeps ever on from fancies to the fact,
> And in this striving, this converting air
> Into a solid he may grasp and use,
> Finds progress, man's distinctive mark alone,
> Not God's, and not the beasts'.'

Even Eliot who professes to be against this 'dissociation' of emotional apprehension from its formulated articulation (which

for him is dogma), even in Eliot's poetry emotion is always a step
ahead of reason – as for example the dim adumbrations of
Christianity provided by the vegetation mythology of *The Waste
Land*, or the disturbance of the Magi that exceeds their understanding, or that ultimate vision in *Marina* the articulation of
which is obscured by the fog.

Not only can the speaker of the dramatic monologue dramatize a position to which the poet is not ready to commit himself
intellectually, but the sympathy which we give the speaker for
the sake of the poem and apart from judgment makes it possible
for the reader to participate in a position, to see what it feels
like to believe that way, without having finally to agree. There
is, in other words, the same split between sympathy and judgment
that we saw at work in our relation to the duke of 'My Last
Duchess'. The split is naturally most apparent in those dramatic
monologues where the speaker is in some way reprehensible,
where sympathy is in conflict with judgment, but it is also at
work where sympathy is congruent with judgment although a
step ahead of it. The split must in fact be at work to some degree,
if the poem is to generate the effect which makes it a dramatic
monologue.

Browning's 'Rabbi Ben Ezra' is a dramatic monologue by virtue of its title only; otherwise it is a direct statement of a philosophical idea, because there is no characterization setting.
Because the statement is not conditioned by a speaker and a
situation, there is no way of apprehending it other than intellectually; there is no split between its validity as somebody's apprehension and its objective validity as an idea. But in 'Abt Vogler',
where the statement is also approved of, it is conditioned by the
speaker's ecstasy as he extemporizes on the organ. His sublime
vision of his music as annihilating the distinction between heaven
and earth has validity as part of the ecstatic experience of extem-
porizing, but becomes a matter of philosophical conjecture as the
ecstasy subsides and the music modulates back into the 'C Major
of this life'. The disequilibrium between the empiric vision that
lasts as long as the ecstasy and the music, and its philosophical
implication, makes sympathy operative; and the tension between
what is known through sympathy and what is only hypothesized

through judgment generates the effect characteristic of the dramatic monologue.

Since sympathy is the primary law of the dramatic monologue, how does judgment get established at all? How does the poet make clear what we are to think of the speaker and his statement? Sometimes it is not clear. The Catholic reader might well consider Tennyson's St Simeon admirable and holy. Readers still try to decide whether Browning is for or against Bishop Blougram. Browning was surprised at accusations of anti-Catholicism that followed the publication of the poem, but he was even more surprised when Cardinal Wiseman[13] (the model for Blougram) wrote in reviewing the poem for a Catholic journal: '*we should never feel surprise at his* [Browning's] *conversion.*' We now know, at least from external evidence if not from more careful reading, that Browning's final judgment is against Don Juan of *Fifine* and Prince Hohenstiel-Schwangau (representing Napoleon III). But the reviewers considered that he was defending the incontinent Don Juan and accused him of perversity; while of 'Hohenstiel-Schwangau', one reviewer said that it was a 'eulogism on the Second Empire', and another called it 'a scandalous attack on the old constant friend of England'.[14]

But these are exceptional cases, occurring mainly in Browning and the result partly of Browning's sometimes excessive ingenuity, partly of a judgment more complex than the reader is expecting, partly of careless reading. Certainly Don Juan's desertion of his wife and return to the gipsy girl in the end – even though he says it is for five minutes and 'to clear the matter up' – ought for the careful reader to show up his argument as rationalizing a weak character, although the argument contains in itself much that is valid. In the same way, the final reference to Gigadibs as starting from the beginning with a plough and the Gospel of St John ought to indicate that he is getting closer to the truth than Blougram. I have tried to indicate that more is involved in our judgment of the bishop than the simple alternatives of *for* and *against*. As the bishop himself says of the modern interest in character, which interest is precisely the material of the dramatic monologue :

Our interest's on the dangerous edge of things.
The honest thief, the tender murderer,
The superstitious atheist, demirep
That loves and saves her soul in new French books –
We watch while these in equilibrium keep
The giddy line midway : one step aside,
They're classed and done with. I, then, keep the line
Before your sages, – just the men to shrink
From the gross weights, coarse scales and labels broad
You offer their refinement. Fool or knave?
Why needs a bishop be a fool or knave
When there's a thousand diamond weights between?

There is judgment all right among modern empiricists, but it follows understanding and remains tentative and subordinate to it. In trying to take into account as many facts as possible and to be as supple and complex as the facts themselves, judgment cuts across the conventional categories, often dealing in paradoxes – the honest thief, the tender murderer. Above all, it brings no ready-made yardstick; but allows the case to establish itself in all its particularity, and to be judged according to criteria generated by its particularity.

In other words, judgment is largely psychologized and historicized. We adopt a man's point of view and the point of view of his age in order to judge him – which makes the judgment relative, limited in applicability to the particular conditions of the case. This is the kind of judgment we get in the dramatic monologue, which is for this reason an appropriate form for an empiricist and relativist age, an age which has come to consider value as an evolving thing dependent upon the changing individual and social requirements of the historical process. For such an age judgment can never be final, it has changed and will change again; it must be perpetually checked against fact, which comes before judgment and remains always more certain.

SOURCE: *The Poetry of Experience* (London, 1957) pp. 75–88, 96–108.

NOTES

1. Ina Beth Sessions in her book, *A Study of the Dramatic Monologue in American and Continental Literature* (San Antonio, Texas, 1933). An extract with revisions appears as 'The Dramatic Monologue', *PMLA* (June 1947). For other examples of this approach, see the only other book-length study: S. S. Curry, *Browning and the Dramatic Monologue* (Boston, 1908); and papers by Claud Howard, 'The Dramatic Monologue: Its Origin and Development', *Studies in Philology*, IV (Chapel Hill, N.C., 1910), and R. H. Fletcher, 'Browning's Dramatic Monologs [*sic*]', *Modern Language Notes* (April 1908).

2. Reviewing Eliot's *Prufrock and Other Observations* in 1917. Reprinted as 'T. S. Eliot', in *Literary Essays*, edited with an introduction by T. S. Eliot (Norfolk, Conn.; London, 1954) p. 419.

3. 'For the eventual writer of the literary history of the twentieth century, Eliot's development of the dramatic soliloquy, a form that has been called "the most flexible and characteristic genre of English verse", cannot be divorced from the impetus furnished by *Men and Women* to *Personae*.' F. O. Matthiessen, *The Achievement of T. S. Eliot* (London, 1935) p. 73.

4. The merging of individual into collective consciousness accounts for Tiresias, who is 'the most important personage in the poem, uniting all the rest. Just as the one-eyed merchant, seller of currants, melts into the Phoenician Sailor, and the latter is not wholly distinct from Ferdinand Prince of Naples, so all the women are one woman, and the two sexes meet in Tiresias. What Tiresias *sees*, in fact, is the substance of the poem'. (Eliot's Notes on *The Waste Land*, III, 218.)

5. M. W. MacCallum, 'The Dramatic Monologue in the Victorian Period', *Proceedings of the British Academy 1924–1925*, p. 276. See also an earlier paper which moves in the same direction, though not nearly so far: G. H. Palmer, 'The Monologue of Browning', *Harvard Theological Review* (April 1918); and the three pages Bliss Perry devotes to the subject in *A Study of Poetry* (Boston, 1920) pp. 267–70. Stopford Brooke makes the pioneering remarks on the dramatic monologue in chap. XIII of *Tennyson: His Art and Relation to Modern Life* (London, 1895). But Brooke in his *Tennyson* and William Lyon Phelps in chap. V of *Robert Browning, How To Know Him* (Indianapolis, 1915), are more concerned with the

content of individual dramatic monologues than with generic characteristics.

6. Quoted in W. C. DeVane, *A Browning Handbook* (New York, 1955) pp. 46–7; (London, 1937) p. 44. Just as the failure of *Pauline* is considered responsible for Browning's reluctance to speak in his own voice, so Tennyson seems to have been similarly wounded by the failure of his 1832 volume, especially by Croker's insulting review of it in the *Quarterly*. Harold Nicolson gives an amusing account of the *Quarterly* review, considering it as 'undoubtedly one of the many causes of the silent and morose decade which was to follow'. *Tennyson* (London, 1949) pp. 112–17.

7. pp. 545–6.

8. To William Carlos Williams, 21 October 1908, *Letters 1907–1941*, ed. D. D. Paige (New York, 1950) pp. 3–4; (London, 1951) p. 36.

9. *ABC of Reading* (New Haven, 1934) p. 33; (London, 1934) p. 31.

10. *A Writer's Diary*, ed. Leonard Woolf (London, 1953) p. 139.

11. *Modern Painters* (London and New York, 1907) IV, 370.

12. For a discussion of Eliot's use of Jungian ideas and symbols, see Elizabeth Drew, *T. S. Eliot: The Design of His Poetry* (New York, 1949; London, 1950).

13. [Editor's Note.] It has recently been established that Cardinal Wiseman did not, in fact, write the review. See Boyd Litzinger and Donald Smalley, *Browning: The Critical Heritage* (London, 1970) p. 185.

14. Quoted in DeVane, *A Browning Handbook* (New York, 1955) pp. 243, 369, 363; (London, 1937) pp. 216, 327, 321.

J. Hillis Miller

FROM *THE DISAPPEARANCE OF GOD* (1963)

The dramatic monologue is not simply a technical discovery or adaptation, chosen because it makes possible vividness and immediacy, or some other objective value. The decision to write dramatic monologues is Browning's way of dealing with his own existential problem. Other men seem to have a single germ of life which can be fulfilled in a single mode of existence. He alone must find some way to indulge all feelings equally, to hear all sides of life. Like other men he is doomed to limitation, and must obey the natural law which says '. . . beyond thee lies the infinite – Back to thy circumscription!' (x, 216).[1] Though Browning cannot ape God's infinitude, there is one way in which he can approach God's fullness, and that is through a certain kind of poetry. The direct way to God has failed. Now Browning must turn to the peripheral way, not the way up, but the way around. He must enter in patient humility the lives of the multitude of men and women who make up the world, and he must re-create these lives in his poems. Only by exhausting in this way the plenitude of the creation can he hope to reach the universality of the creator. There is not time to indulge in reality all the feelings which swarm within him. He must indulge them in imagination, in poetry.

Browning does not fool himself about the powers of poetry. Only God is the perfect poet, and enters completely into his poems. Only God can satisfy all his tendencies and impulses at once, for though the creation is temporal, all times are equally present to God. And only God is creatively autonomous. The earthly poet is dependent on the prior creation by God of the world, and can only imitate in his poems objects or people which already exist, have existed, or could conceivably exist. The mortal poet is bound to time. He cannot act all his creations at once, only one by one. Finally, he does not really enter, body and soul, into his creations. Each one of Browning's dramatic monologues is the playing of a role, the wearing of a mask. It is based on an 'as if'. Browning speaks for a time as if he were Mr Sludge or Bishop Blougram. He is able to 'enter each and all' of his 'men and women/ Live or dead or fashioned by [his] fancy', and 'use their service,/ Speak from every mouth, – the speech, a poem' (IV, 177). But all along we know, and Browning knows, that his playing the role of Sludge is only temporary, that the monologue will soon come to an end, that he will soon be putting on another costume, and performing Caliban, Guido, or Cleon. The juxtaposition of a large number of dramatic monologues betrays the artificiality of any one of them. God actually *is* Guido, Sludge, and the rest (including Browning himself). Browning only pretends to be these men. The least, miserable, sordid gesture of a real flesh and blood man is in a way worth more than all the poems in the world, as a number of Browning's characters affirm. Cleon asks, bitterly: '. . . if I paint,/ Carve the young Phœbus, am I therefore young?' (IV, 168), and Norbert, in 'In a Balcony', speaks with great disdain of poets and painters. It is far better to be himself than merely to watch from a distance the being of others (IV, 204). Bishop Blougram compares himself to Shakespeare, and boasts that what Shakespeare only enjoyed in fancy he has had in reality. Or at any rate he has had some of it, and that little is worth more than all the imagination in the world (IV, 143–5).

Browning, unlike Norbert or the Bishop, is nothing, nothing but unfulfilled desires. To be something in imagination is better than to be nothing at all. In his earliest poems the poet had expressed himself more or less directly. These poems had shocked and bewildered his readers by their morbid introspection and their obscurity. One remembers the reaction of John Stuart Mill to *Pauline*. What these poems really express is Browning's failure to find a way to deal directly with his situation. After the description of his situation in *Pauline*, he proceeds through the dramatization of the failure of Prometheanism in *Paracelsus* to the most obscure and murky poem of all, *Sordello*, finished last of the three. In *Sordello* Browning's attempt to express himself directly and to live his life directly leads him further and more irrevocably back to the primal shapeless mud.

What better escape from this cul-de-sac than the poetry of role-playing? Such poetry, Browning sees, will allow him to organize his diffuse inner energy and give it a momentary plastic form. He will escape from the necessity of seeking an inner drive toward one particular shape. He can depend now on the imitation of forms which already exist or have existed. Since he commits himself only for a time to each life, he will not be petrifying himself in a false self, but will live in a constant process of temporary crystallization, followed by breakup, followed by reorganization in a different form. The difference now will be that the taking of form will be complete: the total patterning of the primitive magma in the shape of a single life. This taking of shape can be more complete precisely because it is based on an 'as if'. The fact that Browning remains uncommitted to any one of these forms will be evident only in the honesty and urgency of his constant disclaimer: 'These are not my opinions or my experiences.' In one sense this is unequivocally true, for these poems were written not by allowing his own unique germ of life to express itself, but by imagining what it is for Pompilia or Fra Lippo Lippi or Aristophanes to be themselves. They are not his opinions, not his experiences, not his life, because he has no opinions, no experiences, no life of his own. But in another way, all of these opinions, experiences, and lives *are* his, and W. C. DeVane is right to insist on the self-expressive side of Browning's poetry. They are all his because each one represents the fulfillment of one impulse of his spirit. Browning has no separate life of his own because he lives his life in his poetry.

Browning would probably have said that his Perseus-like saving of Elizabeth Barrett from her dragon of a father was the definitive private act of his life, the one act which fixed his nature for good, as he says of such an experience in 'By the Fire-Side' (III, 201–11). In 'One Word More' (IV, 173–80) he distinguishes between the public face he turns to the world in his poetry and the private self which is only for his wife, just as, in a very late poem, he says that he has done two things with his life: 'verse-making' and 'love-making' (X, 109). But the very fact that he made verse as well as love, and made verse so indefatigably and at such length, is proof that no single act or commitment, however intense, was enough to satisfy all the needs of his spirit. As he said in a letter to Isa Blagden, his real 'object of life', his 'root' in the strong earth, was poetry.[2] Only there could he assuage his desire to experience 'all the ways' in which human beings have lived or might live.

In one sense Browning sets himself over against a world swarming with people. He is a neutral onlooker, observing what happens, and reproducing it in his verse, like the poet of 'How It Strikes a Contemporary'. He can do this so well because he has a latent possession of all possible forms of life. It is only a matter of letting one of his inner impulses flow out, take form, and he can become Sludge, Guido, or Caliban. Since Browning contains all these lives potentially in himself he can imitate them from the inside, marrying his mind and senses to theirs. This correspondence between what he is potentially and what the world is actually, is the basis of Browning's poetry, and of his intuitive method of comprehension. He knows other people as intimately as he knows himself, and excels in what Du Bos, in another brilliant phrase, called 'the introspection of others', only because he contains the whole world and all its forms of life dormantly within himself. In a passage in *Sordello*, Browning distinguishes between the passive, gentle souls, who yield themselves to external beauty, and the stronger men, the true poets, who see in what is outside themselves the objective revelation of a possibility of their own souls, 'a twin/ With a distinctest consciousness within' (I, 194). Browning is surely of the second sort.

If Browning has all forms of beauty 'dormant within [his] nature all along' (I, 194), then he is a multivocal personality, and there is no way in which he can accede to Elizabeth Barrett's repeated request that, having written so much dramatically, he should now speak in his own person. '*Now* let us have your own voice speaking of yourself . . . ,' she asks, 'teach what you have learnt, in the directest and most impressive way, the mask thrown off however moist with the breath.'[3] He cannot throw off the mask, for there is nothing behind it, or nothing but a face that is all faces at once, and so no face.

Can we not see another manifestation of this inner indistinction in Browning's constant insistence on his rights of privacy, his attempt to destroy his correspondence and his early poetry, and his bitter rejection, in several poems of the *Pacchiarotto* volume, of the idea that the public has any right to know the private life of a poet? Nowadays, in the epoch of Gide and Sartre, we are accustomed to the idea that a man may have no given 'nature', as does a stone or a tree. But in Browning's day, and in England, the idea of the indeterminacy of selfhood was a scandalous notion, contrary to the traditional British conviction that each man has a substantial inner core of self. It was the wavering inner fluidity as well as the morbid self-consciousness of *Pauline* which so shocked Mill and other early readers. Browning's excessive desire for privacy, as well as his decision to write dramatic monologues, may be not so much an attempt to hide the positive facts of his private life as an attempt to keep hidden his secret failure to have the kind of definite, solid self he sees in other people, and feels it is normal to have. Henry James may be perfectly right, in 'The Private Life', to sense a mystery in the disjunction between Browning's poetry and the public life of the man who went to so many dinner parties that people said he would die in his dinner jacket. The disjunction may not be where James saw it, in the contrast between the superficiality of the public life, and the creative depths of the hours when the poetry was written. The real secret may be the central formlessness which is hidden both by the poetry and by the life of party-going. Browning would then be another case of the insubstantiality of the histrionic personality, that blankness behind the succession of roles which James ascribes, in *The Tragic Muse*, to the actress Miriam Rooth. If we turn to Browning's poetry to find a revelation of what he 'really' believes we find ourselves bewildered by a profusion of apparently contradictory assertions, and Browning would affirm that even the poems which seem the most personal are just as dramatic and imaginary as any of the others. Many of the opinions and attitudes which seem most peculiarly Browning's own are put in the mouths of 'villains' like Don Juan or Bishop Blougram.[4] The reader's imagination staggers, and he rushes to the letters to find the 'real' Browning. There he finds, for the most part, Browning in a dinner jacket, the superficial, public Browning who could hardly have written *The Ring and the Book* or 'Porphyria's Lover'. Browning himself, the very pulse of his life and sound of his voice, is more present in the least of his poems, and we are forced to conclude that his 'selfhood' must be defined as the failure to have any one definite self, and as the need to enact, in imagination, the roles of the most diverse people in order to satisfy all the impulses of his being. To be such a self was, in Victorian England, a shameful and reprehensible thing, and it is not surprising to find that Browning should hide it by various means – even, in part, from himself.

Though Browning's three earliest poems are clearly autobiographical, and though he tried his best to suppress *Pauline*, with all the anxiety of a man who regrets an indiscreet self-revelation, nevertheless these poems too are the utterances of 'dramatic persons'. Paracelsus and Sordello are after all historical persons, and *Pauline* is a dramatic monologue, Browning's first. As he tells us, he conceived a plan of publishing anonymously, under different pseudonyms, plays, novels, operas, and poems. The public was not to know that all these works were by the same person, and *Pauline* was supposed to be by the poet of the lot. Even this most personal poem was the expression of an assumed role, as Browning claimed in the preface of 1867 (i, xxi). His resistance to committing himself wholly to one voice was so great that at the age of twenty, before he had developed the theory of the dramatic monologue, he could not bring himself to 'lay bare his heart' without persuading himself that he was only *pretending* to be a Shelleyan poet, full of anguish and nameless sin. Browning could not begin to speak at all unless he convinced himself that he was not speaking in his own voice. Only then would the inner ice melt, and the interminable flow of words begin, the garrulous rumble of his own inimitable voice.

Browning's inability to speak directly in his own voice, the neutrality and pliability of his spirit, link him to a certain aspect of the romantic tradition, an aspect visible not only in German romantic poetry and philosophy, but also in English romanticism. Browning carries just about as far as it can go the Keatsian notion of the chameleon poet who, having no nature of his own, is able to enter into the nature of things around him. One might say that Browning's distinctive contribution to romanticism is his extension of the idea of sympathetic imagination from natural objects to other people. Keats too had claimed to be able to be 'with Achilles shouting in the trenches', as well as to enter into the life of the sparrow pecking the gravel, but in his poetry the sympathetic imagination of natural objects is paramount. Browning, like Keats, feels that he has the power to enter into natural things (I, 24), but clearly dominant in his poetry is the power of the introspection of other people. Both Browning and the romantics have 'A need to blend with each external charm,/ Bury themselves, the whole heart wide and warm, – / In something not themselves' (I, 194). Browning's special gift is his ability to 'bury himself' not only in flower, bird, or tree, but also in the most diverse sorts of human beings.

This gift links Browning to another tradition : historicism. Historicism arises at the same time as romanticism, and has intimate connections with it. Both presuppose a breakdown of the traditional avenues of communication between man and the supernatural. A romantic poet like Hölderlin throws himself sacrificially into the void between man and God, and tries to make himself the vessel in which the divine fire is appeased and made benignant to man. Browning's earliest poems express his experience of the failure of this strategy. Beginning in the same place, with the absence of God, and its concomitant, the loss of selfhood, it is possible to go in another direction : to turn one's back resolutely on God, and to attempt to reach him, if at all, only through a complete inventory of all the diverse forms which human life has taken or could take. This is the strategy of historicism.

The attitude of historicism is humble and modest. It assumes that there is no way to create an absolute system of thought which will allow man to put himself in the place of God and see things *sub specie aeternitatis*. If a man tries to rise to such heights he will suffocate from lack of air, and his system, if he makes one, will lack pith and substance. Reality for man lies in the acceptance of a finite perspective on the world. The difficulty is that the historicist can find no reason to commit himself to any one point of view. He has the old hunger to know everything, but he cannot go directly toward the divine center, for that way is closed. Therefore he must go toward the periphery, the realm of eccentricity. He can approach an absolute vision only by attempting to relive, one by one, all the possible attitudes of the human spirit. He will go through history trying to reconstruct, from the inside, the intimate reasonableness of each age, each point of view, each great thinker or artist. He will try to find out what it would feel like to look at the world with the eyes of Aristophanes, Sordello, or Christopher Smart. Nor will he ignore the lesser people, the Balaustions, Bubb Dodingtons, and Sludges, for such people have also lived, and their unique mode of experience is part of the totality of what is or has been.

Such an attitude will not be sheer relativism, the cynical assumption that since all points of view are equally false, we might as well play capriciously at re-creating them. On the contrary, the historicist assumes that all points of view are true. If these perspectives contradict one another, so much the better, for that opaque, ambiguous, multiple thing, reality, exceeds any one pair of eyes. Only by making use of all historical perspectives, in all their diversity, can we hope to approach it. When we have exhausted history we shall go on into the future, and try to invent new ways of living and feeling, each one contributing its bit to the endless task of the exhaustion of reality. The historicist wants to have experienced all possible feelings, to have seen life from all points of view. Such, in one way or another, is the project of historicism, whether we find it flamboyantly, as in Nietzsche, with the emphasis on the creation of new perspectives, or more soberly, as in Dilthey or Groethuysen, with an emphasis on the comprehension of the historical past, or with a combination of the two, as in Ortega y Gasset. It is to this tradition that Browning belongs. He is England's most distinguished historicist, the one who explored most deeply, in his own way, the implications of the historicist attitude.

The dramatic monologue is par excellence the literary genre of historicism. It presupposes a double awareness on the part of its author, an awareness which is the very essence of historicism. The dramatic monologuist is aware of the relativity, the arbitrariness, of any single life or way of looking at the world. On the other hand, Browning believes that value lies only in energy, vitality, 'life', intense engagement in a finite situation. As he says in 'The Statue and the Bust', 'a crime will do/ As well . . . to serve for a test,/ As a virtue golden through and through' (III, 401). The only real evil, for man, is inaction, 'the unlit lamp and the ungirt loin' (III, 402). What exists for human beings is only the inexhaustible multitude of various lives which have been lived or can be lived, and it is these which the modern poet, the poet of historicism, must attempt to re-create.

So we get the great gallery of idiosyncratic characters in Browning's most famous poems: scoundrels, quacks, hypocrites, cowards, casuists, lovers, heroes, adulterers, artists, Bishop Blougram, Mr. Sludge, Caliban, the Bishop ordering his tomb. Browning has committed himself, like Gide in some of his moods,[5] to the life of the shape-changer, the life of the man who, nothing himself, borrows with the utmost irresponsibility the life of others.

This description of Browning's poetic enterprise must be qualified by a recognition that behind the great crowd of grotesques and idealists there is one constant factor linking them all together: the consciousness of Browning himself. The multitude of eccentrics exists inside the poet as well as outside. In *Pauline* all these feelings and perspectives existed still within Browning himself, as 'impulses', 'tendencies', 'desires', not yet projected into the lives of imaginary persons. Now all these forms of life, all these feelings, all these points of view, will be incarnated in the multitudinous variety of men and women who speak in his poems. The solution of the problem posed in *Pauline* is given in the speech of Aprile, the poet of *Paracelsus*. Paracelsus has sought only knowledge and power. He has haughtily turned his back on his fellow human beings, and has attempted to leap, at once, over the gap separating man from God. But Aprile faces in loving patience toward the multiplicity of the world of time and space, and attempts to re-create all its forms in art. His description of his project in life is a perfect expression of the attitude of Browning himself as a writer of dramatic monologues. What Aprile will use all the arts to attain, Browning will attempt to achieve in a single medium:

Every passion sprung from man, conceived by man,
Would I express and clothe it in its right form,
Or blend with others struggling in one form,
Or show repressed by an ungainly form.
        . . . no thought which ever stirred
A human breast should be untold; all passions,
All soft emotions, from the turbulent stir
Within a heart fed with desires like mine,
To the last comfort shutting the tired lids
Of him who sleeps the sultry noon away
Beneath the tent-tree by the wayside well . . . (1, 78, 79)

*   *   *   *   *

There is another motive for Browning's passionate desire to place himself in the interior of other lives and find out their secrets. He assumes that God exists behind every thing or person, and delights himself in the unique flavor of each life. To reach the real truth behind a person, a flower, or an historical event is to reach not only the particular secret of a particular existence, but always and everywhere to encounter the divine truth itself.

This becomes in Browning a Pascalian or Blakean notion of the special closeness to God of the minuscule. We shall reach God best not by the hopeless attempt to expand ourselves to his size, like the frog imitating the ox, but rather by descending toward ever more minute particulars until below the smallest of the small, rather than beyond the largest of the large, we reach the splendor of God. Every grain of sand is not only irreplaceable and unique; at some moment it reflects the divine sun best of all created things, 'returns his ray with jet/ Of promptest praise, thanks God best in creation's name!' (vii, 184). So 'A sphere is but a sphere;/ Small, Great, are merely terms we bandy here;/ Since to the spirit's absoluteness all/ Are like', 'The Small, a sphere as perfect as the Great' (i, 348), and 'We find great things are made of little things,/ And little things go lessening till at last/ Comes God behind them' (iv, 351).

Every least object, and every least human being, carries a spark of the divine sun in his breast, and if we can really pierce to the center of any one of them we shall reach God himself. Fire under dead ashes, gold under dross, truth hidden behind a surface of lies – Browning devises numerous ways to express this notion. It first appears, appropriately enough, in *Paracelsus*. The idea that God will be found at the center of the soul is an important part of the mystic tradition to which the Swiss alchemist belonged, and it was this tradition which was revived in the eighteenth century by writers like Saint-Martin, Hamann, Von Baader, and Steffens. From these writers it is only a step to Blake and Shelley, and so to Browning, who begins with the double tradition of Protestantism and romanticism, both of which contain this idea of the divine truth at the center of each soul, baffled and hidden by a carnal mesh of lies:

> Truth is within ourselves; it takes no rise
> From outward things, whate'er you may believe.
> There is an inmost centre in us all,
> Where truth abides in fulness; and around,
> Wall upon wall, the gross flesh hems it in,
> This perfect, clear perception – which is truth. (1, 61)

Browning cannot, in isolation, find the tiny point at the center of his own soul where he coincides with God. His only recourse is to bring into existence his inner potentialities one after another by plunging into the lives of other people, in hopes that he may reach the divine spark in that way. His task as poet is to reach and express the infinite enclosed in the finite: 'From the given point evolve the infinite' (VIII, 272). He can free his own infinite depths if he can attain them in what is outside himself.

How does Browning take this plunge into the secret life of another man or woman?

There are two ways to know another thing or person: to make oneself passive and receptive, like an objective scientist, and let the thing reveal itself by displaying itself, or to fight one's way to its center, assaulting its secret places and taking it by storm. Browning's is the second way.

Browning repeatedly describes the poet's knowledge of others in terms of the physical penetration of some object which is hidden or closed in on itself, like a fruit or a shut-up flower (IX, 124;

M.A.W.—F

x, 224). The poet knows the world through his senses and his intuitive power, and these permit him to plunge 'through rind to
pith' (x, 184) of each thing he appropriates. Anything which presents a mysterious surface is an invitation to his insatiable curiosity,
a curiosity both of the senses and of the soul. One suspects that
part of the fascination for him of Elizabeth Barrett was her un-
availability, the way she was immured in darkness and jealously
guarded. Browning's Andromeda would be imprisoned in a cave,
not naked on a promontory, and Browning, as Perseus, would
have to fight his way through solid rock to reach her, as Caponsacchi breaks through all barriers to reach Pompilia.

   Browning's problem is double. He has to batter his way to the
secret center of the life of others, and he also has to express that
experience in words. By naming things and people by the right
words Browning breaks through rind to pith. His model is Christopher Smart, who penetrated from the surface to the center of
each thing, and was thereby able to name things by their proper
names, as did Adam. Adding 'right language' to 'real vision', he
made it possible for us to see things with paradisiacal freshness,
and to possess them wholly, until 'all the life/ That flies or swims
or crawls, in peace or strife,/ Above, below, – each had its note
and name/ For Man to know by . . .' (x, 184, 185).

   The first principle of Browning's poetry is his attempt to make
the words of the poem participate in the reality they describe, for
he seeks to capture the 'stuff/ O' the very stuff, life of life, and
self of self' (iv, 348). He wants his words to be thick and substantial, and to carry the solid stuff of reality. He wants, as he said
in a striking phrase, 'word pregnant with thing' (viii, 294). To
read a poem by Browning should be a powerful sensuous experience, a tasting and feeling, not a thinking. The poem should go
down like thick strong raw wine, 'strained, turbid still, from the
viscous blood/ Of the snaky bough' (ix, 104). It must make the
same kind of assault on the reader that the poet has made on
reality to seize its pith.

   How does Browning manage to make his words pregnant with
things?

   Sometimes he achieves his goal by the plastic re-creation of the
appearances of a scene, after the manner of Goethe or Keats, as

in the deliberately classical frieze in the 'Parleying with Gerard de Lairesse', where Browning is trying to show that he can, if he wants, be as lucid and sculptural as the Greek or Roman poets (x, 226–31). More often he is not satisfied with such a distant vision of a scene. He wants the reader to feel what he describes as if it were part of his own body, and to achieve this he must appeal to the more intimate senses of taste, smell, and touch, and to the kinesthetic sense whereby we make sympathetic muscular movements in response to the motion of things. All the ways in which Browning conveys his sense of being at the center of unformed matter are also used, with appropriate modifications, to express his experiences when he places himself at the interior of particular forms. The pervasive qualities of Browning's poetry are roughness and thickness. There are two opposite, yet related, causes for this texture. It expresses the shapeless bubbling chaos. It also expresses the substantial solidity of realized forms.

Browning wants to make the movement, sound, and texture of his verse an imitation of the vital matter of its subject, whether that subject is animate or inanimate, molten lava, flower, bird, beast, fish, or man. He thinks of matter, in whatever form, as something dense, heavy, rough, and strong-flavored, and there is for him a basic similarity between all forms of life – they are all strong solid substance inhabited by a vital energy. There are everywhere two things: the thick weight of matter, and within it an imprisoned vitality which seethes irresistibly out. The particular forms, however finely developed, are still rooted in the primal mud, and the means of expressing one are not unrelated to the means of expressing the other. It is by imitation of the roughness of a thing that one has most chance to get inside it. Things are not made of smooth appearances, but of the dense inner core which is best approached through heavy language.

Grotesque metaphors, ugly words heavy with consonants, stuttering alliteration, strong active verbs, breathless rhythms, onomatopoeia, images of rank smells, rough textures, and of things fleshy, viscous, sticky, nubbly, slimy, shaggy, sharp, crawling, thorny, or prickly – all these work together in Browning's verse to create an effect of unparalleled thickness, harshness, and roughness. These elements are so constantly combined that it is difficult to demonstrate one of them in isolation, but their simultaneous effect gives Browning's verse its special flavor, and could be said to be the most important thing about it. They are the chief means by which he expresses his sense of what reality is like. No other poetry can be at once so ugly, so 'rough, rude, robustious' (x, 248), and so full of a joyous vitality.

Sometimes Browning achieves his effect by a direct appeal to the kinesthetic sense. The words invite us to imitate with our bodies what they describe, or to react to the poem as if it were a physical stimulus:

> As he uttered a kind of cough-preludious
>   That woke my sympathetic spasm . . . (iv, 7)

>   . . . the pig-of-lead-like pressure
>   Of the preaching man's immense stupidity . . . (iv, 7)

> Aaron's asleep – shove hip to haunch,
>   Or somebody deal him a dig in the paunch! (iii, 386)

Sometimes the chief means is onomatopoeia – language at the level of interjection, exclamation, the sound of the word echoing the reality, often an affirmation of the body's organic life:

> Fee, faw, fum! bubble and squeak! (iii, 385)

> . . . the thump-thump and shriek-shriek
> Of the train . . . (iv, 10)

> He blindly guzzles and guttles . . . (x, 321)

> . . . their blood gurgles and grumbles afresh . . . (x, 324)

Sometimes it is the use of words clotted with consonants, for bunched consonants seem to have power to express not only unformed chaos, but also the sharp texture of particular things:

> . . . slimy rubbish, odds and ends and orts . . . (x, 190)

> And one sharp tree – 't is a cypress – stands,
> By the many hundred years red-rusted,
> Rough iron-spiked, ripe fruit-o'ercrusted . . . (iii, 175)

Sometimes, as in the last quotation, it is the use of verbs of violent action, whether in their primary form or in the form of participles which have become part of the substance of what they modify:

> Yataghan, kandjar, things that rend and rip,
> Gash rough, slash smooth, help hate so many ways . . . (IX, 72)

> If there pushed any ragged thistle-stalk
>   Above its mates, the head was chopped; the bents
>   Were jealous else. What made those holes and rents
> In the dock's harsh swarth leaves, bruised as to baulk
> All hope of greenness? 't is a brute must walk
>   Pashing their life out, with a brute's intents. (III, 408)

Sometimes the chief device giving strength and substance to the line is alliteration, often of explosive consonants:

> Here's John the Smith's rough-hammered head. Great eye,
> Gross jaw and griped lips do what granite can
> To give you the crown-grasper. What a man! (III, 392)

> First face a-splutter at me got such splotch
> Of prompt slab mud as, filling mouth to maw, . . .
> Immortally immerded . . . (VIII, 54)

> No, the balled fist broke brow like thunderbolt,
> Battered till brain flew! (VIII, 56)

> The barrel of blasphemy broached once, who bungs? (X, 277)

Sometimes the chief effect is produced by the quick heavy, often syncopated, rhythm, the heartbeat of the verse helping the reader to participate in the substance of the thing or person and the pace of its life. The rhythm of Browning's poems is internal, vegetative. It is not the mind speaking, but the depths of corporeal vitality, the organic pulsation of life. Browning manages, better than any other poet, to convey the bump, bump, bump of blood coursing through the veins, the breathless rush of excited bodily life, the vital pulse of the visceral level of existence, the sense of rapid motion. No other poetry is more robust in tempo:

I sprang to the stirrup, and Joris, and he;
I galloped, Dirck galloped, we galloped all three . . . (III, 112)

Boh, here's Barnabas! Job, that's you?
Up stumps Solomon – bustling too? (III, 385)

Fife, trump, drum, sound! and singers then,
Marching, say 'Pym, the man of men!'
Up, heads, your proudest – out, throats, your loudest –
'Somerset's Pym!' (X, 248, 249)

Noon strikes, – here sweeps the procession! our Lady borne
    smiling and smart
With a pink gauze gown all spangles, and seven swords
    stuck in her heart!
Bang-whang-whang goes the drum, *tootle-te-tootle* the fife;
No keeping one's haunches still : it's the greatest pleasure
    in life. (III, 158)

Sometimes the effect is produced by a cascade of grotesque metaphors. In Browning's world anything can be a metaphor for anything else, and often he gets an effect of uncouth vitality by piling up a heap of idiosyncratic things, each living violently its imprisoned life :

Higgledy piggledy, packed we lie,
Rats in a hamper, swine in a stye,
Wasps in a bottle, frogs in a sieve,
Worms in a carcase, fleas in a sleeve. (III, 386)

Sometimes, however, it is a more subtle use of metaphor. Browning tends to qualify his description of external events with metaphors taken from the human body. This humanizing of dead objects is so pervasive in Browning's verse that it is easy not to notice it. His anthropomorphizing of the landscape is not achieved by a strenuous act of the imagination which transfers bodily processes to mountains or rivers. Everything in the world is already humanized for Browning, as soon as he sees it, and can be experienced as intimately as if it were his own body. The best proof of this is the casual and habitual way in which body-words are applied to the external world :

Oh, those mountains, their infinite movement!
    Still moving with you;
For, ever some new head and breast of them
    Thrust into view
To observe the intruder; you see it
    If quickly you turn
And, before they escape you, surprise them. (III, 305)

' "Childe Roland to the Dark Tower Came" ' is a masterpiece of this kind of empathy. The effect of this weird poem comes not so much from the grotesque ugliness and scurfy 'penury' of the landscape, as from the fact that the reader is continually coaxed by the language to experience this ghastly scene as if it were his own body which had got into this sad state:

Now blotches rankling, coloured gay and grim,
    Now patches where some leanness of the soil's
    Broke into moss or substances like boils;
Then came some palsied oak, a cleft in him
Like a distorted mouth that splits its rim
    Gaping at death, and dies while it recoils. (III, 411)

Kinesthesia, onomatopoeia, 'consonanted' (VIII, 296) words, verbs of violent action, alliteration, visceral rhythm, grotesque metaphors, pathetic fallacy – by whatever means, Browning's aim is to get to the inmost center of the other life, and working out from it, to express that life as it is lived, not as it appears from the outside to a detached spectator. This power of what Hazlitt called 'gusto' is surely one of Browning's chief qualities as a poet. His ability to convey the 'thingness' of things, in his own special apprehension of it, belongs not at all to the realm of ideas, and yet is at once the most obvious thing about his verse, and, it may be, the most profound. Certain of his very best poems are not at all complicated thematically, but they succeed magnificently in expressing Browning's strong feeling for the density, roughness, and vitality of matter. Such a poem is 'Sibrandus Schafnaburgensis', with its extraordinary description of the adventures of a book he has pitched into the rain-filled crevice of a hollow plum-tree, and later fished up:

Here you have it, dry in the sun,
    With all the binding all of a blister,
And great blue spots where the ink has run,
    And reddish streaks that wink and glister
O'er the page so beautifully yellow . . .
How did he like it when the live creatures
    Tickled and toused and browsed him all over,
And worm, slug, eft, with serious features,
    Came in, each one, for his right of trover?
– When the water-beetle with great blind deaf face
    Made of her eggs the stately deposit . . . ? (III, 122, 123)

Only Browning could have written such a poem, and only he
could have written 'The Englishman in Italy', with its admirable
representation of an Italian landscape on a stormy autumn after-
noon. Perhaps the best lines of all in this splendid poem are those
describing the 'sea-fruit'. All the linguistic devices I have ex-
amined separately here work in concert, and, as in 'Sibrandus
Schafnaburgensis', word is indeed 'pregnant with thing':

– Our fisher [will] arrive,
And pitch down his basket before us,
    All trembling alive
With pink and gray jellies, your sea-fruit;
    You touch the strange lumps,
And mouths gape there, eyes open, all manner
    Of horns and of humps,
Which only the fisher looks grave at,
    While round him like imps
Cling screaming the children as naked
    And brown as his shrimps . . . (III, 301, 302)

*   *   *   *   *

The methods of mimesis discussed so far work for both people
and things. They are appropriate for imitating any matter informed by energy. Man is more than just these, however important they may be to even the most cerebral man. It is spiritual
destinies which most fascinate Browning, and which he most wants

to reproduce in his poems. For this more complicated task of imitation more complicated means are necessary.

The most obvious of these means is the dramatic monologue. Specific notions about human life lie behind this form of poetry and make it possible. Above all, Browning's monologuists are great talkers. An inexhaustible linguistic energy drives them to talk and talk and talk, and in talking to reveal themselves and the unique world they have built around themselves. Let any man, however clever and full of subterfuge, speak long enough, Browning believes, and he will expose his deepest secrets, allow us access all unwittingly to what is most inexpressible in his life – the very mark or note of his unique selfhood.

But we might be forced to wait a long time for this revelation. Browning, in spite of the length of many of his monologues, is anxious to reach the heart of each of his men and women as quickly as possible. Like a world-conqueror moving from city to city, he goes with the utmost rapidity from man to man, always hungry to make new conquests, for his aim is to possess the whole creation. Why does he assume that each town will soon fall to his blitzkrieg?

The assumption is made plausible by one all-important notion about human existence. Browning believes that each man, except perhaps the poet himself, has a permanent node or center of existence, and that his unchanging selfhood persists through all the vicissitudes of his life. If this is the case, then every action of a man, however insignificant, will reveal all of him, if we can understand it. This is another version of the idea that the small sphere is as perfect as the great. God is equally present in every part of the universe, from the fretful midge up to the greatest star; in the same way a man's permanent selfhood is equally present in his least gesture and in his most decisive acts. So Prince Hohenstiel-Schwangau, smoking his cigar in Leicester Square, tells his auditor that she will understand all his actions if she can understand why he connects two inkblots on a scrap of paper in just the way he does it (VII, 97). Browning did not need twentieth-century psychologists to tell him that the inkblot and the doodle reveal all! A man's life, says the Prince, is a strange kind of continuum, in which any point may be the center around which all the rest organizes itself into a pattern of converging rays: 'Rays from all round converge to any point.' This central point is just as complex in structure, has just as many parts, as the whole life from one end to the other. The smallest point is a complete image of the whole: 'Understand one, you comprehend the rest.' Each man lives in time, and must keep moving. But at any moment of time the whole world structures itself around the unchanging center of personality which persists through time, and sees the world always according to a unique perspective, just as the moon casts a uniform circle on the clouds it moves through (x, 120, 121).

If this is man's relation to what is around him, then the whole of a man's life is present in each moment of it, and we can begin anywhere in our attempt to understand him. Browning's dramatic monologues start suddenly in the midst of things. The reader is plunged abruptly into the midst of a consciousness, with its own assumptions and limitations, its own situation, and its own way of looking at things. The first lines of Browning's monologues are of special importance, and at their best they succeed in expressing the immediate pulse of a life, the unique flavor of an existence. To read these monologues one after another is to be thrust suddenly into the thick of a life, then, when one poem is over, in another moment the reader finds himself in another personal world, radically different from the first, but just as real, just as inescapably *given* for the character himself.

Though it may be true that all a man's life is present in every moment of it, nevertheless certain moments express the life more dramatically than others, and make its meaning more manifest to the man himself or to others. Though Browning does not use the word 'epiphany', he anticipates Joyce in his notion that there are certain moments which make the latent meaning of a life visible. Though a man has only one germ of life, that self is at first only an unrealized possibility. Only after a crucial decision, action, or experience does a man surround himself irrevocably with a tight net of circumstances. Then he becomes himself once and for all. Until now the man has been, in a sense, free, free as the shapeless sea. Henceforward he is fixed, trammeled in the results of his choice and act. Liquidity has been poured into a mold:

How the world is made for each of us!
How all we perceive and know in it
Tends to some moment's product thus,
When a soul declares itself – to wit,
By its fruit, the thing it does! (III, 210)

Browning's aim is to get the whole meaning of a life into the most concentrated form. Sometimes this can best be done not by showing the crucial moment of decision itself, but by showing a much later time when a man looks back over his life, sees the pattern fall into place, and recognizes which was the best or most important event. A number of the monologues are like 'Confessions' (IV, 302, 303), in which the speaker, on his deathbed, picks out one moment of his youth as the center of his life. Even 'Porphyria's Lover', which seems so immediate, is written after the murder of Porphyria. This poem, like so many others by Browning, juxtaposes two moments: the present and some time in the past. Each man is always moving forward, and must change to some degree, even if it is only in the sense that each reaffirmation of his all-determining decision is different from all the others. It is impossible to fix life – which is the meaning of 'Porphyria's Lover'.

The best time to choose for a dramatic monologue may be neither the moment of death, nor the moment of repetitive reaffirmation, nor the original moment of choice. It may be simply a time when the character is thrown suddenly into a situation which brings him out strongly as he already is. The monologuist must talk, and to get him to talk it is only necessary to put him in a situation in which he will be stirred into speech to defend himself, and in defending reveal himself. The stimulus to volubility is the ticklish position. When Browning's characters, especially the so-called 'casuists', are put in a situation of stress, a great burst of language rushes forth. So Aristophanes talks when, returning from a drunken party, he hears that his enemy Euripides is dead. So Sludge talks when he is found out in his knavery. So Fra Lippo Lippi talks when he is arrested in the street by the nightguard. So Guido talks in his cell, face to face with death.

SOURCE: *The Disappearance of God* (Cambridge, Mass., 1963) pp. 100–10, 116–27.

NOTES

1. [Editor's note.] All volume and page references are to *The Works of Robert Browning*, 10 vols, ed. F. G. Kenyon (London, 1912).

2. Edward C. McAleer (ed.), *Dearest Isa: Robert Browning's Letters to Isabella Blagden* (Austin, Texas, 1951) p. 201.

3. *The Letters of Robert Browning and Elizabeth Barrett Barrett: 1845–1846* (New York, 1899) II, 181, 180.

4. H. N. Fairchild's article, 'Browning the Simple-Hearted Casuist', *University of Toronto Quarterly*, XVIII (1949) 234–40, though suggestive, does not really solve the problem. Not all the monologues have the giveaways Fairchild describes, and even then we are left with the problem of how to take statements in the body of the poem which, though dramatic, seem as if they might be Browning's 'real' opinions. *Fifine at the Fair*, for example, raises this problem in an acute form. Browning's devils all quote scripture, that is, they speak what seem to be, from the frequency of the reiteration, ideas close to Browning's own heart. The reader is driven to accept the notion that Browning did really want 'to hear all sides', and that all these sides, Guido as much as Pompilia, were aspects of his own 'nature'.

5. Gide was much interested in Browning, and wrote perceptively about him in his notebooks. See his *Journal, 1889–1939* (Paris, 1939), especially the entries for 30 May 1930, and 12 March 1938. Unlike Browning, Gide only changes from one sensual or emotional experience to another. He never places himself in a series of other selves.

Patricia M. Ball

BROWNING'S GODOT (1965)

As the mists clear and it becomes apparent that Victorian poetry
has been the victim of inept criticism and obtuse reading, it becomes even clearer that Browning in particular has suffered to a
crippling degree. It is scarcely too much to say that he has not been
critically considered as a poet at all; in an age which prides itself
on its literary sophistication, comment on his poetry has made the
most naïve assumptions about the 'intentions' which may be dis-
cerned in it and the deductions which may be drawn from it.
Even admiration for his obvious skill in handling his monologues
has coexisted with a complacent denial that these monologues
reveal subtlety of substance and poetic attitude. What may be
termed the 'Rabbi Ben Ezra' approach, which regards Browning
as a brash optimist using poems as banners to cheer the faint-
hearted, has persisted with incredible longevity in the same minds
that will readily praise Donne for being able to create certain
moods and tones in his poems, and will censure as puerile any
reading of him that assumes him personally to be cynic or libertine or whatever else he understands sufficiently to portray poeti-
cally.

The first step towards a maturing criticism can be taken if the
Rabbi is never allowed out on his own; that is, he should not
stray from the company of, at the least, the Bishop ordering his
tomb and the other Bishop setting out his apology. Nor should
Caliban ever be overlooked. This assembly immediately strikes a
blow at the oversimplification of Browning : where is 'his attitude'
in this group? It calls attention at once to an essential factor, the
variety of his creation, and it hints, moreover, that this variety
is not just that of a fortuitous crowd. The presence of Caliban,
moreover, is a reminder of a crucial element in Browning's

imagination : his ironic sense of the grotesque in the person of the natural man. Here in brief are the materials for a criticism which will inject new meaning into the tired old examination phrase 'master of the dramatic monologue', blast away the childish theologizing pronouncements about him, and open routes that reveal a most complex imagination, belonging profoundly to its own day but postulating the world of Samuel Beckett's Estragon and Vladimir.

The poems just mentioned therefore are intended as a microcosm. They all involve human relations with a supernatural world, and if they do so explicitly and centrally, there is hardly a poem of Browning's not in some way concerned with this hypothesis of a context for humanity. But the key word is hypothesis, a point unperceived by the false criticism. Even if the cries of Ben Ezra are not regarded as Browning's first and last views on the universe, it is generally assumed that all the speakers of the monologues are in effect mouthpieces, and that the poet has created them as prejudged beings whose behavior and theories are automatically referred to a central totem of belief. They are either conformists or deviators, and are seen in this light by their creator, with no uncertainties. From this, it is further assumed that when they speak of the best that is to be and the perfect round to come, they bask in the admiring and proselytizing acquiescence of the poet, and when they express worldliness, speculative doubts, or more eccentric views on the way of things, their puppet-master is sorrowfully shaking his head as he pulls their strings. Yet there is no literary reason for these suppositions – only literary prejudice. It is a pleasing detail of this critical situation to see the *Pelican Guide*'s essay on Browning condemning the ambiguities of 'Bishop Blougram's Apology', with the explanation that Browning himself was confused by the argument, and this – in a poet written off long ago as rigidly certain of himself and what he wants to assert – 'this will never do'.

What has to be recognized is the fine balance of Browning's relationship with his creations. It is no help to swing away from the puppet-master view only to deny him any further incentive in the making of monologues than that provided by the patronizing 'he loved human nature' observation. This approach rests content with the title *Men and Women* at its face value, cherishes the portrait-gallery analogy, and never goes on to wonder whether a poet might assemble a gallery for more urgent reasons than the simple desire to suggest that people are various and often odd.

Browning's imaginative nature is to be found between these extremes, and by drawing something from both: his creative attention is engaged by the coincidence in each person of certain common human factors with a unique individual expression of them. From this arises the necessity of seeing his poems as a whole, but of appreciating with equal force, the range they offer. Without this dual awareness, his work is distorted and reduced. There is point in asking the question, why does he create such numerous and various beings, for there is an answer to it; but the answer is not, because he is a poet who has his world-picture cut and dried and wishes to promote this by a series of advertisements displaying success stories and the reverse.

The answer, in brief, is Godot, not God. The common factor that Browning sees is the blinkered human mind which suspects that there is a landscape on either side of the road, but never achieves more than a glimpse, or perhaps hears some sound – music or thunder – that aggravates the suspicion. Fantasies, he observes, may well be erected on slight intimation: the unseen landscape may oust the known realities of the road, and prove an obsession; and there are many other possibilities. The practical horse may concentrate the more intensively on oats in the nosebag, the beauties of the roan mare, the joys of being a thoroughbred, while the sagacious may regard the landscape as a stimulating hypothesis without losing his alertness to the immediate problems and pleasures of the road. Browning's imagination, that is, creates out of its perception of such a universal situation, not out of any personal conceit that it has no blinkers itself. He realizes intensely that questions are only answered out of the brilliant virtuosity of each individual and his equipment, the shapelessness of any given human span being conjured into significance – with heights, depths, and crises – by the indestructible energies of the personal urge to identity. As Estragon and Vladimir wrest their sense of themselves out of the fulfilment of each minute with its dramas of broken boots, questions reaching formulation, spasms of emotion, sudden encounters, and play this off against the vast unformulated and unknown, so Browning's bishops, aristocrats, lovers, artists, and monks enact their scenes of self-creation and combat the silence stretching on either side.

The monologues regarded in this way attain their rightful dignity – a dignity that embraces grotesquerie. Instead of appearing to be feats of a very skilled yet superficial creativity, the work of a poet with a knack rather than an insight, they are shown to be poetry which catches the travail of human self-realization, the sharp focusing of self-experience. In this lies the vital interpenetration of form and substance so often denied to Browning: the monologue is the moment of travail, an act of birth; the speaker delivers his own being through his speaking. This is not just a way of saying that Browning's speakers move towards self-knowledge in the more usual moral sense, or that his skill is to make them reveal more to the reader than they know themselves. Both these things happen in the monologues – Andrea del Sarto sees his nature more ruthlessly by the end of his musing, while the future resident of St. Praxed's remains more comfortably uncritical of his past than some of his readers will be – but bishop and painter alike are brought out of the mists and become themselves as they speak. Whether the character concerned is introspective and self-critical or not, each asserts 'what I am is me – for this I came', and so counters the brooding, or empty, silence of Godot, of which each – however peripherally – is aware.

This is the only philosophy or theology Browning can honestly be accused of. 'Existential' or 'empirical' are terms more relevant than those usually applied to him, from 'nonconformist' to 'optimist'. All the so-called religious sections of the poems stand within this context. Wherever God enters the poems, he comes as a property of the speaker's self-made universe : he is not the poet's ultimate, for Browning's faith rests upon the one certainty – human uncertainty, the ignorance or doubt of any such ultimate. In one sense he does share the ambiguities of Bishop Blougram, and because he can depict that deliberated route-plotting through an enigmatic universe, the more heartily committed voices should be recognized as emerging from little shelters built to keep out the vast and unresponding night.

But it is through the voice of Caliban that Browning makes his own imaginative foundations most clear, and helps to reveal the orientation of the monologues. This poem has rightly been regarded as satiric comment on current religious attitudes, and Berdoe's careful demarcation of its frontiers – 'to rebuke the anthropomorphic idea of God as it exists in minds of a narrow and unloving type' – is only a caricature version of the kind of attention it has universally attracted. It serves to show something of the inadequacy of this approach, with its twofold suggestion that Browning is primarily offering a negative criticism and is doing so from the assured standpoint of his orthodox, wide and loving, Christian faith. This is unwarranted assumption, for if the poem is taken with no preconceived notions about his probable motives for writing it; if, that is, it is read without the handicap of 'Rabbi Ben Ezra' having been arbitrarily chosen as the pole star of Browning's imaginative heavens, then it stands forth with its own claims to be the more positive luminary and the better guide to those heavens. The poem shows Browning moved by the spectacle of the natural man, the human creature with his bare resources making what he can of his situation. Irony remains an essential ingredient in this interpretation too, but the motive is exploratory and the impulse empirical rather than critical. Caliban would settle well beneath the Beckett tree. His life is passed waiting for Setebos, and his strategy for coping with this burden of an enigmatic unknown power has close affinities with the methods of the tramps. He endows it with a character, if not a long white beard; he accommodates his pastimes to its deduced reactions, so that his entire life is a comment on its supposed nature; he receives messages, not from a boy, but from rain, thunder, and earthquake, and these messages leave him exactly where he was before he had them. Like the tramps, that is, he is left with the necessity of invention and interpretation. Estragon is no more mystified, apprehensive, oppressed, or creatively stimulated to realize his own existence than Caliban, Browning's study in basic man.

From this angle, other apparent problems in the poem dis-

appear. The sense of incongruity, for instance, implied in L.
Salinger's description of the poem as 'Shakespeare's savage .
speaking as an exponent of natural religion in the light of D
winism' is no longer an awkwardness. Caliban *is* simultaneou
primitive and don : this is Browning's point about the hum
condition; and all his people, from Abt Vogler to Mr. Slud
illustrate it. Each constructs his Setebos, or his Quiet, each li
in accordance with his conception, each awaits confirmation
his own god, his own universe; and no one in the monolog
achieves more – or less – in this respect than Caliban on
island :

> Saith He is terrible : watch His feats in proof !
> One hurricane will spoil six good months' hope.
> He hath a spite against me, that I know,
> Just as He favours Prosper, who knows why?

It does not throw the poems out of the Godot context h
being claimed as their rightful home, if it is argued that Browni
shows himself very conscious of the idea of revelation. This
indeed an important factor, affecting the poems structurally
well as thematically. But it is not a sign that while some of
poems await Godot, abiding in questions, others are written fr
an orthodox viewpoint, campaigning for the Christian G
Revelation is in fact recognized as a concept of high ambigu
and Browning's imagination is released by this awareness, not
an act of religious assent to it as a single solution or counteri
force to the blind man's buff of natural theology. To put t
another way, Browning is attracted by the concept of revelati
as a feature of the psychological mechanism, with the imme
range of individual variety which this involves, not as the th
logian's implement of revealed truth. In this capacity, it plays
important part in many poems, and is integral to the Godot poe
universe.

This is most readily apparent in such monologues as the 'Epis
from Karshish' and 'Abt Vogler'. Comment on these poems l
implied that the former is Browning as propagandist contributi
to the debate on religious faith, and the latter a vehicle for co
veying his outlook on 'broken arcs' and 'perfect round'. Karsh

has been confronted with living evidence for Christianity, and Vogler does soliloquize on the relationship of earth and heaven; but the imaginative center in each poem is the experience of revelation, that is, a psychological happening, a shift of being from the usual web of habitual assumptions and expectations to a new position and a consequently changed universe. Both Karshish and Vogler undergo this translation. Each reacts in his own way, but as a further result, each is more acutely aware of his usual world, his everyday self. Although from a Christian point of view the poems may bear another kind of significance, this is extraneous to their life as poems, for they are made vital by the poet's concern with a man undergoing his own special kind of revelation, the experience which exposes him to himself by the shock of its unfamiliarity and its demand that he assimilate it into his universe, whether he accepts it or not. Karshish henceforth must live with his memory of Lazarus, and he is no longer unconsciously enclosed in his role of Arab physician: he knows what he is, where his boundaries are, what lies beyond them; and Vogler, after his zenith of creative excitement, knows himself returned to the mundane, the 'C Major of this life' – he has placed normality and its boundaries.

Both monologues seek to record the rhythm of such experiences, to register it seismographically. In this they are not isolated. It is a cliché of Browning criticism to speak of his 'revelations of character', but the term should retain its place only if it is realized that it has far more potency than this tired phrase suggests; that it has within it the sense of the speaker's own discovery of himself, with all the religious force of meaning – the dawning of new light and vision – retained, yet without the narrower theological associations. Thus Lippo Lippi, Mr. Sludge, Andrea del Sarto, the Wife to the Husband all undergo the experience of revelation and their poems record the process, the movement of emotion and perception, as it takes place. This is the ambition of the monologues and it is what happens in *Waiting for Godot*: the play proposes and the monologues more obliquely suggest that this may well be all that can happen. We realize we are in the world, we discover we are Estragon or Andrea del Sarto, and that our history is a saga of broken boots or lifeless pictures; we learn also that we may add to, alter, revise or choose not to revise our ideas of ourselves, our universe, Setebos and Godot, if we meet Lazarus or encounter Pozzo and Lucky. But beyond this, a small clearing in a fog, we cannot experience anything. We make ourselves from within, our Godot attendant on this painfully constructed image.

Beckett's play in its demonstration of human solitude does, however, at the same time show its relativity. Estragon has Vladimir, and displaying the agony and necessity of this bond is a salient factor in the operation of *Waiting for Godot*. To Browning also, the tension of relationships is crucial. The monologue's power is partly dependent on its being a potential dialogue and it is the presence of the listener that brings it to birth, forcing the crisis of utterance, and hence of revelation, the clarity of discovery. Blougram and Gigadibs are the most obvious example of this, as the bishop creates a version of himself expressly for his visitor, but Browning's awareness of relationships is prismatic. He ranges from the fortuitous encounter – Lippo Lippi and the watch – through the 'ghostly' but persistent company of Waring, the lifelong and deathlong rivalries of St. Praxed's bishop and Gandolf, to the formidable intimacies of lover and mistress, husband and wife. In these last is the pattern of Vladimir and Estragon most strikingly approached, in the complexities of revolt and dependence, antagonism and attraction, which are explored – with ruthless analysis in 'James Lee's Wife', the lyrical despair of 'In a Year', the ironic bite of 'Porphyria's Lover', to select only a few from the array of studies and their equal variety of mood. What Beckett displays through the minute to minute shifts of feeling between the tramps, Browning presents in the whole range of the monologues. Human interaction within the context of an unknown concerns them both. Each poet perceives the rhythm of lives most intensely as a continual postponement of results, answers, or conclusions, so that the stuff of experience is the sustained query dominating the immediate procession of exchanges with and adjustment to others. Integral to this is the sensation of arrival at the brink of revelation. Godot is always imminent; he may, he almost certainly will arrive today. And so with Browning's men and women : together with their experience of self-revelation already discussed, there is this further expectation of the ultimate enlightenment.

This is an aspect which has structural influence on the monologues. The final verse of 'In a Year' affords a simple example :

> Dear, the pang is brief.
> Do thy part,
> Have thy pleasure. How perplext
> Grows belief !
> Well, this cold clay clod
> Was man's heart
> Crumble it – and what comes next ?
> Is it God ?

The immediate foreground of the speaker's experience has here suffered disaster : the context of query takes its place, is confronted and moves the poem on to climax by the bald challenge reaching into the silence. The ultimate is invited to answer for itself. But this is essentially the end of the poem; and the word 'God' is not offered doctrinally as an answer in itself but as a term suggesting the enigma and the breadth of the question – to be read as Godot. Browning's sense of the climactic question – either in words or action – rules the construction of many of the monologues, and is a feature of his imagination far more pertinent to his whole poetic universe than the answers he is supposed to have offered in the voice of Ben Ezra and others. 'Artemis Prologuizes' climbs to the pregnant pause of the goddess surveying the restored Hippolytus, expecting resurrection :

> And ye, white crowd of woodland sister-nymphs,
> Ply, as the Sage directs, these buds and leaves
> That strew the turf around the Twain ! While I
> Await, in fitting silence, the event.

This – with less confidence – is the attitude of mind of the human speakers; they live in the hope and the shadow of a possible 'event'. At times, they may feel it has taken place, as in the poems of requited love, but more often, such assumptions are shown to be illusions and the question only presses the more urgently in the deepened silence : 'Is it God?' The step from here to Vladimir and the Boy is a short one :

Vladimir :	You have a message from Mr. Godot.
Boy :	Yes, sir.
Vladimir :	He won't come this evening.
Boy :	No, sir.
Vladimir :	But he'll come tomorrow.
Boy :	Yes, sir.
Vladimir :	Without fail.
Boy :	Yes, sir.
	Silence

The intimate connection between ' "Childe Roland" ' and the other monologues is nowhere better shown than in this structural rhythm of movement to a climax which is always the human challenge, the fear, and the imminence of revelation, and never the avatar himself. The horn sounding, out of the horror of Roland's self-knowledge, into the dark and desolate landscape with its 'round squat turret, blind as the fool's heart', is Browning's fundamental vision transmuted into symbolic form, not at all a stray bastard with a different face and no place in the legitimate assembly of monologues.

'Porphyria's Lover' provides a last example of the importance of the Godot awareness to Browning as a poet. Here again, it supplies him with a climax which at once reaches out to the reader, provoking reaction, and reverberates back through the whole poem, so that its nature is only grasped fully after this detonation :

And thus we sit together now,
    And all night long we have not stirred,
And yet God has not said a word !

As this is one of the two poems headed originally 'Madhouse Cells', the first level of implication here is ironic : God, in the sense of a voice of judgment on the act, has indeed spoken. The murder has been assessed, the murderer labelled and dismissed.

The lover's unconsciousness of this contains a further irony, deflating the high expectations of waiting on the event, the human conceit of assuming its deeds important enough to attract a deity's attention in terms of wrath and thunderbolt. At the same time, as in 'Caliban upon Setebos', the parallel assumption, that the deity may be conniving, and condoning this action, is likewise implied and mocked : he is either with me or against me – such is the human basis in making a god. The force of Browning's feeling for context goes into this poem as into more developed ones – Porphyria's murderer sits forever under the tree with Estragon and Vladimir, inventing his god, exhibiting simultaneously his immunity and his hopeless vulnerability to the facts of the situation, the situation being life itelf.

For Browning with Beckett takes his poetic stand on the perception that for all of us, time is passed thus : creating a Setebos or Godot in our own image, living to a rhythm of endless expectation, clinging to each other and to illusion, yet capable of blowing the only possible horn of revelation, that which discovers us to ourselves, waiting beneath the tree in the silence of Godot's world.

SOURCE : *Victorian Poetry*, III (1965).

PART FOUR

Twentieth-Century Views
2. Essays on Individual Poems

Roma A. King Jr

ECCLESIASTICAL VISION IN STONE: 'THE BISHOP ORDERS HIS TOMB' (1957)

The first clue to the meaning of 'The Bishop Orders his Tomb' is given in the title. Browning originally called the poem 'The Tomb at St. Praxed's', but neither that nor 'The Bishop' appears to have pleased him. In the final version he linked the two and inserted the word *orders*. In what sense does the Bishop 'order' his tomb? The apparent discrepancy between what he requests and what he gets proposes that the title is ironic and suggests an approach to the poem's meaning. The critic's task is largely one of pursuing this suggestion.

The irony of the poem arises from the juxtaposition of two ways of seeing and two standards of values. 'The Bishop Orders his Tomb' is not a persuasive for any point of view or code of behavior, that is, the discrepancies do not exist between Browning's obviously 'right' world and the Bishop's obviously 'wrong' one. In this respect it is different from 'A Modest Proposal', in which Swift establishes the conflict as existing between himself and a somewhat indefinite opposition. We are always conscious of the writer's presence and feel the force of his moral indignation

In 'The Bishop Orders his Tomb', as in 'Andrea del Sarto' and 'Fra Lippo Lippi', Browning's personality has been, to quote Joyce, 'refined out of existence', and the poem is permitted to speak for itself. The result is objective drama rather than subjective didacticism. The discrepancies which produce the irony, then, must exist within the poem itself. They are provided primarily by diverse ways of seeing the Bishop and his world. First, there is the view arising from the facts of the poem; then,

there is the narrower, more subjective one of the Bishop hims
That these two views are not correlative is immediately appare
In 'Andrea del Sarto', the conflicting forces exist within
character, making the poem psychological and tragic; here,
though the Bishop is not entirely without inner struggle,
major discrepancy occurs between his view of himself and
external reality. Of all the characters included in this study,
Bishop of St. Praxed's is the only one not known definitely
refer to an historical personage and not to be given a name. I
the only poem the title of which directs attention more to
action than to a character; in fact, in the original title the na
of the character did not appear at all.

Browning's task was to write the poem so that the two poi
of view would be precisely communicated in an effective, cc
pelling manner. The representation of the Bishop and his object
world was the easier task, accomplished by a selection of sign
cant incident, a use of full, rich details and precise language.
convey the Bishop's subjective view of himself was more diffici
The Bishop was confused, a fact dramatically revealed by
variance between his fully conscious and his semiconscic
speech. In the former, we see the Bishop as he habitually thou;
of himself as he faced the world – 'popes, cardinals, and pries
In the latter, we penetrate a region strange even to the Bishop a
glimpse there the half-formed thoughts, imprecise emotions, a
moral confusion. Browning intended the Bishop's incoheri
speech to be an interpretive comment upon his inner confusi
as he suggests : 'In St. Praxed, the blunder as to the sermor
the result of the dying man's haziness; he would not reveal hi
self as he does but for that.' Communication of this subconscic
level of meaning requires a technique which the poet had be
developing since *Sordello*. I shall say more about it later.

It is easy to underestimate the fullness and complexity
Browning's treatment of the Bishop. As a character, he lives
a smaller world and is less complexly motivated than either I
Lippo Lippi or Andrea del Sarto, lacking the intellectual vi;
and the moral concern of the one, and the inner conflicts of 1
other. In this respect he is more like Jonson's characters th
Shakespeare's. However, his presentation in the poem is co

plete and satisfying. Eliot distinguishes between the 'surface qualities' of Beaumont and Fletcher's work and Ben Jonson's by saying that the formers' is superficial with a vacuum behind it, but that Jonson's superficies are solid. So with Browning's Bishop. His world is limited, but it is fully conceived and convincingly communicated; intellectually and emotionally the Bishop is a logical part of it. He escapes being burlesque, as do many of Jonson's characters, because in relation to his world he is not incongruous. The superficialities, we recognize, are in the Bishop as man, not in the poem.

Pride is a distinguishing characteristic of the Bishop, and an important ironic tension arises from the disparity between his imagined and his obviously real status. The most frequently repeated words in his vocabulary are *I* and *mine*. His sense of exaggerated self-importance isolates him from other people, whom he fails to distinguish from things. Either they are objects to use or barriers to overcome. 'A Jew's head cut off at the nape' is simply a thing to designate the size of a piece of lapis lazuli. He speaks of God as a statue and of himself in his immortal state as a piece of sculpture. The mother and the sons have 'eyes as a lizard's quick'. Conversely, he gives life to the inanimate: 'a sunbeam's sure to lurk', 'impoverished frieze', 'starved design'.

Isolated by his pride, the Bishop feels no great need for human relationships. Andrea, enamoured of Lucrezia, betrays friend and parent, yet he experiences always a real desire for companionship, and his personal failure with people is one of the tragedies of his life. The Bishop, incapable of such tragedy, is, on the other hand, a mere collector. The sons' mother was a major acquisition along with his villas, baths, manuscripts, and art objects. She, of course, was forbidden him by the laws of his church, and the sons were illegitimate; but neither she nor they created for him a moral problem. He regretted only that she was greedy, a charge that has at least two implications. In context, the Bishop seems ironically to accuse her of loving material things. More obviously, having loved and got her body, he rationalizes that she tried to get his soul, a word which itself is ambiguous. At the conclusion of the poem his single comfort is that he won her, not because he loved her but because she was fair and Gandolf envied him.

He shows the same insensitiveness toward his sons. They are pleasant reminders of his triumph over Gandolf, and he hopes to use them to achieve his last great desire. Significantly, I think, with one exception they remain unnamed, impersonal. Their unresponsiveness to their father's request must reflect his long disinterest in them. The lines, 'Nay, boys, ye love me . . .' and 'Sons, all have I bequeathed you . . .' are ironic. The Bishop has felt no need for companionship, and his contempt for people makes his dependence upon the sons at the conclusion of the poem especially meaningful. His appeal to Anselm suggests his desperation, and the son's unfeeling rebuff indicates how little he had cultivated human relationships.

His frustration is not so tragic as Andrea's. In fact, there is an undercurrent of sardonic humor in 'The Bishop Orders his Tomb', a characteristic which became increasingly important in Browning's poetry as he matured. The Bishop's hatred for Gandolf, obviously a threat to his pre-eminence, is so intense that at times it becomes ludicrous. His grotesque pride, objectified in the elaborate tomb, contrasts sharply with the futility of the opening line of the poem, 'Vanity, saith the preacher, vanity!' the meaning of which the Bishop only vaguely apprehends.

His preoccupation in this life has been cultural, materialistic, and sensuous; and his achievements may be viewed from either his own perspective or from the more objective one provided by the whole poem. Eventually, of course, they must be viewed from both, for the poem's meaning lies in the tension created by these disparate views. The Bishop's distorted sense of values, intensely acquisitive spirit, and inflexible will provide another paradoxical contrast both to the first line of the poem and to the situation at the conclusion.

The Bishop is a man of external brilliance, displaying catholic learning in his allusions to ancient literature and art, in his cultivated speech, and in his vocabulary, which is learned rather than colloquial. Characteristically, he uses such words as *limb, carrion,* and *conflagration,* sharp contrasts to Lippo's more homely diction. He has a wide range of artistic interests, admiring the mosaics of angels (and incidentally the sunbeams), the paintings, the statuary in the church, a good line of poetry, the beauty of the ritual. A learned vocabulary, formal tone, rhetorical elegance, balanced and periodic sentences, and Latin syntax give polish and elegance to his speech. All in all, he would have found the suave duke of 'My Last Duchess' socially acceptable.

Appropriately, there are more decorative elements in 'The Bishop Orders his Tomb' than in either 'Fra Lippo Lippi' or 'Andrea del Sarto'. Moreover, they are used in a different manner. In the latter two poems there exists between them and the prose meaning of the line a closer relationship. They are intended to clarify and heighten total meaning. In 'The Bishop Orders his Tomb' the relation is more remote and they are used symbolically rather than presentationally. They communicate the Bishop's surface brilliance, yet at the same time betray an inflexible and uncreative mind. His vision of himself in marble is suggestive : he is a finely shaped, basically inanimate product of his culture. And the Bishop is proud of this.

Among the more obvious decorative devices are rhetorical balance, sound repetition, and a pronounced, regular rhythm. It is important to note that all these are contrapuntal, not harmonic, with the thought of the line. Except in his moments of incoherency, the Bishop uses phrasal and sentence balance and parallelism, sometimes reinforcing these devices with alliteration :

> Big as a Jew's head cut off at the nape,
> Blue as a vein o'er the Madonna's breast.

He frequently uses words in pairs, not to intensify thought by repetition, but to create sensuously pleasing cadence : 'tooth and nail . . .', 'the rare, the ripe', 'rosy and flawless', 'see and burst'.

Similarly, repetition of words, consonants, and vowels appeals more to the ear than to the mind. There is more alliteration than usual, sometimes several letters carrying through a number of lines to form intense emotional and sensuous groups. In addition to repeating vowels and consonants within the line, Browning repeats them also at the end so that they function as rhyme might, for example : *missed–dig, beneath–me, south–same, line–lurk, peach–prize, well–once–was*. The effect, though more subtle than rhyme, is perceptible.

Rhythmically, 'The Bishop Orders his Tomb' is one of the most nearly regular of Browning's dramatic monologues. Every line has ten syllables, and for the most part the stress pattern, though not strictly iambic, is basically regular.

The total effect of the Bishop's rhetorical and sententious style suggests a superficiality of which the divorce of structural devices from thought is symbolic. The sterility of his mind is suggested by his formal sentence structure. He is more fixed than Andrea and less creative than Lippo. Andrea does not suffer from intellectual rigor mortis even if he is incapable of action; Lippo's fertile mind can be expressed only in an erratic and heavily subordinate sentence structure. The Bishop's more limited sphere is communicated appropriately in a stylized and rigid structure. In his normal state, he has neither the emotional nor intellectual impulse to break through the bounds established by rhetorical discipline. It is only when he faces death and frustration that his sentence structure breaks down – of this I shall speak later. His typical sentence is the co-ordinate consisting of two or more unmodified independent clauses with or without a correlative :

Draw round my bed : is Anselm keeping back?

                    I fought
With tooth and nail to save my niche, ye know :
– Old Gandolf cozened me, despite my care;
Shrewd was that snatch from out the corner South
He graced his carrion with, God curse the same !

He also uses the periodic sentence, a construction equally as formal and, in the Bishop's hands, as inflexible. He attempts two long periodics, neither of which he completes for reasons which I shall offer in another connection.

His lack of ingenuity and his subservience to established pattern are further suggested by his Latinisms : his use of the absolute construction; his placement of object before verb, modifier after substantive, and verb at the end of the clause.

The decorative elements of his style, then, perform a double function. They mark him a man of learning and culture, but at the same time, because of their tenuous relationship to the thought of the poem, suggest his lack of intellectual and moral depth. Understanding this enables us to view the Bishop from two perspectives.

Both his materialism and his sensuousness are reflected in his diction. Most of his nouns are concrete. Among the few abstract ones, those which occur most frequently, *God, death, life, peace,* and *world,* are habitually converted into materialistic values. The word *God* appears seven times, five of which are in the form of an exclamation: 'ah, God!' 'God curse the same!' 'God, ye wish it!' He thinks of the Deity as an anthropomorphic being: once by referring to Him as a marble statue, and again by emphasizing the purely physical aspect of the mass. The mass, the candle flames, the incense smoke are all conceived on a sensuous, materialistic level. Eternity is actually an extension of time in which life is continued on a worldly plane – the only apparent difference being the greater advantages it provides the Bishop. One moment he contemplates projection of his political maneuvering on a wider scale, only to be reminded the next of the embarrassment of being humiliated before old Gandolf. He thinks of himself in eternity as a statue which still possesses the sensibilities and passions of a man. His single use of the word *soul,*

> Ever your eyes were as a lizard's quick,
> They glitter like your mother's for my soul,

indicates by the lines which follow that it has some very close relation to his possessions. He uses abstract words, then, as part of the traditional vocabulary of a Bishop, but constantly transmutes them from spiritual to material signs. Even the words which often are used abstractly remain concrete: *church* designates a specific building and *pulpit,* a platform in that building.

There are more adjectives, dominantly sensuous, in this poem than in 'Andrea del Sarto', 'Fra Lippo Lippi', or 'Bishop Blougram's Apology'. Every sense is addressed, but the poem appeals particularly to sight, touch, and smell. It contains some of the most sensuous lines in Browning:

As fresh-poured red wine of a mighty pulse.

And mistresses with great smooth marbly limbs.

The sensuous immediacy of these lines is strengthened by a deft manipulation of movement. In the verse 'And mistresses with great smooth marbly limbs' the voice is held by the long vowels to linger sensuously over each word so that a basic part of the meaning is conveyed structurally. 'Good strong thick stupefying incense-smoke' illustrates another technique. The long vowels slow the speed of the line, and the flanking consonants bring the voice almost to a stop between each word. The line is doubly slowed to give it the requisite ponderousness. 'I fought/ With tooth and nail to save my niche' is given rapid staccato tempo by the dominance of consonants.

It is important to note that Browning's use of adjectives is not merely presentational. There are no passages in 'The Bishop Orders his Tomb' that equal the visual brilliance of Keats's 'The Eve of St. Agnes'. Browning aims at something different – a response that is psychological as well as sensuous. We must exempt this poem from Eliot's charge that Browning and Tennyson 'do not feel their thoughts as immediately as the odour of a rose.' Here Browning does what Eliot says a poet must : in addition to the heart he looks also 'into the cerebral cortex, the nervous system, and the digestive tracts'. The result is a union of thought and sensation. Browning exploits that level of experience on which thought, sense, and emotion cease to be dissociated entities and merge into one pattern. The result is such expressions as 'to revel down', 'impoverished frieze', 'starved design', 'marbly limbs', 'brave Frascati villas', which express a complex experience that must be perceived psychically and physically by the entire nervous and muscular system.

Even the Bishop's qualitative adjectives are sensuous, few of them implying absolute values. He prefers, for example, *great* and *strong* to *good*, and uses *evil* merely to suggest unpleasantness. His quantitative adjectives and most of his adverbs have to do primarily with time and space. He speaks only of the now, of specific units of measurement, and of the future as hours, days, centuries.

He is attracted particularly by the sensuous qualities of both art and religion : the blue vein over the Madonna's breast, the brilliant colorings, the tactile qualities in all forms of art, and the hearing, seeing, feeling, tasting appeal of the ritual :

> And *hear* the blessed mutter of the mass,
> And *see* God made and eaten all day long,
> And *feel* the steady candle-flame, and *taste*
> Good strong thick stupefying incense-smoke

suggests the level of his response. He enjoys the sensuous stimulus which art provides and he judges it by its monetary value or its size. He sneers at Gandolf's tomb because of its clammy paltriness, an antithesis to the rare and costly one which he plans for himself. Typically, he is more impressed by the size than the beauty of the lapis.

The Bishop's imagery, lacking in structural complexity, helps define his limitations. A subconscious expression of his deference to crude force and power ('As fresh-poured red wine of a mighty pulse', 'Like God the Father's globe on both his hands', 'stabbed me with ingratitude'), it is an ironic counterpart to his own weakness. Like other elements of structure, it is primarily sensuous, displaying his fascination with the physiological ('Jew's head cut off at the nape', 'Madonna's breast', 'eyes . . . as a lizard's quick', 'great smooth marbly limbs'), the plastic, the tactile. His concern with these things when he himself is on the point of dissolution provides irony as well as an explanation of his desire to be embodied in a tomblike world.

The scene itself is pictorial and symbolic. The Bishop, arms folded, feet stretched forth, lies on his couch with the bedclothes for a mortcloth dropping around him in laps and folds of sculptor's-work. His sons, like columns, stand round his bed. There is in the situation a rigidity almost as if the old Bishop were actually as well as figuratively dead. As the poem develops, we sense a merging of the symbolic into the actual – with the important reservation that the imaginary tomb will never materialize.

Light is used here to suggest inner drama much as it is in 'Fra Lippo Lippi' and 'Andrea del Sarto'. The Bishop is dying by

slow degrees during the long hours of night, with his bed-bier
lighted by tapers. Whatever vision he may claim is fitful and
uncertain; his phantom-like being may at any moment be lost in
darkness. As his hope wanes and death approaches, the candles
are partly extinguished.

His imagery consists primarily of similes and personifications.
Each serves an immediate purpose and together they express
abstractly subterranean currents in the Bishop's consciousness of
which he is scarcely aware. Yet they fail to unite structurally with
others in a complex relationship such as characterizes 'Andrea
del Sarto'. A more complex pattern would be incongruous, of
course, for the Bishop is incapable of dealing with the intricate
kind of symbolism which Andrea's awareness opens for him;
indeed, the Bishop's lack of self-understanding renders impossible
such integration. It is his single vision which forms the ironic
pattern of the poem. His imagery must operate within the narrow
limits imposed by his intellectual and emotional awareness. He
is concerned about life, success, and some ultimate destiny, and
having found his *summum bonum* in the material and sensuous,
he arrives at what to him is a satisfactory solution to his problem.
Until the very end, he is disturbed neither by the frustrating
knowledge that he has failed, nor by the more perplexing and
unsolved problems which might stimulate a more sensitive
individual.

In the passages spoken in semiconsciousness an inner superficiality parallels his surface brilliance. He seems only vaguely
aware of the meaning of his quotations until circumstances force
upon him the fact that life is vanity and man is mortal. The
most revealing passage in the poem is

> The bas-relief in bronze ye promised me,
> Those Pans and Nymphs ye wot of, and perchance
> Some tripod, thyrsus, with a vase or so,
> The Saviour at his sermon on the mount,
> St. Praxed in a glory, and one Pan
> Ready to twitch the Nymph's last garment off,
> And Moses with the tablets. . . .

Here pagan and Christian elements are indiscriminately brought together in a manner which to the moral judgment appears incongruous. The confusion seems largely to cancel what might otherwise appear the import of the questions, spoken also in semiconsciousness. The Bishop, however, apparently recognizes no inconsistency, accepting all as appropriate subjects for art. Thus the projected bas-relief is a symbolic expression of his standard of values, suggesting the superficial hold Christianity had on him. That it appears confused is consistent with the traits which I have already noted in his conduct. It should be stated again that Browning is not discussing morals didactically. Here, as in 'The Statue and the Bust', he is concerned with a standard of values primarily as a psychological stimulus which produces action revelatory of character and situation.

That the Bishop created for himself a character and a world opposed to objective reality is clear. Before turning to the ironic pattern which brings these together in artistic form, I should like to note Browning's means of communication – through which, it seems to me, he made a distinctive contribution to poetic art.

In addition to presenting incident, narrative, and statement, he also communicates symbolically the complex emotions, sensations, and thoughts not yet formulated into rational phrases. The latter are expressed directly in their preconscious state unshaped by the rationalizing mind. The result is a disruption of normal syntax and an incoherency implicit in matter itself. Had the Bishop seen clearly enough to rationalize his confusion, his communication would have been different: a reflection upon, rather than an immediate sensuous and emotional expression of, experience. In using linguistic signs to express symbolically an area of experience not yet rendered totally conscious, Browning points toward the stream of consciousness technique of twentieth-century literature. Browning maintains the dramatic form, implying in the Bishop's speech a state which Joyce reports directly; it seems apparent, however, that each writer, in his own way, draws from a common source of experience. Browning's use of this method in much of his work beginning with *Sordello* accounts partly for what the Victorians called his obscurity.

Browning used this method for a number of reasons. Here the two levels of communication parallel the two strata of meaning

and make the reader more immediately conscious of discrepancies which form the basis of the poem's irony. The technique
dramatizes the tensions between the cultured, superficial structure of the Bishop's own creation and the deeper reality of life
itself. For Browning, it permitted a more precise expression of
the actual experience he was trying to communicate. He struggled
in all his poetry to find the exact structural equivalent for a
complex poetic experience, and in his best works he succeeded.
Marred as it is by immaturities, *Sordello* is yet one of Browning's
poems with which we cannot dispense. His attempt to make
structure a sensitive expression of meaning foreshadows what he
later realized more successfully. His syntactical elements, fragments, associational items, and rapid transitions actually indicate
the sensitive response of structure to matter in the joint task of
expressing poetic meaning. The promises of *Sordello* are fulfilled
in 'The Bishop Orders his Tomb'.

Let us note how the technique actually works in the poem.
The Bishop makes a statement, but we understand by a complex
of structural devices that there are other levels of meaning. In
addition to reading words in normal syntactical order, we must
read also word choice and distribution, sentence structure, omissions, punctuation, sound patterns, and rhythm; we must be
responsive to emotional and sensuous stimuli; we must take the
whole structural pattern as symbolic of a meaning not explicitly
stated.

I have already shown how sound, diction, and imagery are
immediately communicative. So are the incomplete sentences,
associational fragments, and ellipses. There are two types of in-
completions. One communicates experience directly in anacolu-
thic structure in order to gain imaginative, emotional, and sensuous immediacy :

> – That's if ye carve my epitaph aright,
> Choice Latin, picked phrase, Tully's every word,
> No gaudy ware like Gandolf's second line –
> Tully, my masters?

In addition to communicating ideas, these lines give also a direct impression of the rapidly changing flow of the Bishop's thoughts and feelings.

The other type of incompletion is the unfinished periodic:

> My sons, ye would not be my death? Go dig
> The white-grape vineyard where the oil-press stood,
> Drop water gently till the surface sink,
> And if ye find . . . Ah God, I know not, I! . . .
> Bedded in store of rotten fig-leaves soft,
> And corded up in a tight olive-frail,
> Some lump, ah God, of *lapis lazuli*,
> Big as a Jew's head cut off at the nape,
> Blue as a vein o'er the Madonna's breast . . .
> Sons, all have I bequeathed you, villas, all, . . .

> And as yon tapers dwindle, and strange thoughts
> Grow, with a certain humming in my ears,
> About the life before I lived this life,
> And this life too, popes, cardinals and priests,
> Saint Praxed at his sermon on the mount,
> Your tall pale mother with her talking eyes,
> And new-found agate urns as fresh as day,
> And marble's language, Latin pure, discreet,
> – Aha, ELUCESCEBAT quoth our friend?

In neither case did the Bishop forget what he began to say. Either he realized that, having communicated his meaning, he needed say no more, or he was diverted by a more powerful stream of thought stimulated by association of ideas or by a response from his audience. Taken as a whole, the statements accurately express psychological phenomena even though their logic is faulty.

For example, he is reminded of the tragedy of possibly losing his lapis, which he would give his 'all' to preserve. Impulsively he reminds his sons:

> Sons, all have I bequeathed you, villas, all,
> That brave Frascati villa with its bath,
> So, let the blue lump poise between my knees.

Again, in the sons' inattention, the Bishop suddenly realizes the

futility of his hopes and abruptly ends his description of the tomb
in an ellipsis that expresses more than words.

The associational fragment is an incompletion, but it differs
from the others in that it is more fragmentary, less communicative on the language level, and is differently related to adjoining
elements :

Nephews – sons mine . . . ah God, I know not ! Well –

Peach-blossom marble all, the rare, the ripe
As fresh-poured red wine of a mighty pulse.
– Old Gandolf with his paltry onion-stone,
Put me where I may look at him ! True peach,
Rosy and flawless : how I earned the prize !

'Do I live, am I dead ?' There, leave me, there !
For ye have stabbed me with ingratitude
To death – ye wish it – God, ye wish it ! Stone –
Gritstone, a-crumble ! Clammy squares which sweat
As if the corpse they keep were oozing through –
And no more *lapis* to delight the world !

The unity of these sentences rests upon the associational relationship between their elements, or between their elements and some
object, emotion, or sensation suggested by them. In the third
example, for instance, the unity of the two sentences is emotional.
The grief suggested by the first line links together the loss of the
jasper and the baths. Their meaning encompasses the whole of
the inner experience which they objectify. There are many such
examples in 'The Bishop Orders his Tomb'.

The ellipsis functions also to communicate subconscious experience. In some cases it is indicated orthographically, but often
it is not. In the poem, there are Browning's usual omissions of
functional words, and of even more important elements in the
associational fragments. These, however, are not particularly dis-
turbing to the reader. Readers who find 'The Bishop Orders his
Tomb' cryptic do so largely because of the omitted lines and
paragraphs. They fail to see that the meaning may be emotional
and sensuous, not always rational, and that much of it can be
expressed better by what is not said than by what is. Browning

might have gained readier intelligibility had he expanded, but in that case he would have done what Ruskin did – written thirty pages of prose. The real poem here is not contained within the one hundred and twenty-five lines, but rather in the complex world of thought, emotion and experience which they represent. Through this manner of communication, a forerunner of the stream of consciousness, Browning gains immediacy of expression without entering the poem in his own person. The reader not only understands what is said but comes to feel and sense the Bishop's world.

Irony serves in 'The Bishop Orders his Tomb' the unifying function which imagery accomplishes for 'Andrea del Sarto'. It provides a means of bringing together the diverse ways of seeing. The central ironies result from a juxtaposition of the Bishop's high evaluation of himself and his actual insignificance when he comes to die; his illusion that he has controlled great wealth and the final discovery in the defection of his sons that his ownership is only temporary; his materialistic one-dimensional view of life and his grotesque desire for a kind of immortality; his pride in the exercise of authority and the realization of the ineffectualness of his 'order'.

Like so many other of Browning's poems, 'The Bishop Orders his Tomb' is marked by a dialectical movement between juxtaposed opposites : from a stricture on vanity to a description of the elaborate tomb; from the peace of St. Praxed's to the tooth and nail fight with Gandolf; from the angels in the aery dome to the cursed carrion of old Gandolf in the tomb; from oozing corpse to lighted tapers. The direction of the poem is toward an ultimate identification by which the Bishop gains a surprising, ironic self-realization.

It is questionable whether at the beginning of the poem the Bishop realizes the full significance of the words 'Vanity, saith the preacher, vanity!' for with apparent unawareness he proceeds directly to describe plans for an elaborate tomb. Both the title and the opening line counterpoint the Bishop's illusion against the reality. In the first, he is unaware of his limited power; in the second, of his own weakness. The poem provides the dramatic development of his discovery of both.

One of the ironic devices used throughout is the Bishop's quotations. They are precisely applicable to him, but any real meaning which they might have has been so submerged that it fails to operate on a conscious level. Like the priestly blessing which he gives his sons, they are echoes of ecclesiastical duties performed emptily in the past. Appearing only during his semiconscious moments, they convey more truth than he is able or willing to admit. The lines

> Swift as a weaver's shuttle fleet our years :
> Man goeth to the grave, and where is he?

are followed directly by

> Did I say basalt for my slab, sons? Black –
> 'T was ever antique-black I meant!

However, he does not yet realize how much death really will end for him. He displays a characteristic attitude in his reference to his sons' mother :

> . . . she is dead beside,
> Dead long ago, and I am Bishop since.

Weakness and death belong to his mistress and Gandolf, strength and life to him. He may confuse himself with God ('Like God the Father's globe . . .') but never with other men. It is an embittering blow, therefore, when he is brought at last to acknowledge the common tie, death, with his mistress and Gandolf. His frustrating impotency in the presence of death causes him to wonder whether life has not been a dream after all. For to him life had meant 'tooth and nail' fighting, having his orders respected and obeyed. Now, in contrast, his strength and power are gone. 'Do I live . . .?' he asks. Passivity is certainly death. The Bishop's concept of life as activity is counterpointed by his actual powerlessness. We have both the Bishop of endless striving and animal activity, and the Bishop fossilized symbolically in marble.

The latter is the more basic and eventually predominates. Appropriately, therefore, there are in the poem fewer active verbs, more passive, than in either 'Andrea del Sarto' or 'Fra Lippo Lippi'. Faced with the inevitability of death and fearing extinction, he turns to the tomb as a means of preserving his superiority and places his 'order' with his sons.

From this point, the tension increases until the Bishop comes partly to realize about himself and the tomb what the reader has known from the beginning. The poem is a dramatic presentation of a self-revelation which forces the Bishop to accept a reality paradoxical to the illusion under which he has lived. More striking than the discrepancy between the tombs is his changing relationship with people and things, particularly with Gandolf. In the beginning he is triumphant and Gandolf is humiliated; in the conclusion the Bishop has been humbled and Gandolf relatively elevated. Gandolf won a minor triumph by dying early and securing for his tomb the best niche in the church, even though his resting place was marked by paltry onion-stone. 'Put me where I may look at him,' the Bishop gloats. In contrast, he muses, his tomb will be magnificent, his triumph final and complete : 'For Gandolf shall not choose but see and burst !' Only gradually does he realize that he will not have his wish. Instead of lapis to delight the world, there will be only

> ... Stone
> Gritstone, a-crumble ! Clammy squares which sweat
> As if the corpse they keep were oozing through –

Instead of reposing in luxury, he will

> ... gasp
> Bricked o'er with beggar's mouldy travertine
> Which Gandolf from his tomb-top chuckles at !

The last line is the important one. The relative positions of the Bishop and his old enemy have been reversed.

Further, the imagined tomb was a symbol of values which the Bishop had considered enduring. It was to be an appropriate summation of his achievements, embodying his cultural and material wealth. But instead, he receives the same cheap gritstone that marked Gandolf's grave. After being feared and obeyed

all his life, the Bishop issues his last 'order' only to discover that he
has no power to command. He tries to bribe his sons but finds
that what he offers has already passed from his hands to theirs.
Contrary to his supposition, power of action lies with his sons, not
with himself. At last he discovers what earlier had existed only
vaguely in his subconscious : all, indeed, is vanity.

The final irony is in the line 'Well go! I bless ye'. The Bishop
has one thing in mind and makes the statement lightly. It has
been part of his ecclesiastical duty to give empty blessing, but
unwittingly, it is no longer empty. What he had once given
nominally he now gives actually. Dying, he leaves 'all' to his sons,
and by his own definition of the good life he bestows on them the
greatest blessing. It is doubly ironic that this, the first genuine
blessing he has ever given, brings him no spiritual comfort.

SOURCE : *The Bow and the Lyre* (Ann Arbor, 1957) chapter IV.

W. O. Raymond

'THE STATUE AND THE BUST' (1959)

With the possible exception of *Fifine at the Fair*, there is no other poem of Browning whose ethics have provoked such controversy as 'The Statue and the Bust'. The two poems have frequently been linked both in hostile criticism and in eulogy. In the *Scottish Art Review* for December 1889, Mr. Mortimer asserted that *Fifine at the Fair* and 'The Statue and the Bust' showed that Browning 'prescribes action at any price, even that of defying the restrictions of the moral law'. Swinburne, on the other hand, enthusiastically admired both works. Lord Bryce has recorded how at a meeting of the Old Mortality Society in Swinburne's rooms at Oxford in 1858, the Pre-Raphaelite poet 'repeated, or rather chanted, to his friends, a few of Browning's poems, in particular "The Statue and the Bust", "The Heretic's Tragedy", and "Bishop Blougram's Apology" '.[1] Again, shortly after the publication of *Fifine at the Fair*, Swinburne said, 'This is far better than anything Browning has yet written. Here is his true province.'[2]

In one respect, at least, the ethical problem involved in 'The Statue and the Bust' was more disquieting to many of Browning's Victorian readers than that in *Fifine at the Fair*. In *Fifine*, Don Juan is the speaker throughout, and his defence of his immoral delinquencies could be interpreted as the utterances of a libertine casuist rather than the poet's own sentiments. But in 'The Statue and the Bust', although Browning is relating an old legend, 'this story . . . our townsmen tell', the comment is his own; and, moreover, in the last verses he defends his poem against the criticism which he foresees it will evoke and definitely states his personal convictions. This defence at once differentiates 'The Statue and the Bust' from the so-called casuistical mono-

logues of Browning, such as 'Bishop Blougram's Apology', 'Mr.
Sludge, The Medium', *Fifine at the Fair*, and 'Prince Hohenstiel-
Schwangau'. If there is casuistry in the ethical thesis of 'The
Statue and the Bust' it is casuistry in which the poet himself is
directly involved; it cannot be palmed off as the dramatic sentiments of any imaginary characters. What may be called the Epilogue to 'The Statue and the Bust' is therefore of special importance. Although the dramatic disguise is very thin in many of
Browning's monologues, it is seldom that he casts it off altogether
and avowedly speaks in his own person.

In the body of the poem, the two lovers are criticized for the
procrastination and infirmity of will which prevented them from
eloping and gratifying their unlawful love. Does the poet then
maintain that adultery may be laudable under certain circumstances? It is this charge which Browning strives to defend himself against in the Epilogue. At its outset he voices the foreseen
adverse criticism.

> I hear you reproach, 'But delay was best,
> For their end was a crime.'

The reference to adultery as a *crime* is in itself significant as
evidence that Browning does not condone it. He then proceeds
with his defence. What he singles out and dwells upon is the
weakness and cowardice of the lovers' procrastination and lack of
resolution. Had they repented of their sinful passion and been
deterred from eloping by moral considerations, he would have
commended them. But they were deterred only through lack of
courage and the fear of worldly consequences. Their sinful motives and desires, the lust of their hearts, remained unchanged.
Consequently the poet holds that they simply added to their original sin the vice of procrastination.

The method of Browning's argument in this poem may be
illustrated by a comparison between it and the biblical parable
of the Unjust Steward. After his dismissal from his position, the
steward set about making friends for himself by dishonestly reduc-
ing the bills owed by his master's clients. Then we read: 'And
the Lord commended the unjust steward, because he had done

wisely.' Are we to assume that Christ's teaching was that the
steward was to be praised on account of his dishonesty? It is
clearly the energy, pains, and forethought of the steward in securing friends for himself after his dismissal which are singled out for
commendation, abstracted, so to speak, from his dishonesty. His
diligence and sagacity are contrasted with the slothfulness and
ineptness of people whose ends are moral, but who are lukewarm,
half-hearted, and negligent in their pursuit of these. 'The children of this world are in their generation wiser than the children
of light.' What Browning says, in effect, in the concluding verses
of 'The Statue and the Bust' is that he has illustrated the weakness
of procrastination, 'the unlit lamp and the ungirt loin', through
characters who were sinful rather than virtuous. Finally, in the
last two lines of the poem, with a swift probing thrust, he rounds
upon people who plume themselves upon their virtue but are
slothful in pursuing it :

> You of the virtue (we issue join)
> How strive you? *De te, fabula.*

Yet the ethical problem of the poem is not fully solved by
Browning's concentration on the weakness of procrastination and
infirmity of will. He has to defend his ethics on two grounds, the
one specific, the other general.

In the first place he has maintained that the duke and the
lady are as guilty in cherishing their unlawful love as they would
have been had they committed the crime of adultery. He judges
them by their motives, and in this respect we are reminded of
Christ's words in the Sermon on the Mount : 'But I say unto you,
That whosoever looketh on a woman to lust after her hath committed adultery with her already in his heart.' It is characteristic
of Browning that he lays such stress on inner motive, and that he
should be primarily concerned with the soul of the individual
rather than with the individual in his nexus of social relationships.
Throughout his poetry the worth of the individual is estimated
not by outward achievement, but by aim and motivation. Often,
as in 'A Grammarian's Funeral', he extols characters whose
worldly accomplishment has amounted to little, in order to throw

into relief the loftiness of their aspiration. As he writes in 'Rabbi Ben Ezra' :

> For hence, – a paradox
> Which comforts while it mocks, –
> Shall life succeed in that it seems to fail :
> What I aspired to be,
> And was not comforts me. . . .

There is a sharp contrast between Browning's judgment of the duke and the lady and their position in the eyes of the law. From a legal point of view the secret love of the two would have escaped censure. The law, which is concerned with individuals as members of society, would not have condemned them until they had actually committed adultery. From an individualistic standpoint the poet is justified in regarding sin in motive as quite as culpable as sin in act. Yet it may be asked whether, since man is a social animal, it is entirely legitimate to abstract him from the society which helps largely to shape and mould him, and of which he is an organic part. Can an open violation of the restraints imposed by the standards, codes, even the conventions, of civilized society, the translation of sinful thought into act, fail to enhance individual guilt? As Berdoe puts it in his comment on 'The Statue and the Bust' : 'If every woman flew to the arms of the man whom she liked better than her own husband, and if every governor of a city felt himself at liberty to steal another man's wife merely to complete and perfect the circle of his own delights, society would seem to be thrown back into barbarism.'[8]

In the specific instance of 'The Statue and the Bust', Browning has maintained that if motives are evil, it is better to act on these with vigour and resolution, than to be deterred by weakness of will and cowardice. It is, however, his generalization of this into a universal standard of conduct which has provoked most hostile criticism :

> Stake your counter as boldly every whit,
> Venture as warily, use the same skill,
> Do your best, whether winning or losing it,

If you choose to play ! – is my principle.
Let a man contend to the uttermost
For his life's set prize, be it what it will !

It is clear that to the poet the most hopeless state of human nature
is that of indifference and inaction. As Henry Jones has written :
'It is under the guise of warfare that morality always presents
itself to Browning.'⁴ The development of man's soul can be
achieved only through conflict. Therefore, let truth and false-
hood, good and evil grapple :

No, when the fight begins within himself,
A man's worth something. God stoops o'er his head,
Satan looks up between his feet, – both tug –
He's left himself, i' the middle : the soul awakes
And grows. . . .
('Bishop Blougram's Apology', 693–7)

In view of the supreme importance of the moral conflict, to evade
it is, in a sense, the worst of sins. It is better, Browning holds, to
act evilly than to lapse into atrophy of soul.

The situation in 'The Statue and the Bust' is one of many illus-
trations in Browning's poetry of the importance he attaches to a
climactic moment in the lives of individuals. In the 'Epilogue' to
Dramatis Personae he represents the spiritual powers of the universe as concentrating in some critical moment on the life of every
man to challenge him to an all-important decision involving not
merely temporal but eternal consequences. On a person's response
or lack of response to this challenge his destiny depends. An individual at this crux is like a point of 'central rock' in 'Arctic
seas' towards which all the waters converge for a moment before
they 'hasten off to play elsewhere'. In 'Cristina' Browning writes
of moments

When the spirit's true endowments
Stand out plainly from the false ones
And apprise it if pursuing
Or the right way or the wrong way
To its triumph or undoing.

In the majority of instances this is what Browning calls 'the good minute'. His poems dealing with it fall into two classes. In the first, the good choice which the moment offers is made, and the result is beneficent. In the second, the good choice is missed or neglected, and the result is baneful. A fine example of the first class is the happy choice of the lovers in the beautiful semi-dramatic lyric 'By the Fire-Side'. The heaven-sent opportunity of the 'moment one, and infinite' is grasped, the positive decision made, and the fruitage is eternal.

> I am named and known by that moment's feat;
>   There took my station and degree;
> So grew my own small life complete,
>   As nature obtained her best of me –
> One born to love you sweet!

Finally, in 'By the Fire-Side', as in 'The Statue and the Bust', Browning generalizes a specific incident in order to stress a general truth :

> How the world is made for each of us!
>   How all we perceive and know in it
> Tends to some moment's product thus,
>   When a soul declares itself – to wit,
> By its fruit, the thing it does!

'Dîs Aliter Visum' and 'Youth and Art' exemplify the second class of Browning's poems dealing with 'the good minute', in which the failure to use its opportunities is disastrous. These poems are complementary to 'By the Fire-Side' in that they are concerned with the destiny of potential lovers at a crucial moment of their lives, but contrasted in the results that ensue. Love is blasted by a failure, through weakness of will and worldly prudence, to act, and the lives of the lovers are irretrievably marred. As the woman in 'Youth and Art' laments :

> Each life unfulfilled, you see;
>   It hangs still, patchy and scrappy :
> We have not sighed deep, laughed free,
>   Starved, feasted, despaired, – been happy. . . .
> This could but have happened once,
>   And we missed it, lost it for ever.

Neither of these poems involves any ethical problem. It is indisputable that a failure to achieve a good end because of unworthy motives is morally wrong and culpable.

There are, however, in 'The Statue and the Bust' and other poems of Browning, climactic moments of another order than that of 'the good minute'. In these, if the opportunities are embraced, the end is a crime not a virtue. Yet the poet holds that if a failure to grasp them is due only to infirmity of will, cowardice, or procrastination, and not to any moral restraint, it would be better for the sinners to act with decision and energy, and commit the contemplated crime. As Dr. Westcott writes of Browning's ethical teaching : 'No room is left for indifference or neutrality. . . . A part must be taken and maintained. The spirit in which Luther said "Pecca fortiter" finds in him powerful expression.'[5]

In the poem 'Before', the speaker maintains that even for the wrong-doer in a quarrel it would be preferable to fight the issue out in a duel rather than add cowardice to his guilt by avoiding it. Even in the event of his being the victor, there is more hope that remorse of conscience will ultimately redeem him than if he had shrunk from accepting the challenge :

> Better sin the whole sin, sure that God observes ;
> Then go live his life out ! life will try his nerves. . . .
>
> And the price appears that pays for the misfeasance.

In 'Too Late', where again the lives of a man and woman are ruined by a failure to avow love, the man declares that even violent action to take possession of 'Edith' would have been worthier than his inaction :

> Why better even have burst like a thief
>   And borne you away to a rock for us two,
> In a moment's horror, bright, bloody, and brief.

In 'The Worst of It', the sin of the woman in being false to her husband ultimately becomes the means of his redemption. In 'The Lost Leader', the speaker maintains that it would be better for the leader, after his defection from the people's cause, to follow his wrongful course with energy and decision rather than to vacillate weakly and return to the party he has betrayed :

> Best fight on well, for we taught him – strike gallantly,
> Menace our heart ere we master his own. . . .

In Browning's defence of his ethical standards in 'The Statue and the Bust', the argument of the poems I have been considering is definitively summed up :

> Let a man contend to the uttermost
> For his life's set prize, be what it will !

It is the poet's fervent stress on action, and above all on action as preferable to inaction, if the latter is due to unworthy motives, even when the end pursued is immoral, which has been assailed. At the same time there is a distrust, and indeed a dislike, of Browning's aggressive and unqualified emotional optimism, and a conviction of the inadequacy of his concept of evil. A portion of this criticism is, it seems to me, justifiable; but a larger portion has led to a grave misapprehension of his outlook on life and his ethical and spiritual tenets.

In his essay on 'The Poetry of Barbarism', Santayana has declared that for Browning 'the crude experience is the only end, the endless struggle the only ideal, and the perturbed "Soul" the only organum of truth'. Browning's temperament is such that for him 'life is an adventure, not a discipline', and 'the exercise of energy is the absolute good, irrespective of motives or of circumstances'.[6] In similar vein, Professor Fairchild writes concerning Browning's poetry :

At a time of deep uncertainty as to life's ultimate aim, the transference of value from the thing sought to the mere seeking provided a potent emotional lift. Since one did not know what the prize was, it was heartening to be assured that 'The prize is in the process'. The thing done, since it is never done, must be less important than the courage and vigor of the doing.[7]

It is undeniable that the militancy of Browning's temperament and the robustness of his optimism cause him to over-stress the value of action *per se*. The conquest of evil by discipline, self-control, and the restraints of reason is minimized. For him the

crux of life is moral struggle, whose essence is not the overcoming
of evil by self-denial or the avoidance of temptation but the overcoming of evil with good. Moreover, he welcomes the strenuous-
ness of moral conflict. After paraphrasing the clause in the Lord's
Prayer 'Lead us not into temptation', the Pope in *The Ring and
the Book* exclaims:

> Yea, but O Thou, whose servants are the bold,
> Lead such temptations by the head and hair,
> Reluctant dragons, up to who dares fight,
> That so he may do battle and have praise! (x, 1189–92)

'The kingdom of heaven suffereth violence, and the violent take
it by force'; and Browning has never more poignantly expressed
his ideal of heroic moral achievement than when in utter scorn
of the cowardice and procrastination of the duke and the lady
in 'The Statue and the Bust', he writes:

> Only they see not God, I know,
> Nor all that chivalry of his,
> The soldier-saints who, row on row,
>
> Burn upward each to his point of bliss –
> Since, the end of life being manifest,
> He had burned his way thro' the world to this.

One cause of a biased and warped criticism of Browning's
ethical and spiritual convictions has been, I believe, a concentration on his intellectual scepticism, especially in his so-called
casuistical poems, and a neglect of his unswerving faith in the
sovereign virtue of love. His gnosticism in the sphere of feeling
and emotion, where the intuitions and revelations of the heart are
concerned, is surely as much to be reckoned with as his rational
agnosticism.

In order to evaluate the ethics of Browning in 'The Statue and
the Bust', it is necessary to consider his general concept of the
nature of evil, and its function in the moral conflict. As an absolute idealist the poet believes that God is omnipotent and all-

loving; and, as a corollary to this, he has, as Professor Jones puts it, 'a conviction of the ultimate nothingness of evil, and of the complete victory of the good'.[8] Yet how can such a faith be reconciled with the presence and power of evil on earth? Browning's attempt to solve this age-old problem has many facets; but his main argument is that the supreme purpose of God for man is the formation of his character; and that this can be achieved only through a moral struggle, centring on a choice between good and evil. 'This dread machinery of sin and sorrow' must be designed to develop 'the moral qualities of man' and 'to make him love in turn and be beloved'.[9] In this connection, however, the poet's distrust of reason involves him in a difficulty. So far as knowledge is concerned, he maintains that every man is confined to his own subjective experience. He cannot be sure that this has any objective validity. Even though he himself is conscious of a moral law, he has no assurance, through knowledge, that the moral law of which he is aware corresponds with a moral law in the universe without, or is in harmony with the ultimate purposes of the Absolute. Such thorough-going scepticism might make it seem a matter of indifference whether an individual follows a good or evil course. If man has no knowledge that his moral or immoral choice has any confirmation in objective reality, the only ethical value that remains lies in the qualities of energy and will evoked in the struggle. As the poet himself says, from the point of view of knowledge, 'the prize is in the process'. The justice of Santayana's criticism that for Browning 'the exercise of energy is the absolute good, irrespective of motives or of circumstances' might seem to be confirmed.

Actually, however, this description of the tenor of Browning's poetry is far from being accurate. Lack of confirmation of its objective reality never makes the poet swerve from the conviction that man should act in accordance with the intuitions and promptings of his conscience which urge him to follow good rather than evil. These are, rationally, subjective, confined apparently to each individual's private experience, but they are an absolute for him. A man's ignorance of their ultimate worth the poet regards as part of his probation on earth. Even though he may not know until the Day of Judgment that they are in accord with divine reality, he must act in obedience to their guidance.

> Ask thy lone soul what laws are plain to thee,
> Thee, and no other; stand or fall by them!
>
> ('A Camel-Driver', 54–5)

> . . . I do
> Discern and dare decree in consequence,
> Whatever prove the peril of mistake.
>
> ('The Pope', 1250–2)

> . . . Man's part
> Is plain – to send love forth, – astray, perhaps :
> No matter, he has done his part.
>
> ('The Sun', 136–8)

> . . . I have one appeal –
> I feel, am what I feel, know what I feel;
> So much is truth to me.
>
> (*Sordello*, vi, 439–41)

The poet's belief that he is a moral agent, even though this may be only a pious hope, is his

> . . . solid standing-place amid
> The wash and welter, whence all doubts are bid
> Back to the ledge they break against in foam.
>
> ('Francis Furini', x, 161–3)

Like Kant, Browning holds that it is impossible to prove the reality of the supersensible or the existence of God through knowledge. But, again like Kant, the rational subjectivity of man's experience is for him no warrant for disregarding the intuitions of the moral consciousness. The choice of duty and goodness which it enjoins is as much a 'categorical imperative' for the poet as it is for the philosopher.

Moreover, the moment Browning passes from the negations of knowledge to the sphere of intuition and feeling, his intellectual scepticism is replaced by emotional gnosticism.

> I trust in my own soul, that can perceive
> The outward and the inward, nature's good
> And God's....
> ('A Soul's Tragedy', I, 256–8)

Above all he bases his emotional gnosticism on the sovereign
virtue of love. Were knowledge all man's faculty he would be
compelled to confess that 'the prize is in the process'. The poet,
however, immediately adds, 'But love is victory, the prize itself'.
'God! Thou art Love! I build my faith on that!' Browning
wrote in *Paracelsus*, and this statement is the corner-stone of his
belief and spiritual conviction. It follows that, despite the
apparent contradiction between the testimonies of the heart and
the head, the loving purposes of God must be working themselves out in the life of man and in the external universe.

> Is not God now i' the world His power first made?
> Is not His love at issue still with sin,
> Visibly when a wrong is done on earth?
> ('A Death in the Desert', 211–13)

There is not, from the point of view of love, any gulf between
subjective and objective, between the moral ideal in the heart of
man and its absolute reality in the nature of the being of God.

> Were knowledge all thy faculty, then God
> Must be ignored : love gains him by first leap.
> ('A Pillar at Sebzevar', 134–5)

Consequently, in the light of Browning's concept of love, the
worth of the moral conflict cannot be confined to the mere processes of subjective experience. Its motivation and its goal have
an ethical and spiritual objective value and reality.

At this juncture, however, Browning has to grapple with the
most perplexing and darkest aspect of the problem of evil. It is
not difficult to comprehend that, since the development of the
soul is dependent upon a moral struggle, the existence of evil is
necessary in order that in combating it man's character may be
shaped and God's purpose for him realized. But what can be said

in the case of a sinner who makes the wrong choice and follows
the path of evil? How can evil, in this connection, be reconciled
with the omnipotence and infinite love of God, or be regarded
as subject to his power?

In dealing with this problem, Browning does not qualify the
optimism of his absolute idealism. If God has absolute authority
over evil as well as good, and if his purposes of infinite love cannot be thwarted by evil, then evil through being transmuted must
be instrumental in the working out of his divine plan. There is
no sin so vile, no evil so grim, as to be incapable of *ultimate*
transmutation. As he writes:

> Of absolute and irretrievable
> And all subduing black, – black's soul of black
> Beyond white's power to disintensify, –
> Of this I saw no sample....
>
> ('A Bean-Stripe', 200–3)

For Browning, 'all things ill' are not, as Milton regarded them,
merely 'slavish officers of vengeance' in the service of 'the Supreme Good'; they are rather, through being finally transmuted,
the slavish officers of God's love. Ultimately, since God is omnipotent as well as all-loving, every sinner, through remorse, repent-
ance, atonement, and divine mercy, must be redeemed. Such a
belief involves the rejection of the doctrine of eternal punishment.
Confronted with an appalling aftermath of evil in the bodies of
three suicides lying in the Paris morgue, Browning writes in
'Apparent Failure':

> My own hope is, a sun will pierce
> The thickest cloud earth ever stretched;
> That, after Last, returns the First,
> Though a wide compass round be fetched;
> That what began best, can't end worst,
> Nor what God blessed once, prove accurst.

It is in connection with Browning's belief in evil as 'stuff for
transmuting' that his ethical standards in 'The Statue and the
Bust' must be evaluated. Whenever good and evil grapple there

is no hesitation whatever in his praise of the choice of virtue and his condemnation of the choice of vice. This indeed is the very core of his moral credo. No other poet has been a more militant champion of virtue. In *The Ring and the Book* there is no measure in the contrast between his extolling of the good as represented in Pompilia and Caponsacchi and his denunciation of evil as represented in Guido. Yet, because he does regard evil as 'stuff for transmuting', he holds that the shirking of the moral conflict is the worst sin of all.

If the will is alive, if a man acts with energy and courage even in pursuit of an evil end, there is hope for him. The poet believes that the punishment which sin entails, the prickings of conscience, the realization on the part of the sinner that he is hopelessly contending against the will of God and is betraying his better nature, must, in conjunction with divine love and mercy, ultimately redeem him either on earth or in a life hereafter. But if a man's will is dead, if through inertness or cowardice he refuses to act at all, his passivity is a graver sin than that of an active evil-doer. Since he has shunned the moral conflict, no development of his soul is possible, not even through the transmuting of evil-doing.

> Let a man contend to the uttermost
> For his life's set prize, be it what it will!

To play a part in the moral struggle with will and decision is for Browning the primary requirement of all. In *Christmas-Eve and Easter-Day* he rejoices that he can

> Be crossed and tempted as a man,
> Not left in God's contempt apart,
> With ghastly smooth life, dead at heart,
> Tame in earth's paddock as her prize.
> (*Easter-Day*, xxxiii, 16–19)

In *The Ring and the Book*, the Pope denounces Pietro and Violante for their timidity and double-dealing in vacillating between right and wrong:

... Go,
Never again elude the choice of tints,
White shall not neutralize the black, nor good
Compensate ill in man, absolve him so :
Life's business being just the terrible choice.
('The Pope', 1234-8)

Browning's contempt for faint-heartedness and paralysis of will is, as Pigou notes, reminiscent of Dante's scorn for him 'who made through cowardice the great refusal', and pines forever in the outskirts of the Inferno, 'hateful to God and to his enemies'.[10]

As has been stated, Browning believes that even a sinful course of action is ultimately transmuted to become an instrument for the realization of the good ends of a God of infinite power and love. In 'By the Fire-Side' he maintains that hate as well as love may have a function in the development of individual souls, and consequently in the evolution of the human race :

Be hate that fruit or love that fruit,
    It forwards the general deed of man,
And each of the Many helps to recruit
    This life of the race by a general plan;
Each living his own to boot.

It must be acknowledged that the poet's argument here, and in kindred passages, skates perilously close to the verge of the pernicious casuistry of 'Let us do evil that good may come'. As a matter of fact it is twisted into such sophistry by Don Juan, Sludge the Medium, and other protagonists of Browning's casuistical poems. It must also be conceded that the poet's intellectual agnosticism beclouds, at times, his speculative thought on moral and spiritual problems. Yet the whole tenor and purport of his poetry, when he is voicing his own convictions, refute the assertion that for him 'the exercise of energy is the absolute good, irrespective of motives or of circumstances'. To maintain that evil by being transmuted is ultimately overruled by God for good, is very different from an acceptance of the casuistical precept 'Let us do evil that good may come'. In this respect Browning's belief may be compared with the Christian doctrine of the Atonement. Faith in the potency of the Atonement is in harmony with his conviction that evil is 'stuff for transmuting', that no sinner is beyond the pale of final redemption; but it does not imply that evil *per se* is ever good, or that the following of it is ever justified. Browning would have echoed St. Paul's impassioned protest, 'Shall we continue in sin, that grace may abound? God forbid.'

There is no other concept in Browning's ethics which has been more adversely criticized than his belief that evil is illusory. Yet there is an important element of truth in his contention. If evil and good are not coequal, evil cannot have the same degree of reality as good. Evil is rebellion, negation, imperfection, the consciousness of the gulf between man's moral ideal and his present state of being. Having served its end in the moral conflict it will be overthrown, since the purpose of a loving God for his universe must be the final and complete victory of goodness. The conviction that evil is relative rather than absolute has been nobly voiced by Milton :

> Yea, even that which Mischief meant most harm
> Shall in the happy trial prove most glory.
> But evil on itself shall back recoil,
> And mix no more with goodness, when at last
> Gathered like scum, and settled to itself,
> It shall be in eternal restless change,
> Self-fed and self-consumed. If this fail
> The pillared firmament is rottenness,
> And earth's base built on stubble. . . .
>   (*Comus*, 591–9)

Milton's concept of the relativity of evil does not, however, imply that he regards it as *mere* semblance or illusion.

Unfortunately, Browning's representation of this aspect of evil is warped by his intellectual agnosticism. An extreme instance is his argument that although evil is an illusion, it is necessary for man to regard it as real in order to preserve the worth of the moral struggle. This would seem to make man's moral effort dependent on ignorance and delusion, or to hold, as Professor Jones writes, that 'the world is a kind of moral gymnasium, crowded with phantoms, wherein by exercise man makes moral muscle'.[11] As I have stated, the confusion of thought engendered by Browning's sceptical theory of knowledge seems to me responsible for much misunderstanding regarding his ethical standards. The poet exposes himself to this because he fails to realize that even from an absolute point of view evil has a relative degree of reality, and is not mere semblance and illusion.

There is also, I feel, on another ground, a residuum of truth in the hostile criticism of the poet's concept of evil. Often as Browning is preoccupied with the problem of evil, he never, even while condemning it, feels that loathing and horror of evil which characterizes the prophets of the Old Testament. He does not, as *The Ring and the Book* is ample testimony, shut his eyes to it as Emerson did. One would hesitate to say of him, as it has been said of Milton contrasted with Dante, that in his representation of Hell 'he never saw the damned'. Yet the gulf between Dante's utter abhorrence of evil and Browning's reaction to it is wide.

The explanation lies in Browning's temperamental and emotional optimism. Its sources are both physical and psychical. A statement of Carlyle concerning the poet may be cited :

> But there's a great contrast between him and me. He seems very content with life, and takes much satisfaction in the world.
> It's a very strange and curious spectacle to behold a man in these days so confidently cheerful.[12]

As William James has written :

> In many persons, happiness is congenital and irreclaimable. 'Cosmic emotion' inevitably takes in them the form of enthusiasm and freedom. . . . We find such persons in every age, passionately flinging themselves upon their sense of the goodness of life. . . .[13]

Such people are 'animally happy', and spiritually their religion is that of 'healthy-mindedness'. They know little of the divisions of 'the sick soul', or the agonizing struggle of those who through conversion must be 'twice born' to achieve their ultimate salvation.

Intellectually there is pessimism in Browning's attitude towards the world as it is. In 'Reverie' and elsewhere he laments, 'Earth's good is with evil blent : / Good struggles but evil reigns.' Yet, the poet's emotional optimism is far more potent than his intellectual pessimism. Psychologically this optimism is reflected in the buoyancy and positiveness of his temperament, morally and spiritually in his conviction that, since God is a being of infinite love, the whole scheme and framework of his creation must be flawlessly good from an absolute point of view, in which the transient and illusory appearances of evil and discord are resolved and transmuted into the eternal harmonies of God's all-loving purposes. While it is somewhat arbitrary to wrench the lines in Pippa's song from their dramatic context ('God's in his heaven – / All's right with the world!'), there can be no doubt that they voice the poet's belief. So also do the lines in 'At the "Mermaid" ', although dramatically attributed to Shakespeare :

> I find earth not grey but rosy.
>   Heaven not grim but fair of hue.
> Do I stoop? I pluck a posy.
>   Do I stand and stare? All's blue.

Browning's representation of evil is conditioned by his optimism and the militancy of his temperament and conflict-loving nature. Evil is not in his eyes primarily horrible and loathsome, but rather 'stuff for transmuting'. Like Roderick Dhu in Scott's *The Lady of the Lake* he confronts it with eagerness, 'and that stern joy which warriors feel in foemen worthy of their steel'. As 'stuff for transmuting' he must even show that 'there is a soul of goodness in things evil'. There is nothing in the world which

> But touched aright, prompt yields each particle its tongue
> Of elemental flame, – no matter whence flame sprung
> From gums and spice, or else from straw and rottenness,
> So long as soul has power to make them burn. . . .
>   (*Fifine at the Fair*, LV, 12–15)

It cannot be denied that such tenets do tend to stress the worth of the moral struggle *per se* rather than the black-and-white opposition of its elements, sin as Dante saw it in its loathsomeness and virtue in its crystalline purity.

Yet this distinction is only relatively valid, and often more theoretical than actual. As I have pointed out, no speculative doubts regarding the confirmation in objective reality of his subjective experiences prevent Browning from deeming it imperative that he should be loyal to the guidance of his conscience. For him the choice between good and evil is an all-important decision. He takes his stand for virtue along with 'the famous ones of old' who, in the 'Epilogue' to 'Ferishtah's Fancies', his imagination pictures 'thronging through the cloud-rift' as witnesses of his own moral conflict. They are an evidence to him that his choice of good rather than evil, so far from being a matter of indifference, has supreme value and significance.

> 'Was it for mere fool's play, make-believe and mumming,
>   So we battled it like men, not boylike sulked or whined?
> Each of us heard clang God's "Come!" and each was coming :
>   Soldiers all, to forward-face, not sneaks to lag behind!'

Despite the approach to casuistry and the confusion of thought in which Browning is frequently befogged through his nescient theory of knowledge and distrust of reason, there is no real ground for the assertion that he is indifferent to ethical ends, or that for him 'the exercise of energy is the absolute good, irrespective of motives or of circumstances'. His belief that, if God is omnipotent and all-loving, evil must finally be transmuted, by no means implies that he is blind to the moral distinction between good and evil, or in any way counsels 'Let us do evil that good may come'.

Above all, when Browning turns from the evidence of the head to that of the heart in what has been called 'the richest vein of pure ore' in his poetry, his view of the nature and function of love, he attains a certainty of good which convinces him of its objective as well as subjective validity. 'But love is victory, the prize itself.' Who can doubt that in the noble utterance of the Pope in *The Ring and the Book* the poet is attesting his own assurance :

... I
Put no such dreadful question to myself,
Within whose circle of experience burns
The central truth, Power, Wisdom, Goodness, – God :
I must outlive a thing ere know it dead. ...

So, never I miss footing in the maze,
No, – I have light nor fear the dark at all.
                                        (x, 1631–5, 1659–60)

SOURCE : *The Infinite Moment,* 2nd ed. (1965) chap. 12. Originally published in the *University of Toronto Quarterly,* XXVIII (1959) 239–49.

NOTES

1. Edmund Gosse, *Life of Algernon Charles Swinburne* (New York, 1917) pp. 39–40.
2. W. H. Griffin and H. C. Minchin, *The Life of Robert Browning,* 3rd ed. (London, 1938) p. 258.
3. Edward Berdoe, *The Browning Cyclopedia,* 6th ed. (London, 1909) p. 519.
4. Henry Jones, *Browning as a Philosophical and Religious Teacher* (Glasgow, 1892) p. 111.
5. Cited in ibid. p. 118.
6. George Santayana, *Interpretations of Poetry and Religion* (New York, 1924) pp. 212, 206.
7. Hoxie Neale Fairchild, *Religious Trends in English Poetry,* IV (New York, 1957) 154.
8. Jones, *Browning,* p. 119.
9. *The Ring and the Book,* x, 1375–81.
10. See A. C. Pigou, *Robert Browning as a Religious Teacher* (London, 1931) p. 111.
11. Jones, *Browning,* p. 240.
12. Quoted in Jones, *Browning,* p. 45.
13. William James, *The Varieties of Religious Experience* (New York, 1920) p. 79.

Richard D. Altick

'ANDREA DEL SARTO': THE KINGDOM OF HELL IS WITHIN (1968)

Andrea del Sarto was called 'The Faultless Painter'. If it were not that in Browning's poem the epithet falls short of being an unqualified term of praise, one might apply it to 'Andrea del Sarto', probably the poet's greatest short dramatic monologue. Certainly few of his poems approach it in sheer intensity, fidelity, and mounting horror of psychological portraiture. The received interpretation, that Andrea is simply the victim of timidity or weakness, seems to me to fall far short of the whole truth. Has anyone yet sought to express in print the full measure of Browning's achievement in this picture of a man whose capacity for self-deception is tragically insufficient for even his momentary comfort?

Andrea's condition, as this essay proposes to demonstrate, is terrible beyond the reach of irony. Ordinarily in Browning's dramatic monologues we are superior to the speaker : we are able to see him as he does not, or at least we see more than he is aware of. But Andrea has an insight into himself that approaches our own, for he recognizes as soon as we do, perhaps earlier, the illusoriness of what he calls Lucrezia's love for him, and more than that, his moral inadequacy which is manifested both in his weakness as a man and in his failure as an artist. Our response in this poem therefore is not governed by irony – irony such as we feel, for example, over the ignorance of Pictor Ignotus, who rationalizes to his own satisfaction his refusal (actually his inability) to compete with the bright new stars of Renaissance painting, not knowing that the secret of great art lies in the artist's unfettered realisation of a passionate personal vision, and that he is the slave of outmoded conventions. Although incidental

M.A.W.—H

ironies abound in 'Andrea del Sarto', our response is chiefly one
of pity, dictated not by the painter's ignorance but by his very
lack of ignorance. He knows himself too well to find solace; no
soothing balm of deception can alleviate his stark awareness of
his nature and present situation. Browning elsewhere (as in 'A
Death in the Desert') celebrates God's mercy in providing clouds
or eyelids by which man, a finite creature who cannot tolerate the
absolute, is spared the blinding sun-rays of God's pure truth. In
a similar manner, self-deception is a psychological device by
which a human being is enabled to avert the whole intolerable
truth about himself; it makes life, however less honest, a little
more endurable. Andrea's tragedy is that he has no such refuge.

If this is the poem's implicit statement, it is worth repeating a
few critical commonplaces to enlarge our realisation of the extra-
ordinarily close relationship in this poem between technique and
content. In 'Andrea del Sarto' Browning's artistry intensifies the
ultimate psychological revealment : to a degree seldom matched
in dramatic poetry, the two are inseparable. Only when we comprehend the full emotional depth of his portrait of Andrea can
we appreciate the degree to which poetic means here is the vehicle
of poetic meaning.

As one of the finest examples of Browning's stream-of-con-
sciousness technique, the poem has no logical progression. The
speaker's thoughts wander, double back upon themselves. The
setting as evening descends on Florence, his own weariness,
Lucrezia, the fatality of God, his paradoxical triumph as a drafts-
man and failure as an artist, the cuckolding cousin, the superior
gifts and fortunes of Rafael, Leonardo, and Michelangelo, the
golden year at the French court and its sordid consequence when
Andrea fraudulently converted to Lucrezia's pleasure the money
the King entrusted to him to buy more art for Fontainebleau, a
flicker of sexual passion not wholly spent – all these are inter-
woven in the natural involution of reverie. But this seeming aim-
lessness is actually reducible to one recurrent emotional movement. Andrea, brooding over the sterility of his life and the nullity
of his prospects, clutches at a straw; he assumes confidence, attributes blame, or otherwise seeks peace in finding a reason, however untenable, or hope, however frail, only to have each com-

forting thought crumble as he grasps it. Only the disconsolate resignation born of weariness remains.

A second constant is the poem's pervasive tone, which has always been taken to suggest the technical perfection of Andrea's painting – even, lifeless, and dull – as well as his mood as he reflects on the failure of his life and seeks to divert responsibility from where he knows it really resides. The diction is no less colloquial than that of, say, Browning's other poems spoken by artists : but here is heard no lovely (and slightly tipsy) 'I am poor brother Lippo, by your leave!/ You need not clap your torches to my face./ Zooks, what's to blame?' The music hath a dying fall. Andrea's cadences have a sad dignity which reduces our awareness of their colloquial nature; they are spoken, for the most part, in a monotone; and the fact that they belong to a soliloquy rather than a monologue – for Lucrezia can scarcely be called an auditor in the literal sense – further drains them of animation. The very exclamations seem muted. Yet beneath the lethargy and the surface placidity, beneath the gray ashes of Andrea's resignation the fires of restlessness still smolder, and once in a while they burst into momentary flame. There is not much suggestion of physical movement to relieve the prevalent mood of enervation. Once Andrea makes a gesture of still unmastered physical desire as he reaches out his hands to 'frame your face in your hair's gold,/ You beautiful Lucrezia that are mine!' And at another juncture he suddenly rises to correct a false detail of anatomy in a sketch by Rafael. But the impulse soon spends itself, is quenched indeed by his ready awareness of its futility : 'Ay, but the soul! he's Rafael! rub it out!'

As in Andrea's painting, so in his present mood – 'I often am much wearier than you think,/ This evening more than usual' – and so in the poem : 'A common greyness silvers everything'. There is a Tennysonian perfection of sober, melancholy ambience in the lines

> There's the bell clinking from the chapel-top;
> That length of convent-wall across the way
> Holds the trees safer, huddled more inside;
> The last monk leaves the garden; days decrease,
> And autumn grows, autumn in everything. (41–5)

(One may believe that Tennyson would particularly have admired the choice of verb in the first line : a toneless, choked-off *clink* rather than a full-voiced, resonant, freely echoing *ring*.) The dominant colour throughout is the silver grayness of twilight. But it too, like the prevailing silver tone of Tennyson's 'Tithonus', a poem of perpetual dawn rather than of twilight, is momentarily broken on several occasions. As in 'Tithonus', gold and fire intrude, symbolic here of two influences which led Andrea to prostitute his gift – the celebrity and fortune he won as a painter at Francis I's court and the irresistible attraction of the golden-haired Lucrezia – and in addition ironically symbolic of the fire of pure internal inspiration, the divine gift which belongs to the true artist but was denied him, or perhaps, as he suspects, which he threw away. The surface calm, a 'perfection' of mood corollary to the technical perfection and the neutral wash of gray and silver tones that characterizes Andrea's art, thus proves to be, like his rationalisations, illusory. Underneath, in the succession of quickly extinguished bursts of passion as he recalls what was and what might have been, there is poignant disturbance. The whole poem, so quiet in superficial impression, is in fact made dramatic by the sustained tension between Andrea's wish to live out what life remains to him in a sort of drugged repose and the uncontrollable devil-pricks of his self-knowledge.

One thinks of Shakespeare's seventy-third sonnet :

> In me thou see'st the twilight of such day
> As after sunset fadeth in the west,
> Which by and by black night doth take away,
> Death's second self, that seals up all in rest.
> In me thou see'st the glowing of such fire
> That on the ashes of his youth doth lie,
> As the deathbed whereon it must expire,
> Consumed with that which it was nourish'd by.
>   This thou perceivest, which makes thy love more strong,
>   To love that well which thou must leave ere long.

But Andrea has no such comfort as is expressed in the last couplet. Accompanying his awareness of his artistic and spiritual failure, as his soliloquy continues its inexorable course, is the equally bitter

knowledge that, if he ever possessed Lucrezia's love, he does not
have it now. The very first lines begin with a sigh, and the true
nature of their relationship as husband and wife is at once plain :

> But do not let us quarrel any more,
> No, my Lucrezia; bear with me for once :
> Sit down and all shall happen as you wish.
> You turn your face, but does it bring your heart? (1–4)

The possessive 'my' of the second line, here so unremarkable a
monosyllable, will acquire its own burden of irony as the situation is revealed, beginning in the very next line after these : 'I'll
work then for your friend's friend, never fear.'

Unlike most of the attending figures in Browning's dramatic
monologues, Lucrezia is not a mere casual witness, a fortuitous
occasion for the speaker's revealment : she is the central figure in
his tragedy. None of Browning's unspeaking auditors is more
silent than she, and in none is silence more eloquent. Her
Gioconda smile tells more about her, about Andrea, and about
their history and present situation than could pages of dialogue.
It is the smile of a woman confident of her power over men, and
at the same time contemptuous of the man to whom she belongs,
not in fact but in name and in the transparent illusion to which he
so desperately clings. She has no interest in his art; she carelessly
smears with her robes a still-damp product of his brush. Nor
does she listen as he pours out his soul. She merely smiles, and
awaits the 'cousin's' whistle.

Lucrezia's relation to her husband, as the first ten lines of the
poem make clear, is limited to the interest defined by her very
name, which is etymologically suggestive of profit and riches. She
tolerates him, in his tired age, solely for the money he can earn
her through the dogged exercise of an admired but empty art.
Because of her, he suffers the ultimate degradation as both man
and artist. Not only is he reduced to painting frescoes, portraits,
and assorted artistic make-weights to order for a wealthy patron
('Treat his own subject after his own way,/ Fix his own time,
accept too his own price') : the commissions came through the
'cousin', her lover, and the money he is paid will be devoted to

liquidating – through the euphemism of 'loans' – that same lover's gambling debts.

Except for the moments when he frames her hair and essays to correct Rafael's line, Andrea's hand presumably encloses Lucrezia's throughout most of the monologue. If so, it sustains an irony initiated in the early stages of the poem. In lines 8–9, 14, 21–2, and 49, there occurs a hand-within-hand image normally suggestive of security and comfort. But the symbolic meaning is determined by whose hand holds whose or what, and in this case God's hand encloses Andrea (49), whose hand encloses Lucrezia's (14, 21–2), which will enclose the money Andrea expects from the patron (8–9) and which she in turn will hold for the cousin. Here we have no such firm belief in God's wise beneficence as is conveyed by the use of the same figure in 'Popularity' – the image of 'God's glow-worm', the unrecognized poet-genius, being held tightly in 'His clenched hand' until the time comes for God to 'let out all the beauty'. Nor does 'Your soft hand is a woman of itself,/ And mine the man's bared breast she curls inside' have its ordinary implication of quiet, trusting intimacy. It is belied not only by the serpent-suggestion of 'curls', but by the whole emotional context.

Nor, we are invited to believe, do the lover and the patron represent the limits of Lucrezia's sphere of influence. In lines echoing Dryden's 'Your Cleopatra;/ Dolabella's Cleopatra; Everyman's Cleopatra' (*All for Love*, IV i, 297–9), Andrea celebrates

> My face, my moon, my everybody's moon,
> Which everybody looks on and calls his.
> And, I suppose, is looked on by in turn,
> While she looks – no one's. . . . (29–32)

In a declension characteristic of Browning and far more devastating than Dryden's single line, the 'my' gives way to the ambiguous 'my everybody's', and thence to the brutal truth of the succeeding lines. Lucrezia is public property, at least so far as her superlative beauty is concerned; but she maintains the strategic distance, the cool lack of sole commitment, which is part of the

desirable woman's armory of fascination. She has attributes of
the *femme fatale* : her hand, inside his, represents her whole
woman-self, curling snake-like against his breast; her hair is 'ser-
pentining beauty, rounds on rounds'; and her low voice is like
a fowler's pipe' which the bird 'follows to the snare'. Physically
she is the walking objective correlative of his art : she too is technical perfection, and as a work of art she too lacks the redeeming,
crowning element of soul. She has 'perfect brow,/ And perfect
eyes, and more than perfect mouth', and perfect ears into which
she places pearls – jewels of the same grayness which 'silvers
everything' in the present setting as it does in her husband's art.
'There's what we painters call our harmony!' Andrea exclaims;
but it is a harmony limited to the eye, one that has no counterpart in their spirits.

Andrea seeks another kind of harmony, an acceptable simple
interpretation of his life which will explain as it consoles :

> . . . the whole seems to fall into a shape
> As if I saw alike my work and self
> And all that I was born to be and do,
> A twilight-piece. (46–9)

And so begins the tortuous course of reflexions on his failure.
Initially he is confident of his scope as artist. He

> can do with my pencil what I know,
> What I see, what at bottom of my heart
> I wish for, if I ever wish so deep – (60–2)

the last clause reminding us of the similar bold and unsupported
claim of Pictor Ignotus : 'I could have painted pictures like that
youth's/ Ye praise so.' But boasts are cheap, and, unlike the
forgotten painter whose success lies in his ability to construct
tenable rationalisations for his failure, Andrea cannot delude
himself for long. What begins as an assertion of superiority ends
as an admission of inferiority. He is, beyond question, a facile
artist, one with dazzling skills. He can do things 'easily', 'perfectly', 'no sketches first, no studies' – 'do what many dream of,

all their lives'. They strive, agonise, and in the end fail; he suc-
ceeds. The truth, however, as he realises, is that his is a lower
order of accomplishment, the product of a 'low-pulsed forthright
craftsman's hands'. The striving he attributes to the rivals who
envy him his effortless command of technique is not, in the end,
toward outward perfection but toward a quasi-religious vision
that transcends colour and line.

> Their works drop groundward, but themselves, I know,
> Reach many a time a heaven that's shut to me,
> Enter and take their place there sure enough,
> Though they come back and cannot tell the world.
> My works are nearer heaven, but I sit here. (83–7)

True fulfilment in art occurs not in the creation but in the creator.
The act of striving, stirred by the 'truer light of God . . . / In
their vexed beating stuffed and stopped-up brain,/ Heart, or
whate'er else', results in no tangible evidence of success, but in an
experience as supernal and ineffable as that of Lazarus or the
mystics.

We have, then, the paradox that the closer a work of art comes
to physical perfection, the wider the gap that separates it from
true, or spiritual, perfection; and so with the artist himself. Perfection, as Browning asserts so often in his poetry, may be beyond
the possibility of human achievement, but ceaselessly to struggle
toward it is the impulse and deed that distinguishes man from
beast, and artist from mere craftsman. 'Even if the longed-for
goal be never reached, even though the violence of the striving
consume the soul utterly, yet it is enough that it should burn so
nobly.' So remarked Giordano Bruno, a philosopher of the generation just after Andrea's. In Browning's view, such struggle will
strengthen, not consume, the soul. A man reaches in order 'that
heaven might so replenish him,/ Above and through his art.'
But, overweighted with his special earth-bound powers, Andrea
never reaches, never dares; he prefers the safety of a limited art,
the perfectness, as Ruskin put it in *The Stones of Venice*, of the
lower order. Unlike true artists with their fierce pride in their
work, he is indifferent to praise or blame; he has no 'sudden

blood'. His temperament is emblematised by the 'length of convent-wall across the way' which 'Holds the trees safer, huddled
more inside'; he is, he says later, 'the weak-eyed bat [a painter
with weak eyes!] no sun should tempt/ Out of the grange whose
four walls make his world'.

> In this world, who can do a thing, will not;
> And who would do it, cannot, I perceive :
> Yet the will's somewhat – somewhat, too, the power –
> And thus we half-men struggle. At the end,
> God, I conclude, compensates, punishes.
> 'Tis safer for me, if the award be strict,
> That I am something underrated here. . . . (137–43)

But can the man who values safety ever be said to struggle? The
answer implicitly nullifies Andrea's momentary assurance. He is
not entitled to number himself even among the 'half-men' (those
with the will but not the power, and those with the power but not
the will). For he has not striven heroically, even in the face of
certain futility, to round himself off into a whole man; therefore
he will not earn God's grace. 'In heaven, perhaps, new chances,
one more chance', he says later – but the 'perhaps' is a true
measure of his confidence. The only struggle of which we have
positive evidence that he is capable is the present one – the pursuit
of extenuation – and it is not likely to be rewarded. Far from being attuned to divine inspiration his soul is 'toned down' to the
low seductive call of a callously selfish woman. On the one occasion in the poem when he looks upward, it is a physical gesture
prompted by tired eyes, not a symbolic manifestation of inner
desire; and the resulting vision is not of the New Jerusalem but
of the walls of his 'melancholy little house' cemented with the
misapplied 'fierce bright gold' of Francis I. He is a mercenary
in a profession whose true *dévots* have a priestly vocation. At the
same time – and this is the final turn of the screw – he knows that
those same dedicated painters with whom he must constantly
compare himself have in fact won a far greater measure of worldly
fame than he has. At the end of a wasted life he has nothing to
show for his ambitions but a certain ephemeral reputation for

facility, while Rafael, Leonardo, and Michelangelo have enjoyed
both fulfilment of spirit and ample earthly reward.

Faced with this bitter maldistribution of fortune, Andrea seeks
to lay it to divine decree :

> Love, we are in God's hand.
> How strange now, looks the life He makes us lead;
> How free we seem, so fettered fast we are !
> I feel He laid the fetter : let it lie ! (49–52)

But the admission that men strive, and through struggle achieve
a glimpse of heaven, disposes of a foreordaining God as a scape-
goat. We are not 'fettered fast' : man's will is free. God not serv-
ing his need, Andrea seeks some other reason for his failure – and
Lucrezia is at hand. In passages laden with past conditionals
(the subjunctive is the grammatical mode of regret), he considers
what he might have been and done :

> I know both what I want and what might gain,
> And yet how profitless to know, to sigh
> 'Had I been two, another and myself,
> Our head would have o'erlooked the world !' No doubt.
>
> (100–3)
>
> Had you . . . given me soul,
> We might have risen to Rafael, I and you !
> Nay, Love, you did give all I asked, I think –
> More than I merit, yes, by many times.
> But had you – oh, with the same perfect brow,
> And perfect eyes, and more than perfect mouth,
> And the low voice my soul hears, as a bird
> The fowler's pipe, and follows to the snare –
> Had you, with these the same, but brought a mind !
> Some women do so. Had the mouth there urged
> 'God and the glory ! never care for gain.
> The present by the future, what is that ?
> Live for fame, side by side with Agnolo !
> Rafael is waiting : up to God, all three !'
> I might have done it for you. (118–32)

But this supposition is another product of a half-man. He has the power to make it, but not the power to believe it. Its frailty is summarised by 'might have', and it is totally demolished by what follows : 'So it seems : / Perhaps not'. This bleak concession is neutralised for an instant by a return to the former theme : 'All is as God over-rules'. But, having been destroyed earlier, this assumption will no longer serve, and Andrea must face the truth : 'incentives come from the soul's self;/ The rest avail not'. And the great painters he envies did not have wives, not even incomplete women like Lucrezia.

Nevertheless, this truth is not to be borne, and in his search for another incentive which would have availed him, he recalls one which indeed did once serve : 'that long festal year at Fontainebleau !' This was, in retrospect, the Browningian 'great moment' in Andrea's life. 'I surely then could sometimes leave the ground,/ Put on the glory, Rafael's daily wear.' (*Could* : but did he ? Rationalization is often assisted by the merciful filters of memory.) 'A good time, was it not, my kingly days ?' As he describes it, however, his success even then was not of the order of a Rafael's or a Michelangelo's. He basked in the 'humane great monarch's golden look'; but certain details of his description of the King suggests that Francis' favour is as irrelevant to the true source of Andrea's tragedy as is Lucrezia's lack of soul and the premise that 'All is as God over-rules'. The King's 'curl' and 'smile' link him with Lucrezia, and 'his gold chain' recalls God's fetters. To be sure, there was a 'fire of souls/ Profuse' in those halcyon days at the court; but as far as we can tell it was in other souls, those of his admiring onlookers, not his. He was not a Rafael, 'flaming out his thoughts/ Upon a palace-wall for Rome to see'. No : he was Lucrezia's husband, and in the end the gold of her hair worked more potently upon him than the gold of the King's patronage. 'You called me, and I came home to your heart.'

But was her heart – if she has one – really ever his ? Certainly he does not possess it now. For as Andrea talks on, Lucrezia continues to smile, and as she smiles, the utter hollowness of his confidence becomes more pronounced. It is increasingly apparent that she dominates him absolutely, and that all he wins from her

presence is the grim pretence they are bound by mutual love. His
only concern in life is to satisfy her, so that she will continue to
play what he well knows to be merely the meaningless simulacrum
of a role. Whether or not Michelangelo was right when he told
Rafael that Andrea would one day 'bring the sweat into that brow
of yours', all he now cares for

> Is, whether you're – not grateful – but more pleased.
> Well, let me think so. And you smile indeed !
> This hour has been an hour ! Another smile?
> If you would sit thus by me every night
> I should work better, do you comprehend?
> I mean that I should earn more, give you more. (202–7)

Candid about his art as about his place in Lucrezia's life, he recognizes that he is deliberately prostituting the unique talents he does
possess. But he persists in trying to persuade himself that the purchase is worth the sacrifice. 'Come from the window, love', he
pleads in phrases oddly prophetic of 'Dover Beach' : 'Let us but
love each other'. It is an empty wish, and he knows it, for he un-
dercuts it at once with 'Must you go?/ That Cousin here again?'
    His meditations in this latter part of the poem are a comming-
ling of rationalisation, realisation, and inadvertent self-reveal-
ment, all of which belie his assertion that 'I am grown peaceful
as old age to-night'. Not all passion is spent, for beneath the
surface, his feelings remain turbulent and conflicting. 'Clearer
grows/ My better fortune, I resolve to think' – but whatever
confidence is implied by the first five words is cancelled by the
succeeding revelation that it is generated by an act of will rather
than a sincere conviction. The subjunctive 'would' and 'should'
of lines 205–6, 'If really there was such a chance' (201), and the
'Well, let me think so' (203) reinforce the contrary-to-fact tone
seen earlier in the use of frequent conditionals. 'Well, let smiles
buy me!' (223), however, ruthlessly dispels the general ambival-
ence. Against such a blunt admission of his helplessness before
her, the succeeding platitudes – 'Let each one bear his lot' (252)
and 'No doubt, there's something strikes a balance' (257) – are
impotent.

The image of the walls of the New Jerusalem at the poem's end is the culmination of a process that began in the early lines. The 'length of convent-wall' enclosing its safe huddled trees (42–3) became 'the grange whose four walls' make Andrea's – the 'weak-eyed bat's' – world (170), the idea of safety thus acquiring the additional suggestion of cowardice and retreat. Later, the walls turned into those of the house built with Francis' money; their drabness gone, they were 'illumined' with 'fierce bright gold' (216–17) and thus, by implication, tainted. Finally, the walls are transformed into those of 'the New Jerusalem' upon which Leonardo, Rafael, Michelangelo, and Andrea (as he momentarily allows himself to believe) will fulfil their ultimate aspiration as artists (261–3). The concurrent expansion and alteration of the image from beginning to end of the poem is both illusory and ironic. Andrea's present confinement, symbolised by the convent wall, gives way to a vision of freedom and fulfilment. But we quickly realise, with him, that this seeming prophecy is but another futile dream.

These last ten lines of the poem contain a terrible sequence of truths, most of them ironic. There is heavy significance in the past tense of line 258: 'You loved me quite enough, it seems to-night.' The tense of 'loved' is a slip of the tongue which adds substance to our conviction that he has a deeper subconscious awareness of the truth than his words normally express, and it renders additionally false the ensuing statement that, while Andrea's hypothesised co-workers on the celestial frescoes are without wives, 'I have mine!' Neither the present tense of the verb nor the possessiveness of both verb and pronoun, we are certain by now, has any justification in fact. But the pretence persists. 'There's still Lucrezia' (she is indeed still present – in the flesh) 'as I choose.' In this ultimate denial of the predestination he had earlier sought to embrace, he confesses that he has freely devoted himself to her, the embodiment of soulless physical perfection, rather than to the high, sacramental art to which the other three artists are dedicated. The choice may have been indefensible, as it surely was disastrous, but he alone made it.

'Again the Cousin's whistle! Go, my Love.' Toward these last three monosyllables the whole poem has pointed. They are charged with the meaning of all that has gone before, as Hamlet's 'Good night, Mother' is heavy with memory of the conflicting passions he has experienced in the closet scene. The verb, the possessive pronoun, and the noun : each has its bitter burden. His only comfort, and a cold one she is – the woman for whom he sacrificed his integrity as man and artist, in contemplating whom he saw mirrored at twilight the full failure of his life and character – no longer affords him even her physical presence. She leaves to keep a rendezvous with livelier company, and he resignedly watches her go ('my Love' !). He is left alone with himself, an awful fate. Like all men cursed with too much self-knowledge and lacking the saving grace of rationalisations that will stick, he carries the kingdom of hell within him.

SOURCE : *Brownings's Mind and Art*, ed. Clarence Tracy (Edinburgh and London, 1968) pp. 18–31.

PART FIVE

Two Parodies

I had o' course upo' me – wi' me say –
(*Mecum*'s the Latin, make a note o' that)
When I popp'd pen i' stand, scratch'd ear, wiped snout,
(Let everybody wipe his own himself)
Sniff'd – tch ! – at snuffbox; tumbled up, he-heed,
Haw-haw'd (not hee-haw'd, that 's another guess thing :)
Then fumbled at, and stumbled out of, door,
I shoved the timber ope wi' my omoplat;
And *in vestibulo*, i' the lobby to-wit,
(Iacobi Facciolati's rendering, sir,)
Donn'd galligaskins, antigropeloes,
And so forth; and, complete with hat and gloves,
One on and one a-dangle i' my hand,
And ombrifuge (Lord love you !), case o' rain,
I flopp'd forth, 'sbuddikins ! on my own ten toes,
(I do assure you there be ten of them),
And went clump-clumping up hill and down dale
To find myself o' the sudden i' front o' the boy.
Put case I hadn't 'em on me, could I ha' bought
This sort-o'-kind-o'-what-you-might-call toy,
This pebble-thing, o' the boy-thing? Q. E. D.
That's proven without aid from mumping Pope,
Sleek porporate or bloated Cardinal.
(Isn't it, old Fatchaps? You're in Euclid now.)
So, having the shilling – having i' fact a lot –
And pence and halfpence, ever so many o' them,
I purchased, as I think I said before,
The pebble (*lapis, lapidis, -di, -dem, -de* –
What nouns 'crease short i' in the genitive, Fatchaps, eh?)
O' the boy, a bare-legg'd beggarly son of a gun,
For one-and-fourpence. Here we are again.

Now Law steps in, bigwigg'd, voluminous-jaw'd;
Investigates and re-investigates.
Was the transaction illegal? Law shakes head.
Perpend, sir, all the bearings of the case.

At first the coin was mine, the chattel his.
But now (by virtue of the said exchange

C. S. Calverley

THE COCK AND THE BULL

You see this pebble-stone? It's a thing I bought
Of a bit of a chit of a boy i' the mid o' the day –
I like to dock the smaller parts-o'-speech,
As we curtail the already cur-tail'd cur
(You catch the paronomasia, play 'po' words?)
Did, rather, i' the pre-Landseerian days.
Well, to my muttons. I purchased the concern,
And clapt it i' my poke, having given for same
By way o' chop, swop, barter or exchange –
'Chop' was my snickering dandiprat's own term –
One shilling and fourpence, current coin o' the realm.
O-n-e one and f-o-u-r four
Pence, one and fourpence – you are with me, sir? –
What hour it skills not: ten or eleven o' the clock,
One day (and what a roaring day it was
Go shop or sight-see – bar a spit o' rain!)
In February, eighteen sixty nine,
Alexandrina Victoria, Fidei
Hm – hm – how runs the jargon? being on throne.

Such, sir, are all the facts, succinctly put,
The basis or substratum – what you will –
Of the impending eighty thousand lines.
'Not much in 'em either,' quoth perhaps simple Hodge.
But there's a superstructure. Wait a bit.

Mark first the rationale of the thing:
Hear logic rivel and levigate the deed.
That shilling – and for matter o' that, the pence –

And barter) *vice versa* all the coin,
Per juris operationem, vests
I' the boy and his assigns till ding o' doom;
(*In sæcula sæculo-o-o-orum;*
I think I hear the Abate mouth out that.)
To have and hold the same to him and them. . . .
Confer some idiot on Conveyancing.
Whereas the pebble and every part thereof,
And all that appertaineth thereunto,
Quodcunque pertinet ad eam rem,
(I fancy, sir, my Latin's rather pat)
Or shall, will, may, might, can, could, would or should,
(*Subaudi cætera* – clap we to the close –
For what's the good of law in a case o' the kind)
Is mine to all intents and purposes.
This settled, I resume the thread o' the tale.

Now for a touch o' the vendor's quality.
He says a gen'lman bought a pebble of him,
(This pebble i' sooth, sir, which I hold i' my hand) –
And paid for't, *like* a gen'lman, on the nail.
'Did I o'ercharge him a ha'penny? Devil a bit.
Fiddlepin's end! Get out, you blazing ass!
Gabble o' the goose. Don't bugaboo-baby *me!*
Go double or quits? Yah! tittup! what's the odds?'
– There's the transaction view'd i' the vendor's light.

Next ask that dumpled hag, stood snuffling by,
With her three frowsy blowsy brats o' babes,
The scum o' the kennel, cream o' the filth-heap – Faugh!
Aie, aie, aie, aie! ὀτοτοτοτοῖ,
('Stead which we blurt out Hoighty toighty now) –
And the baker and candlestickmaker, and Jack and Gill,
Blear'd Goody this and queasy Gaffer that.
Ask the schoolmaster. Take schoolmaster first.

He saw a gentleman purchase of a lad
A stone, and pay for it *rite*, on the square,
And carry it off *per saltum*, jauntily,

Propria quæ maribus, gentleman's property now
(Agreeably to the law explain'd above),
In proprium usum, for his private ends.
The boy he chuck'd a brown i' the air, and bit
I' the face the shilling : heaved a thumping stone
At a lean hen that ran cluck clucking by,
(And hit her, dead as nail i' post o' door,)
Then *abiit* – what's the Ciceronian phrase? –
Excessit, evasit, erupit – off slogs boy;
Off like bird, *avi similis* – (you observed
The dative? Pretty i' the Mantuan!) – *Anglice*
Off in three flea skips. *Hactenus,* so far,
So good, *tam bene. Bene, satis, male –,*
Where was I with my trope 'bout one in a quag?
I did once hitch the syntax into verse :
Verbum personale, a verb personal,
Concordat – ay, 'agrees,' old Fatchaps – *cum*
Nominativo, with its nominative,
Genere, i' point o' gender, *numero,*
O' number, *et persona,* and person. *Ut,*
Instance : *Sol ruit,* down flops sun, *et* and,
Montes umbrantur, out flounce mountains. Pah !
Excuse me, sir, I think I'm going mad.
You see the trick on't though, and can yourself
Continue the discourse *ad libitum.*
It takes up about eighty thousand lines,
A thing imagination boggles at :
And might, odds-bobs, sir ! in judicious hands,
Extend from here to Mesopotamy.

SOURCE : *Fly Leaves* (1872).

[Editor's note] Although this parody was occasioned by *The Ring and the Book,* it catches (and exaggerates) the tricks of Browning's style so well as to justify its inclusion.

J. K. Stephen

THE LAST RIDE TOGETHER (FROM HER POINT OF VIEW)

When I had firmly answered 'No',
And he allowed that that was so,
I really thought I should be free
For good and all from Mr B.,
    And that he would soberly acquiesce:
I said that it would be discreet
That for a while we should not meet;
I promised I would always feel
A kindly interest in his weal;
I thanked him for his amorous zeal;
    In short, I said all I could but 'yes'.

I said what I'm accustomed to;
I acted as I always do;
I promised he should find in me
A friend, – a sister, if that might be:
    But he was still dissatisfied:
He certainly was most polite;
He said exactly what was right,
He acted very properly,
Except indeed for this, that he
Insisted on inviting me
    To come with him for 'one more last ride'.

A little while in doubt I stood:
A ride, no doubt, would do me good:
I had a habit and a hat
Extremely well worth looking at:
    The weather was distinctly fine:

My horse too wanted exercise,
And time, when one is riding, flies :
Besides it really seemed, you see,
The only way of ridding me
Of pertinacious Mr B. :
  So my head I graciously incline.

I won't say much of what happened next :
I own I was extremely vexed :
Indeed I should have been aghast
If any one had seen what passed :
  But nobody need ever know
That, as I leaned forward to stir the fire,
He advanced before I could well retire,
And I suddenly felt, to my great alarm,
The grasp of a warm unlicensed arm,
An embrace in which I found no charm;
  I was awfully glad when he let me go.

Then we began to ride : my steed
Was rather fresh, too fresh indeed,
And at first I thought of little, save
The way to escape an early grave,
  As the dust rose up on either side.
My stern companion jogged along
On a brown old cob both broad and strong :
He looked as he does when he's writing verse,
Or endeavouring not to swear and curse,
Or wondering where he has left his purse :
  Indeed it was a sombre ride.

I spoke of the weather to Mr B. :
But he neither listened nor spoke to me :
I praised his horse, and I smiled the smile
Which was wont to move him once on a while;
  I said I was wearing his favourite flowers :
But I wasted my words on the desert air,
For he rode with a fixed and gloomy stare :

I wonder what he was thinking about :
As I don't read verse, I sha'n't find out :
It was something subtle and deep, no doubt,
 A theme to detain a man for hours.

Ah! there was the corner where Mr S.
So nearly induced me to whisper 'yes' :
And here it was that the next but one
Proposed on horseback, or would have done,
 Had his horse not most opportunely shied;
Which perhaps was due to the unseen flick
He received from my whip : 'twas a scurvy trick,
But I never could do with that young man :
I hope his present young woman can.
Well, I must say, never, since time began,
 Did I go for a duller or longer ride.

He never smiles and he never speaks :
He might go on like this for weeks :
He rolls a slightly frenzied eye
Towards the blue and burning sky,
 And the cob bounds on with tireless stride.
If we aren't at home for lunch at two
I don't know what Papa will do;
But I know full well he will say to me
'I never approved of Mr B. :
'It's the very devil that you and he
 'Ride, ride together, for ever ride.'

SOURCE : *Lapsus Calami* (1891).

SUGGESTIONS FOR FURTHER READING

The best *Life* of Browning is still that of W. H. Griffin and H. C. Minchin, first published in 1910 (rev. ed., Methuen, 1938). More controversial is Betty Miller's *Robert Browning, A Portrait* (John Murray, 1952), a psychological study which deals with Browning's relationships with women in particular; chatty and readable are the two volumes of Maisie Ward's *Robert Browning and His World: The Private Face* (Cassell, 1968) and *Two Robert Brownings?* (Cassell, 1969).

A complete edition of Browning's work, with full textual and scholarly apparatus, is in process of publication by Ohio University Press under the general editorship of Roma A. King Jr. The first volume appeared in 1969. Until its completion, there is the ten-volume centenary edition by F. G. Kenyon (Smith, Elder, 1912), and other more convenient volumes: Ian Jack's *Browning: Poetical Works, 1833–64* (Oxford U.P., 1970) prints the poems of these years in their original groups. Editions with helpful notes include Paul Turner's *Men and Women, 1855* (Oxford U.P., 1972) and the selections of Browning by Donald Smalley (Riverside Press, 1956) and Jacob Korg (Bobbs-Merrill, 1971). The letters of the Brownings' courtship are edited by Elvan Kintner as *The Letters of Robert Browning and Elizabeth Barrett Barrett, 1845–1846* (Harvard U.P., 1969). The remainder of Browning's letters are scattered about in various volumes, and there is a great need for a collected edition.

The most useful single book on Browning is W. C. DeVane's *A Browning Handbook* (rev. ed., John Murray, 1955). This contains a short life of Browning, and essential information on each poem, though its critical assessments are only gestures. As the preface to this present book shows, the *Browning* volume in the 'Critical Heritage' series, edited by Boyd Litzinger and Donald Smalley (Routledge & Kegan Paul, 1970), is an excellent assemblage of reviews and other contemporary criticism. Browning is seen with acuteness and accuracy against the background of the temper of his time in the works by J. Hillis Miller and E. D. H. Johnson, sections from which are printed above. The approach through genre is also of great interest, and Robert Langbaum's *The Poetry of Experience* (Chatto & Windus, 1957) should be consulted by all Browning students. Other critical studies of Browning tend to fall into fragments, articles stuck together between hard covers: this is true of the two notable works from which essays have been taken for this casebook, those by W. O. Raymond and Roma A. King Jr. Others include Barbara Melchiori's *Browning's Poetry of Reticence* (Oliver & Boyd, 1968), and Philip Drew's *The Poetry of Browning* (Methuen, 1970), an important book for the advanced student because of its rigorous questioning of received critical ideas.

Written with more specific themes in mind are Park Honan's *Browning's Characters* (Yale U.P., 1961), a study of the development of Browning's art of character; W. David Shaw's *The Dialectical Temper* (Cornell U.P., 1968), a study of Browning's rhetoric; and Donald S. Hair's *Browning's Experiments with Genre* (Oliver & Boyd, 1972), which deals with Browning's modifications of traditional literary forms.

Perhaps because Browning criticism has been at its best in the essay, there are three notable collections of articles on Browning:

Boyd Litzinger and K. L. Knickerbocker (eds), *The Browning Critics* (University of Kentucky Press, 1965).
Philip Drew (ed.), *Robert Browning, a Collection of Critical Essays* (Methuen, 1966).
Clarence Tracy (ed.), *Browning's Mind and Art* (Oliver & Boyd, 1968).

The first of these includes a fine essay by F. E. L. Priestley, 'Blougram's Apologetics', and W. C. DeVane's 'The Virgin and the Dragon', a remarkable article which traces Browning's fascination with the Andromeda myth in his life and his poetry. This is also reprinted in Drew's collection, together with a penetrating short essay by Edwin Muir, and, among others, a good article by Richard D. Altick, ' "A Grammarian's Funeral": Browning's Praise of Folly?'. Altick's study of 'Andrea del Sarto', printed above, comes from Tracy's collection, which also contains a distinguished and humane essay on Browning by Geoffrey Tillotson.

More detailed suggestions for further reading will be found in two annotated guides to Browning studies: Ian Jack's entry for Browning in *English Poetry, Select Bibliographical Guides*, ed. A. E. Dyson (Oxford U.P., 1971), and Park Honan's section in *The Victorian Poets, a Guide to Research*, ed. Frederic E. Faverty, 2nd ed. (Harvard U.P., 1968). A comprehensive bibliography will be found in *Robert Browning, a Bibliography, 1830–1950*, by L. N. Broughton, C. S. Northrup, and Robert Pearsall (Cornell U.P., 1953). This is supplemented by a bibliography of works published on Browning from 1945–69, in Norton B. Crowell's *A Reader's Guide to Robert Browning* (University of New Mexico Press, 1972).

NOTES ON CONTRIBUTORS

RICHARD D. ALTICK is Professor Emeritus of English, Ohio State University. His publications include *Browning's Roman Murder Story* (with J. F. Loucks, 1968), the Penguin edition of *The Ring and the Book* (1971) and *Victorian People and Ideas* (1973).

PATRICIA M. BALL is the author of *The Central Self* (1968), a study of the Romantic and Victorian imagination, and *The Science of Aspects* (1971), a study of works of Coleridge, Ruskin and Hopkins, and of the changing role of fact within them.

C. S. CALVERLEY was a fellow of Christ's College, Cambridge, classical scholar and translator (1831–34). He was author of *Verses and Translations* (1862) and *Fly Leaves* (1872) and was noted for his parodies, and for his light verse ('O Beer! O Hodgson, Guinness, Allsopp, Bass!').

G. K. CHESTERTON (1874–1936) was a poet, novelist and critic.

E. D. H. JOHNSON, formerly Professor of English at Princeton University, is the author of *The Alien Vision of Victorian Poetry* (1952) and editor of *The World of the Victorians* (1964) and *The Poetry of the Earth* (1965).

ROMA A. KING JR, Professor of English at Ohio University, is the author of the complementary studies of Browning, *The Bow and the Lyre* (1957) and *The Focusing Artifice* (1968), and chief editor of the Ohio *Complete Works* edition of the poet (1969–   ).

ROBERT LANGBAUM is James Branch Cabell Professor of English at the University of Virginia. He is the author of *The Gaiety of Vision: A Study of Isaac Dinesen's Art* (1964), and essays on nineteenth- and twentieth-century literature, collected in *The Modern Spirit* (1971).

J. HILLIS MILLER is Professor of English and of Comparative Literature at Yale. His publications include *Charles Dickens: The World of His Novels* (1958), *The Disappearance of God: Five Nineteenth-Century Writers* (1963), *The Form of Victorian Fiction* (1968) and *Fiction and Repetition* (1982).

W. O. RAYMOND was Professor of English, Bishop's University, Quebec. His many essays on Browning are collected in *The Infinite Moment* (1959; enlarged edition, 1965).

J. K. STEPHEN was a Fellow of King's College, Cambridge, parodist and wit (1859–92). Author of *Lapsus Calami* (1891) and *Quo musa tendis* (1891), he was most celebrated for his poems on English writers ('When the Rudyards cease from kipling / And the Haggards ride no more.').

GENERAL INDEX

INDEX TO BROWNING'S POEMS